The Making of
Pro-life Activists

Morality and Society Series

EDITED BY ALAN WOLFE

RECENT TITLES:

Heartwood: The First Generation of Theravada Buddhism in America
WENDY CADGE

Moral Communities in Medical Science: Managing Risk in Early Human Experiments
SYDNEY HALPERN

Soft Patriarchs, New Men: How Christianity Shapes Fathers and Husbands
W. BRADFORD WILCOX

Citizen Speak: The Democratic Imagination in American Life
ANDREW J. PERRIN

The First Year Out: Understanding American Teens after High School
TIM CLYDESDALE

God and Government in the Ghetto: The Politics of Church-State Collaboration in Black America
MICHAEL LEO OWENS

The Catholic Social Imagination: Activism and the Just Society in Mexico and the United States
JOSEPH M. PALACIOS

FOR A COMPLETE LIST OF SERIES TITLES, PLEASE SEE THE END OF THE BOOK.

The Making of Pro-life Activists

How Social Movement
Mobilization Works

ZIAD W. MUNSON

The University of Chicago Press   Chicago and London

ZIAD W. MUNSON is the Frank Hook Assistant Professor of
Sociology at Lehigh University. He received his PhD from Harvard
University in 2002.

The University of Chicago Press, Chicago 60637
The University of Chicago Press, Ltd., London
© 2008 by The University of Chicago
All rights reserved. Published 2008
Printed in the United States of America

17 16 15 14 13 12 11 10 09 08   1 2 3 4 5

ISBN-13: 978-0-226-55119-7 (cloth)
ISBN-13: 978-0-226-55120-3 (paper)
ISBN-10: 0-226-55119-9 (cloth)
ISBN-10: 0-226-55120-2 (paper)

Library of Congress Cataloging-in-Publication Data

Munson, Ziad W.
   The making of pro-life activists : how social movement mobiliza-
tion works / Ziad W. Munson.
       p. cm.
   Includes bibliographical references and index.
   ISBN-13: 978-0-226-55119-7 (cloth : alk. paper)
   ISBN-13: 978-0-226-55120-3 (pbk. : alk. paper)
   ISBN-10: 0-226-55119-9 (cloth : alk. paper)
   ISBN-10: 0-226-55120-2 (pbk. : alk. paper)
   1. Pro-life movement—United States—History. 2. Pro-choice
movement—United States—History. 3. Social action—United States—
History. 4. Social movements—United States—History. I. Title.
   HQ767.5.U5M86 2008
   363.46—dc22

                                              2008024436

For Amy

Contents

Illustrations

Acknowledgments

Writing does not come easily to me. I am therefore especially grateful to all the people who have been generous with their time, expertise, and support over the several years in which I have been working on this project. The book began as my doctoral research in Harvard's Sociology Department. I thus continue to owe thanks to members of my original dissertation committee: Theda Skocpol, Kathy Newman, Andy Andrews, and Bob Wuthnow. Each helped me turn the loose collection of sometimes half-baked ideas I brought them into a completed study. Several other scholars also took the time to listen to my ideas and share their advice, especially in the beginning stages of the project. Thanks to Nancy Ammerman, Dallas Blanchard, Kristen Luker, and Rhys Williams for their feedback on my many proposals, memos, and draft chapters. Mike Beers, Bayliss Camp, Susan Dumais, Kate Ellis, Gaby Gonzalez, Liz Gorman, Heather Johnson, Andy Karch, Monica McDermott, Omar McRoberts, and members of the department's Social Movement Workshop all provided helpful comments on different pieces of this work. Irene Bloemraad was especially helpful in her willingness to read, reread, and re-reread iterations of my writing. A special thanks to Andy John and Judy Lasker for their careful reading of the entire manuscript. Doug Mitchell at the University of Chicago Press helped me enormously in his shepherding of the manuscript through the many stages of the revision process.

I also wish to thank Cherie Potts for all her help in the monumental task of transcribing my interview tapes.

Ruth and Eric Oser in Charleston, South Carolina, and Paul Samuels in the Twin Cities of Minneapolis/St. Paul, Minnesota, generously opened their homes to me for months at a time while I was conducting my fieldwork in those cities. And the hundreds of people in each of the four cities I visited, both inside and outside the pro-life movement, require a special thanks for making this research possible. I have learned a great deal from their willingness to give their time and share their experiences and beliefs with me.

I was fortunate to receive funding for this project from a number of sources. Thanks to Harvard's DeWolfe Howe Fund for the Study of Civil Liberties and the Hauser Center's Doctoral Fellowship, and the National Science Foundation Dissertation Improvement Grant for their financial support while I was collecting data, and to Lehigh's Faculty Research Grants and Franz Fellowships for support while I wrote and revised the manuscript.

My wife, Amy, has been thoroughly supportive throughout the project, not only with kind words and deeds but also with the keen eye of an editor. Thank you. Thanks, too, to Willow and Elliot, who endured this book as a regular excuse for not playing with trains or going to the playground. And thank you as well to my friend Burt Ditkowsky, who always knew when to call and reassure me I was on the right track. Having a cheerleader in your camp makes an enormous difference.

ONE

Explaining Mobilization in the American Pro-life Movement

"It's a shocking thing when you come to the realization of what they're doing and how many women are maimed, let alone the kids that are killed. And the fact that they feel every bit of that abortion. Every bit of pain, just like we feel, they feel, you know, while you're slicing and dicing and sucking them out of the womb. There's no nice way to do it." Tim,[1] a pro-life activist in Oklahoma City, is explaining his view of abortion. "I more than 100 percent believe that abortion is killing an innocent human being. No amount of research or anything else will ever change my mind that from the time of conception, there's a child there. I mean my mind is set and it isn't gonna change." Tim sees abortion not only as wrong in and of itself but also as tied to many other issues. He believes, for example, that the controversy over so-called partial-birth abortion[2] is really about "the selling and buying of body parts for kids, the billion-dollar industry that it is, you know, UPS and FedEx shipping body parts all over the country and saying they don't know what's going on."

In Tim's mind, these problems can ultimately be traced to the country's turn away from God. "If you don't believe in a Creator and you don't believe anything is created, then why does it matter if human life is destroyed, or if it's a fetus or a baby or whatever?" Tim asks rhetorically.

"Who cares? All you care about is, you know, your next meal or your next drink or your next roll in the hay with hopefully somebody from the opposite sex." For Tim, God is the only solution to our moral decline. "This country is going to go south if God doesn't turn it around. That's the bottom line."

In Charleston, South Carolina, Jerome also thinks abortion is wrong. "I believe that there are some foundational truths that are eternal foundational truths," says Jerome, "and murder—killing babies, abortion—is one of them." Like Tim, Jerome has a dualistic worldview that he roots in his faith in God. Abortion "is not about politics, is not about choice," Jerome says, "it's about truth and what is right and wrong. And killing a baby, killing anybody, is not right." Jerome, too, draws a connection between the abortion issue and a larger moral decline in America. "The way that our country has gone? . . . People are getting what they deserve, unfortunately."

Both men are similar in other ways as well. Jerome is a forty-four-year-old married father of five, and Tim is a thirty-eight-year-old married father of four. Both grew up in rural areas, attended small colleges, and married shortly after graduation. They were both raised as Methodists, and both have since become members of more conservative churches—Tim in a nondenominational church and Jerome in an evangelical Presbyterian congregation. An important difference between Tim and Jerome, however, is that Tim is an activist in the pro-life movement and Jerome is not. Tim is regularly involved in pro-life activity and sits on the board of directors of a major pro-life organization in Oklahoma City. Although Jerome also believes that abortion is simply murder by a different name and even knows many people who are involved in the movement, he himself has never become involved.

This book seeks to explain this important difference between Tim and Jerome. How did Tim become an activist? Why hasn't Jerome ever "put his money where his mouth is"? I answer these questions by developing a model of how people get involved in the pro-life movement.[3] The model focuses attention on the *process* by which people become activists rather than on any different individual attributes they might have. Ultimately, the explanation of how Tim's and Jerome's stories differ shows how beliefs about social and moral issues are as much the product of social movement participation as they are the impetus for such involvement. The analysis here thus questions our conventional understanding of the relationship between ideas and action, and in doing so builds on and refines what we already know about how people become involved in all kinds of different social and political activities.

Who Becomes a Pro-life Activist?

The stories of Tim and Jerome highlight a question scholars and prac-
titioners have asked repeatedly in the study of social movements: why
do some people become mobilized into a social movement while others do not? Scholars have generally addressed this question by focusing on how individual attributes of activists differ from those of nonactivists. Doug McAdam (1986), for example, takes this approach in his
classic study of participants in the 1964 Freedom Summer civil rights
campaign. He found that the participants had greater numbers of organizational affiliations, higher levels of previous civil rights experience,
and more extensive ties to other participants than those who withdrew
from the campaign. David Meyer (2007) summarizes the research on
the attributes of activists since McAdam's study by noting that activists
in most movements are more politically active, better educated, and
wealthier than the population as a whole.

In the case of the abortion debate, research has focused on comparing the characteristics of pro-life activists with their counterparts
in the pro-choice movement. In terms of demographics, both Donald
Granberg (1981) and Kristin Luker (1984) found pro-life activists are
less educated, less wealthy, and more likely to be married, Catholic, and
live outside of major cities than pro-choice activists. This same research
also found those involved in the pro-life movement to be more religious and have more traditional views of sex, marriage, and the family
than do those involved in the pro-choice movement. These generaliza-
tions about the demographic and attitudinal characteristics of pro-life
activists have been echoed and reinforced, albeit with less empirical
data, by subsequent influential work (Tribe 1990; Faludi 1991).

The focus on individual attributes begins to paint a picture of pro-
life activists, but it is ultimately inadequate for understanding why Tim
mobilized into the movement while Jerome did not. First, the empirical evidence that the individual characteristics of those in the pro-life
movement differ substantially from the general population is weak.
More recent studies of the abortion debate in Fargo, North Dakota
(Ginsburg 1989/1998), and direct-action activists in St. Louis, Missouri
(Maxwell 2002), found little evidence of demographic differences between pro-life and pro-choice activists. Moreover, much of the research
on activism around abortion has focused on comparing pro-life and
pro-choice activists rather than comparing activists and *non*activists.[4]
These studies are thus of limited help in answering the question being
posed here.

There is also a strong theoretical reason to develop a deeper understanding of who becomes an activist. The problem lies in the inability of any explanation based on differences in attributes to account for the vast majority of people who share the same attributes as pro-life activists and yet are not part of the movement. One would be hard-pressed, for example, to find differences in the characteristics of Tim and Jerome that could explain why one is so active in the movement while the other is entirely uninvolved. This problem parallels a similar one in criminology: no matter how many individual traits are correlated with criminal behavior, there will always be *more* people who share those traits who are *not* criminals (Sampson and Laub 1993). Logicians call this problem the fallacy of affirming the consequent. We may identify a whole set of characteristics we attribute to pro-life activists, but not all activists will ever share all of those characteristics. Moreover, many nonactivists will have these same attributes. The causal connection between individual attributes and activism will therefore always be weak, no matter how many individual characteristics we identify or how many people we include.

In this study, I focus on developing a model of the process by which individuals come to participate in the pro-life movement. Becoming an activist is a dynamic, multistage process, not a singular event or discrete decision (Klandermans 2004; Schussman and Soule 2005). We thus need a rich description and theoretical focus on this process, how it develops, and how it affects those who get involved. Individual attributes are important, but my emphasis here is on understanding *how* individuals come to participate in order to develop a deeper, fuller account of becoming an activist than just the different attributes of people can provide. My goal is to offer an explanation that accounts not only for why Tim has become an activist and Jerome has not but also for the full range of different paths to activism followed by the tens of thousands of others in the movement.

How Do Pro-life Beliefs Matter in the Movement?

In answering the question of how individuals become pro-life activists, it is necessary to address a second important question regarding the movement they are joining: what role do personal ideas and beliefs about abortion play in the mobilization process? Tim and Jerome have very similar views on abortion, at least on the surface. What more do we need to know about their beliefs to differentiate the beliefs of activists from those of nonactivists? Is there even a difference between the two? How are beliefs important for understanding how people become activists?

Scholars typically treat the role of beliefs in social movements in one of three different ways. The standard approach is to look at the role of ideas in social movements under the rubric of frame analysis (Snow et al. 1986; Snow and Benford 1992; Benford and Snow 2000), in which the focus lies on the ties between the beliefs of the individual and the ideology of the movement. Ideas are seen as possessing mobilizing potential to the extent that they can be made to resonate with the beliefs of potential recruits.[5] The second way is to see ideas as *the* central offering of a social movement: a social movement's core task is to reflect and affirm the identities and beliefs of its members. This view is common in new social movement theory (Inglehart 1977; Melucci 1989; Larana, Johnston, and Gusfield 1994). Rationalist explanations offer still a third approach, incorporating ideas and beliefs as a component of motivation. Beliefs are the impetus for people to get involved; activism is a way in which people express and act on their ideas (Lichbach 1994; Mason 1984; Muller and Opp 1986).

These approaches share a common assumption that individual beliefs logically and causally precede social movement participation. They conceptualize the link between belief and action in terms of individuals who have ideas about social issues, and only after these ideas are consistent with the ideology of a social movement is mobilization possible. In the case of the framing literature, for example, the challenge is to understand how movements frame issues in a way that will appeal to or draw in conscience adherents—that is, those who already have ideas consonant with the movement's cause. The task, then, is to understand how movements convince those who share their beliefs and goals to take action (Benford 1993).

One of the central claims I make in this analysis is that the common assumption underlying these three approaches is incorrect. In the pro-life movement, at least, many individuals get involved in the movement before they develop meaningful pro-life beliefs. Action in the movement actually precedes commitment to pro-life ideas or the development of pro-life "frames." The data I present contest the notion that social movements draw their members primarily from larger constituencies of those who already have sympathetic beliefs about an issue. The pro-life movement draws on people with a remarkably wide range of preexisting ideas about abortion for its potential recruits; those who already consider themselves "pro-life" are not the only ones who get involved. My data show that many individuals who become activists are at best ambivalent, and in many cases decidedly pro-choice, in their views on abortion before getting involved. Their views change during the actual process of becoming activists—that is, in the process of becoming mobilized.

Becoming an activist does not, however, have the same implications for the beliefs of each person who gets involved. The movement is not rooted in a single worldview, nor does it possess a unified "master frame" (Snow and Benford 1992; Benford and Snow 2000). As a result, the beliefs about abortion that new activists encounter are often fragmented and contradictory. Activists' beliefs develop differently depending on how they get involved in the movement and which organizations they encounter.

Tim understands abortion as the natural, evil consequence of a fallen society. "I mean, really, abortion is perfect for this day and age," he says. "I mean it really is what *should* be happening. As sinful as the rest of society is, abortion is really in vogue for the general society." He also sees conspiracy in abortion—conspiracy to keep it legal, conspiracy to sell human body parts, conspiracy to make money—ideas that parallel his larger worldview, in which conspiracies are rampant in politics, the economy, and society. Although his views are not unusual among pro-life activists, they are far from representative.

Robert, an activist in the Twin Cities of Minneapolis and St. Paul, provides a much different view of pro-life activist belief. Like Tim, he believes that abortion is the killing of a child and therefore wrong. But Robert understands the issue in much different terms and situates it in a much different worldview from Tim's. Robert, a forty-four-year-old married father of three, first became involved in social movement activism as a student leader of the antiwar movement in the 1960s and later was part of the Central American peace movement of the 1980s. He understands abortion as a "capitalist plot that has to do with integrating women into the workforce." "The people who gave you napalm and Agent Orange," Robert says, "are now giving you abortion at home." Although he describes himself as a spiritual person, he is not religious and neither was raised as a churchgoer nor attends today. Although Robert finds common cause with Tim on the issue of abortion, they disagree on virtually every other social issue. "Part of my concern is that there is a resurgence of cultural conservatism in this country," Robert tells me, "and there is no resurgence of what I'd like to see: pro-life, left-wing radicalism, you know, that isn't there at all."

The views of Tim and Robert in many ways represent the two poles of pro-life beliefs. They demonstrate the surprisingly broad spectrum of ideas about abortion among those involved in the movement. These ideas fracture the movement into different social movement streams, consisting of mutually exclusive sets of organizations, people, and activities. Activists find themselves involved not in some singular and homogeneous movement but instead in particular streams of the movement that seldom work with or interact with the groups or individuals in other streams. Streams are defined and maintained by differences in beliefs about the abortion issue and, in particular, differences in beliefs about appropriate forms of activism. If I am right about the importance of the mobilization process in the development of individual beliefs, then these streams are enormously consequential in how people come to understand the abortion issue. The kinds of beliefs activists hold about the abortion issue are a function of the stream in which they become active.

Beliefs about abortion, beliefs about appropriate moral and political action, and beliefs about the movement matter to the movement, but they matter in different ways from what we would traditionally expect. Opposition to abortion is rooted in very different moral understandings among activists. These understandings cannot be collected in a single, coherent worldview. In fact, they are often in considerable tension with one another. Perhaps most important, different understandings of abortion structure both the movement and the process by which people become activists and adopt a pro-life view of the world. In part, this study is thus about more carefully specifying how and (especially) when beliefs matter in the mobilization process.

What Is the Relationship between Religion and the Pro-life Movement?

This pro-life worldview often, although not universally, includes a strong commitment to a religious faith. The common stereotype of the pro-life movement has it deeply enmeshed in religion—an outgrowth of conservative religious faith and commitment. Certainly Tim's story fits this view. His understanding of abortion is rooted firmly in a Christian faith in God. "God's laws have been around forever. . . . The absolute truth is the absolute truth, and it ain't gonna change. And that's exactly where all this pro-life abortion stuff is. You're killing a human being whether you want to say it or not." Robert is also an activist but uncomfortable with this kind of religiosity. One example he gives is prayer at sporting events: "One of my reactions, being from a prosecular background, I mean, they used to have prayers before football games. And that always struck me as so idiotic. I mean, as if God cared about this damned football game." Based on his "prosecular" background and suspicion of religious invocations, Robert does not see the abortion issue in religious terms. He bristles at the suggestion that it is a religious issue. The contrast between Robert on the one hand and Tim and Jerome on the other reveals a kind of division within the movement that suggests a third question I address in this book: what is the relationship between religion and the pro-life movement?

The question arises because many have held out religion as the key explanatory variable in understanding the pro-life movement. Kerry Jacoby (1998) sees pro-life activism as more of a religious movement than a social or political one. She therefore analyzes the history of the movement as a series of religious ideas that were incorporated first as Catholics founded the initial organizations and then as Protestant fundamentalists and evangelicals began to fill in the ranks of the movement beginning in the 1980s. A proliferation of journalistic accounts has also contributed to the view that the movement is an outgrowth of religious faith. The titles of the volumes themselves tell the story: *Articles of Faith* (Gorney 1998), *Wrath of Angels* (Risen and Thomas 1998), *Live from the Gates of Hell* (Reiter 2000), *Absolute Convictions* (Press 2006).

The religious picture of the movement, however, is complicated by division among activists over precisely what role faith should play in activism—a division highlighted by the different attitudes of Tim and Robert toward religious faith. Tim sees it as the central issue; Robert sees faith as something completely separate from abortion beliefs. The story becomes even more complex when you consider that activists are frequently either Roman Catholics or Protestant evangelicals—religious traditions that have a long history of animosity and conflict with each other in the United States. Indeed, the tension continues to be divisive within the movement. One priest in Charleston explained the relative lack of Catholic clergy involvement in the area as due to priests' "being so busy trying not to piss off the Baptists." Conflict arises between Catholics and Protestants over who will lead different organizations and campaigns, the kinds of prayers said, the songs that are sung, and the understandings of why abortion is wrong and what must be done to stop it.

In this study, I find (not surprisingly) that pro-life activists are more religious on the whole than the general population. Robert's views notwithstanding, activists tend to have stronger religious beliefs, attend church more often, and be more involved in religious activity outside of the church. At the same time, however, I find that churches' getting directly involved in the movement or exhorting congregants to protest in the streets is the exception rather than the rule.

Individual activists seldom understand their activism as a consequence of some prior religious faith. Instead, the relationship between religion and the pro-life movement is better understood if we consider the two as overlapping spheres of action. My focus on the mobilization process provides an opportunity to analyze not only the role that religion plays in how some individuals become activists but also the surprising frequency with which activism affects religious faith. Activists who participate in discussions, meetings, events, and campaigns of the pro-life movement are not simply influenced by religion. They are also simultaneously reinforcing the vitality of religious faith in their own lives and in their social worlds. Social movement action among pro-life activists is often simultaneously and irreducibly both religious practice and social movement practice. As a result, the relationship between religion and the movement is not a one-way street. On the individual level, religious choices are being made on the basis of pro-life commitments. On the organizational level, individual pro-life activists and pro-life groups put pressure on clergy, congregations, and denominations to become more vocally and actively pro-life in their theologies, teachings, and activities. Thus, not only does religion affect the pro-life movement, but the movement can also affect religion (as it certainly *tries* hard to do).

This analysis of religion and the pro-life movement builds on a growing body of work that documents the rich and nuanced relationship among religion, politics, and people's everyday lives (Bender 2003; Moon 2004; Ammerman 2006). It suggests that we need to break out of the long-standing tendency in much of sociological research to treat religion solely as an independent (and largely immutable) variable. The relationship between religion and the pro-life movement suggests that the process of becoming an activist is a conversion process comparable to a religious conversion (Lofland and Stark 1965). Most important, conversion to the movement can itself be the catalyst for a religious conversion.

Studying Activists

Starting with the puzzle of why Tim has become a activist and Jerome has not, I have now introduced the three questions important for understanding that puzzle: Who becomes an activist? How do beliefs matter when a person gets involved in pro-life activism? What role does religion play in such activism? I address these questions through data drawn from the contemporary pro-life movement in the United States. My approach to studying pro-life activists was to balance the twin goals of conducting a national study and examining grassroots mobilization at the local level. To accomplish these goals at the same time, I organized data collection around four cities: Oklahoma City, Oklahoma; Charleston, South Carolina; the Twin Cities of Minneapolis/St. Paul, Minnesota; and Boston, Massachusetts. I chose these cities, each in a different region of the United States, to maximize variation on two potentially important dimensions: level of activism and religious composition. Because I am interested in explaining mobilization in the movement, it is necessary to focus on places where the overall level of mobilization varies. Oklahoma City and the Twin Cities are metro areas that have witnessed a great deal of pro-life movement mobilization; in Charleston and Boston the movement is less visible. Because I am interested in exploring the role of beliefs and the role of religion in the mobilization process, it is also necessary to focus on places in which the religious culture varies. The Twin Cities and Boston both have large Catholic majorities; Oklahoma City and Charleston, by contrast, are dominated by evangelical Protestant populations.

Ultimately, the variation on these two dimensions plays only a very small role in the model of how people become activists. The mobilization process, as well as the role of pro-life beliefs and the relationship between religion and the movement, turns out not to depend very much on the overall level of mobilization or religious composition of individual communities. However, inclusion of different cities allows for greater confidence in the representativeness of the data and the generalizability of the findings than would be possible with data drawn from only one community or region of the United States.

Organizational Data

I spent between three and five months in residence in each of the four cities collecting data on the movement. In each location, I first identified every pro-life organization involved in any kind of movement activity. Organizations were identified through a review of newspaper archives, interviews with local journalists, yellow pages searches, talking with protesters in front of abortion clinics, and referrals from other pro-life groups. Organizations were considered part of the pro-life movement if they self-identified the bulk of their activity as a part of the "pro-life cause."

I interviewed the executive director or president of every organization and in some cases held additional interviews with other key informants within the group. I collected information on each organization's founding and development; structure; principal activities, events, and projects; size in terms of leaders, staff, volunteers, and members; funding (amount and sources); and relationship to national pro-life organizations and other local pro-life groups, churches and other religious organizations, and various political groups. I also collected all brochures, pamphlets, newsletters, press releases, audio- and videotapes, training guides, conference handbooks, and any other material available that was produced directly by the organization. A total of thirty-two major organizations were eventually identified and studied in this way across the four cities.

The organizational data are an important part of the research design for answering each of the three questions posed here. First, answering the question of who gets involved in the pro-life movement requires some understanding of the organized groups in which they are getting involved. After all, formal organizations are the primary vehicles through which pro-life social movement activism takes place. Second, organizations play a crucial role in the link between beliefs and action, as they are key venues in which individual beliefs about the abortion issue are developed and shaped. Finally, evaluating the impact of religion on the movement requires that we know something about the kinds of organizations that make up the movement. For example, were they founded by religious institutions? Are they run by religious leaders? We also need to know about the sources of organizational support. For example, do the organizations receive funding from religious bodies? Do they hold meetings in churches? The organizational data provide a solid starting point for tackling each of the central questions of this book.

Individual Data

The bulk of the data for this study comes from in-depth life-history interviews conducted with activists and nonactivists in each of the four cities. Activists in each city were initially found through a search for individuals who had published a pro-life editorial in the major local newspaper in the last five years, referrals from pro-life organizational leaders, and referrals from individuals I met while observing pro-life protest events and attending other movement activities such as fund-raisers, chapter meetings, banquets, and so forth. Additional activists were subsequently identified through these initial contacts. From names gathered with this snowball technique, I then selected individuals to be interviewed, with a focus on ensuring I had a wide range of ages, religious backgrounds, levels and types of commitment, and involvement in the different streams of the movement—what Anselm Strauss and Juliet Corbin (1990) call a theoretical sample.

Nonactivists were identified by asking activists for names of friends, acquaintances, neighbors, or colleagues who they thought might be pro-life and yet were not actively involved in the pro-life movement. Choosing nonactivists in this way ensures a pool of individuals who are demographically similar to the activists and therefore a reasonable comparison group. I define nonactivists for the purpose of this study as individuals who have never regularly attended pro-life meetings or rallies and have never regularly donated their time or money to a pro-life organization. Activism is measured across a person's entire life, so that an individual who was once active for a considerable period but no longer contributes or participates in any way is still considered an activist here. By contrast, making a single donation to a pro-life organization, or writing one letter about the issue to a political representative, does not qualify an individual as an activist in my study.

I was initially concerned that it might be difficult to draw a clear distinction between activists and nonactivists. Where, after all, do you draw the line? In practice, however, I found that individuals either are very involved for a period in their life or have never been involved at all. The boundary between the two groups is thus empirically very clear. Kristin Luker (1984, 250) similarly found in her study that people either were involved in the movement "as a consuming passion" or were no more involved than having their name on a mailing list.

Comparing activists and nonactivists with similar stated opinions and social ties is an important element of my research design. Much has been written about pro-life activism solely on the basis of information from individuals already deeply involved in the movement (Ginsburg 1989/1998; Luker 1984; Blanchard and Prewitt 1993; Maxwell 2002). In order to fully understand the boundary between mobilization and nonactivism, however, it is important to know something about those who stand just to each side of the dividing line. Rather than comparing pro-life with pro-choice activists, which is the way in which the movement has been analyzed in the past, the present study seeks to understand the pro-life movement through a comparison with those who are most like pro-lifers but who nonetheless remain uninvolved in any sustained way.

In addition to approximately 50 interviews with organizational leaders, I conducted a total of 111 individual life-history interviews, 82 with activists and 29 with nonactivists. Roughly one-quarter of these interviews were completed in each of the four cities. The sample includes individuals in every major racial category, ranging in age from fourteen to eighty-five; three-fifths of the respondents were Catholic and two-fifths Protestant. Of those I contacted for an interview, only 10 declined to participate, making for an excellent response rate of 92 percent. Interviews were conducted in a semistructured format designed to collect detailed information about the participants' personal biography, relationship to the pro-life movement, involvement in other social movements and political and civic organizations, ideas and beliefs about abortion, and relationship to religious institutions and ideas. The interview format and content were pretested in interviews with several activists in Orange County, New York, and then modified for use with actual study participants.

The interviews were a compromise between the shorter, structured interviews that typify large interview projects with a staff of interviewers and hundreds of participants and the much longer life-history interview projects that often include no more than a handful of participants. This compromise has a number of advantages. Unlike with structured interviews, I was able to adapt each interview to the individual biography of the participant. Rather than trying to force respondents into predefined categories by using prewritten questions, I allowed participants to provide narrative responses to open-ended queries. They were thus able to use their own vocabulary and ways of thinking in providing answers to each of my questions. I adopted this approach with an eye toward understanding the process of becoming an activist rather than just collecting lists of covariates of activism. This semistructured interview format is ideally suited to answering questions about social processes (Weiss 1994; Maxwell 1996; Seidman 1998), which is exactly how becoming an activist is conceptualized here.

At the same time, however, the interviews were briefer and considerably more focused than more anthropological life-history interviews. Such interviews, often lasting five hours or more and in some cases

spanning multiple days, are an onerous prospect for potential interviewees and would have yielded minimal additional value for this
study. The most common reservation I encountered in asking people
for interviews was the three-hour time commitment involved. Of the
ten people who ultimately refused to be interviewed, seven of them
gave time as the primary reason. By decreasing the time commitment
of potential participants, I increased the number of people willing to
participate in the study. Shorter interviews also helped ensure that individuals less committed to the movement were willing and able to
participate. More complete information on the study's methodology
can be found in the appendix.

Looking Ahead

The goal of this book is to provide a new model for understanding how
individuals become social movement activists. In doing so, I build on
and refine arguments made in the study of social movements, the sociology of religion, and civil society. The central argument here is that
we can do better than simply enumerating a set of static individual attributes that predict activism. Becoming an activist involves a process,
the steps of which can be empirically identified and analyzed. A focus
on the mobilization process reveals that beliefs about controversial issues are as often a product of mobilization as they are a motivation
for getting involved in the first place. Beliefs about abortion are developed and reproduced by the movement and transmitted primarily to
those who get involved. Beliefs structure and segment the movement,
and ideas about abortion lead people to adopt or rethink core religious
commitments. Each of these arguments is developed in detail in the
chapters that follow.

The structure of the argument I develop here differs somewhat from
that used in many studies of social movements. My analysis is not organized around the standard perspective of an omniscient analyst,
with each chapter building on the one that precedes it, to an ultimate
"punch line" in the final chapter. Instead, the book is organized around
the trajectory of an ideal-typical activist into the movement. Thus, the
book's organization reflects the order in which activists themselves are
likely to encounter different issues as they become mobilized into the
movement. I begin by looking at people's beliefs about the abortion
issue before they get involved and trace the process by which they be-

come mobilized. I then move to an examination of how activists, once involved, relate to others in the movement and the larger terrain of the movement of which they have become a part. Finally, I consider the effects participation in the movement has on a particularly salient part of the lives of many pro-life activists—religion. This activist's-eye orientation allows me to meld the theoretical arguments of the analysis with the rich empirical data I have drawn from the many interviews with both activists and nonactivists.

Chapter 2 begins with the question of what leads an individual into pro-life activism in the first place. In exploring this question, the chapter fully develops one of the key claims of the book—that individuals actually get involved in the movement before they develop clear pro-life beliefs. We commonly understand participation in social movements as motivated by concern over a cause. Although this understanding holds true for those already involved in a movement, the biographies of pro-life activists show that concern over abortion was not what brought them to the movement in the first place. In other words, movement action commonly *precedes* the formation of strong pro-life sentiments among activists.

Chapter 3 then looks at the mobilization process in detail. I argue that becoming an activist is characterized by a series of specific steps: contact with the movement at a life turning point, initial activism, the development of pro-life beliefs, and finally full movement participation. The chapter demonstrates that, consistent with much previous research, organizational affiliations and social networks are critical to this overall process. Organizational and relational ties are most often responsible for bringing potential activists into contact with the movement for the first time, thereby making further stages of the mobilization process possible.

The following two chapters describe and analyze the movement terrain activists face once they become a part of the pro-life movement. Chapter 4 provides a short history of the abortion debate in the United States, showing how the past development of the movement affects the way new activists today come to understand the abortion issue and their own pro-life activism. Abortion has attracted the attention of grassroots activists only in the last few decades, and the historical unfolding of the issue has important implications for the debate right up to the present. Chapter 5 then gives a more detailed overview of the movement today, including a focus on the variety of organizations and beliefs that compose it. The particular constellation of different beliefs about abortion present within the movement proves to be important to those becoming activists. Although the organizations and activists that make up the movement agree on a common goal for the movement, they differ strongly in their beliefs about the most efficient and morally appropriate means to achieve that goal. The movement is in fact structured by these differences in belief into separate and mutually exclusive social movement streams. These same streams exist in all four of the cities I studied and help to both provide a picture of how activist beliefs develop and suggest how new recruits into the movement ultimately reenact and reinforce the existing cleavages within the movement.

I return to a central focus on the beliefs of the movement in chapter 6, where I analyze the pro-life moral universe. Pro-life activists, once mobilized, do not all accept a singular worldview. Activists share a common opposition to abortion, but this opposition is often rooted in very different values and understandings of the issue. The views of Tim and Robert that I have already outlined foreshadow the wide range of beliefs about abortion present in the movement, beliefs that are frequently in tension with one another. These tensions tend to diminish sustained activism and efforts to achieve the common goal of the larger movement.

The pro-life movement does not homogenize the worldviews of those who participate, but this is not to say that activists' beliefs are static or uninfluenced by their participation. Chapter 7 addresses the third central question of the book, regarding the relationship between religion and pro-life activism. Analyzing the way in which many social movement activities are simultaneously religious and political, it shows that the pro-life movement is an important influence on religious institutions and faith. After activists have been involved in the movement, they are prone to reorient their religious belief system in massive and sometimes surprising ways. The process of becoming an activist thus does not stop once a person is involved in the movement; activism can bleed out into other aspects of a person's life and worldview.

Together, these chapters reveal the contemporary pro-life movement in action through the eyes of the activists themselves and demonstrate the rich connections that exist between beliefs and the trajectory of social movement participation. Modeling the process of becoming a pro-life activist does not just speak to issues related to the abortion debate or even social movement participation. It also forces us to address more abstract concerns of long-standing interest in the social sciences:

the relationship between social structure and individual agency, the tie between beliefs and action, and the role of traditional religious faith in contemporary society. Understanding how people become pro-life activists offers us a window into a much larger set of concerns about our social world.

TWO

Learning to Care

I met Linda at her home in one of the endless cul-de-sac neighborhoods that surround the Twin Cities. At fifty-three, Linda is a homemaker and mother of two children. Linda has what many would describe as an alpha personality. She has tremendous energy and confidence, which came through in how she narrated her life and experience with the pro-life movement. She is the woman who always organized the neighborhood block parties, led the local PTA, and volunteered to head the raffle at her church's fund-raiser. She is proud of her accomplishments as a mother, wife, neighbor, and pro-life activist and is happy to talk about them. In fact, I was not the first sociologist to interview her. As a young woman, she was interviewed by Luther Gerlach (1970) as part of his study of social movement dynamics.

Linda became involved in the pro-life movement even before the famous *Roe v. Wade* decision in 1973 that legalized abortion in the United States. Her road to activism started in a very mundane way: a regular visit to her obstetrician. Her doctor was Fred Mecklenburg, who happened to be one of the early leaders of the pro-life movement in Minnesota and the country. Over the course of their conversation that day, Mecklenburg explained that the Minnesota legislature was currently holding hearings on liberalizing the state's abortion law. He urged her to attend the hearings and even offered her a ride to the statehouse; Linda agreed to go.

She agreed but was not in fact opposed to abortion at the time. As she explains, she went out of a sense of personal obligation to Dr. Mecklenburg, a man who had helped her through a difficult pregnancy and someone she considered a "casual" friend. In other words, she agreed because she wanted to please someone she knew personally, not because she considered herself pro-life. In fact, Linda had spent much of her life predisposed to the pro-choice point of view: "By the time I knew what abortion was, I was already sensitive to the feminist movement. I think that I was always a bit of a feminist in the sense that girls can do anything boys can do, and probably better. And so, when they were talking about abortion in terms of women's rights, I wasn't closed to it; I wouldn't have objected." As a young woman, Linda was committed to many of the causes championed by the civil rights and peace movements. As a teenager, she used to send the money she earned babysitting to the ACLU to help it fight racism, and as an adult, she had refused to pay her telephone taxes to protest the Vietnam War.

Linda began to rethink her views on abortion after attending the state legislative hearings. Sitting with Mecklenburg and several other early pro-life activists, she understood proponents of liberalizing abortion law to be arguing that abortion is needed to "eliminate" disabled children and those conceived when a black man rapes a white woman: "I'd never been to the state capitol, except for a tour when I was in the eighth grade. And I went over, . . . and I heard them frame this issue in terms of those things. Rape by a black man, I mean, things like that. And I thought, 'How awful.' This is not only a tragedy in terms of human life but a tragedy in terms of the whole political system." Linda continued to stay in touch with the activists she met at those hearings. Soon she began attending meetings with other pro-life activists and—after *Roe v. Wade*—organized her own local chapter of Minnesota Citizens Concerned for Life (MCCL), the state's largest pro-life group. Although the intensity of her activism has ebbed and flowed over the last thirty-five years, she remains active in the pro-life movement even today.

Linda's trajectory into the movement is typical of many pro-life activists. Her biography, even in this bare-bones retelling, also suggests a need to question the standard story we tell of how social movements recruit new members. Conventional wisdom suggests that social movements are forms of expressive behavior. People get involved because they care about the environment, women's rights, the exploitation of wage laborers, peace, or abortion. Preexisting beliefs, in other words, are understood to motivate and underlie commitment to the cause. From this perspective, the task of understanding pro-life activism is to understand why some people come to regard the abortion issue as so important that they are willing to contribute time and resources, or risk arrest, to end it.

My data on the pro-life movement challenge this conventional wisdom. The link between beliefs and action in social movements must be turned on its head: real action often precedes meaningful beliefs about an issue. Demographic and attitudinal differences between activists and nonactivists cannot explain why some people join the pro-life movement and others do not. Instead, mobilization occurs when people are drawn into activism through organizational and relational ties, not when they form strong beliefs about abortion. Beliefs about abortion are often undeveloped, incoherent, and inconsistent until individuals become actively engaged with the movement. The "process of conviction" (Maxwell 2002) is the result of mobilization, not a necessary prerequisite for it. Linda first took action—she attended a political event at the personal behest of someone she already knew and respected. Only after that experience, and in no small measure because of it, did her pro-life beliefs develop.

This chapter first presents the conventional wisdom in more detail, especially as it has been applied to pro-life activists in the past, and shows the limitations of that perspective. I then use comparisons of activists and nonactivists to show that abortion beliefs are seldom what motivate people to first get involved. Like Linda, most activists begin their involvement without abortion being the explicit focus of attention. Even more surprisingly, this initial involvement often occurs when their position on abortion is ambivalent or even pro-choice. Nonactivists' understanding of the abortion issue confirms the importance of the movement itself for shaping and developing pro-life beliefs. Nonactivists express incoherent and vague beliefs about the issue. They can seldom articulate even basic pro-life ideas, such as why abortion is wrong or whether abortion should be illegal. Pro-life activists learn to care, a learning process that begins with activism instead of activism being the culmination of commitment to any particular belief system.

The Conventional Wisdom

Beliefs precede action—this is a basic assumption in the study of collective action and politics. As Sidney Verba, Kay Lehman Schlozman, and Henry Brady's influential study of civic voluntarism notes (1995, 12),

"Citizens have complex preferences across a myriad of issues; they hold these preferences with varying degrees of intensity; and they can express these preferences by engaging in any of a variety of participatory acts." This common assumption carries with it a causal argument; namely, that individuals first form ideas (or preferences) and then act on those preferences by getting involved in various forms of collective action. Alexis de Tocqueville was using this same assumption more than a century earlier when he wrote about the associational spirit of Americans—forever forming associations to act on their (preexisting) needs and beliefs.

The social movement literature proceeds from the same starting point: a social movement recruits from that subset of the population who already believe in its core ideas. In the jargon of social movement scholarship, movements draw their activists from those who are already "conscience adherents." Bert Klandermans provides an example of this kind of analysis that directly addresses the issue of individual mobilization:

Generating attitudinal support—the process through which a social movement organization "tries to obtain support for its viewpoint" (Klandermans 1984, p. 586)—we will call "consensus mobilization"; generating behavioral support—the attempt to "[call] up people to participate" (Klandermans 1984, p. 586)—we designate "action mobilization." . . . Successful consensus mobilization generates a pool of potential supporters, people who sympathize with the movement, and are willing to support it one way or another but are not necessarily prepared to participate in every kind of collective action. Successful action mobilization in its turn converts large proportions of those sympathizers into participants in specific movement activities. (1997, 7)

Here Klandermans makes an analytic division: movements must first generate sympathetic beliefs—consensus mobilization; only after such sympathetic beliefs are generated can people be mobilized to act on those beliefs. In a much different theoretical tradition, James Jasper (1997) attaches great importance to "moral shocks" as motivating social movement action. In both cases the underlying conceptualization is the same: visible violation of someone's existing beliefs about the world leads him or her to activism.

Previous work on the pro-life movement also adopts this causal argument. "In the beginning," writes Jacoby (1998, 79) in describing the origins of the movement, "there was only a vast, untapped sea of abortion opponents." The imagery here is of a movement responding to the beliefs of a constituency. The movement then gives collective voice and organizational power to these individual beliefs, the "untapped sea" of those outraged by legalized abortion. Consistent with this conventional wisdom, the usual way of explaining pro-life activism is to identify certain attitudes—or demographic correlates of such attitudes—that set pro-life activists apart from the general population.[1] These attitudes or demographic characteristics are then said to "account" for activism.

Attributes of Pro-life Activists

The earliest research on the pro-life movement was conducted by Donald Granberg (1981) in a study of both pro-choice and pro-life activists. He sent an eight-page questionnaire to a random sample of dues-paying members of the National Right to Life Committee (NRLC) in thirty-one states. He found that pro-life activists held more "traditional" views than the general population on premarital, extramarital, and homosexual sex; sex education in the schools; and contraception. More than 90 percent of his pro-life respondents opposed the Equal Rights Amendment, an important political issue at the time. Granberg concluded that "a conservative approach to personal morality appears to explain opposition to abortion" (p. 158). In other words, a particular set of personal beliefs leads to pro-life activism.

Scholarship since Granberg's study has continued to rely on the notion that preexisting beliefs can explain the mobilization of activists. Kristin Luker's 1984 study—perhaps the best-known analysis of the pro-life and pro-choice movements to date—used measured differences in the beliefs of pro-life and pro-choice activists regarding a variety of social and moral issues to argue that abortion activism is rooted in "two very different orientations to the world and that these orientations in turn revolve around two very different moral centers" (p. 186). More recently Carol Maxwell (2002, 90) looked at direct-action activists within the movement and concluded that their mobilization was a "linear process beginning with abortion disapproval and at some point reaching the conclusion that the most appropriate response to legal abortion was direct action." In both cases activists are seen in the same way as activists in many other studies: people who first formulate beliefs, then act on them.[2]

Even when the pro-life movement is studied in terms of the basic demographic or human capital correlates of activism, the basic causal inference is the same, rooted in the logic that demographic characteris-

Table 2.1   Demographic characteristics of activists, by study

	Luker	Granberg	Maxwell	Jacoby
Data collection year	1979	1980	1991	1992
Sample size	106	426	80	104
White (%)	n.a.	98	99	n.a.
Male (%)	38	37	40	54
College degree (%)	71	58	51	>50
Catholic (%)	75	70	29	39
Married (%)	76	87	68	n.a.
Average number of children	3.1	3.4	3.0	n.a.
Average age	42	43	41–50	34
Average household income ($)	27,410	31,700	35,000	n.a.
Income as % of national mean	130	151	83	n.a.

Sources: Granberg 1981, Maxwell 2002, and Jacoby 1998. Luker data are from the study's original interview face sheets.
Note: N.a. = not available.

tics produce different attitudes, which are then responsible for people's beliefs about abortion and hence their activism. Education, for example, might expose individuals to more diverse viewpoints and give them more life options, thus making them more accepting of abortion as a woman's personal choice. Catholics might be more likely to actively oppose abortion than mainline Protestants because of the official Catholic teaching that abortion is wrong. Demographic variables such as education and religion are thus markers for different underlying values and priorities.

Table 2.1 reports the basic demographic findings from the main studies that have been done on pro-life activists. Granberg found that almost two-thirds of the NRLC members at the time of his study were female, the vast majority were married, and they had an average of 3.4 children. Respondents were almost universally white, 70 percent were Catholic, and almost 60 percent had finished college. Luker's results were similar: 62 percent of the activists she interviewed were women, and three-quarters were married, with an average of 3.1 children. They were also mostly Catholic (75 percent), and a large majority (71 percent) had college degrees. Maxwell's and Jacoby's more recent results are similar in many respects, although their respondents were more likely to have college degrees and less likely to be Catholic than in the previous studies.[3]

So what do all the results from these different studies mean? None of the studies are truly representative of the pro-life movement as a whole. The Granberg study surveyed only members of one organization. Luker's sample comes entirely from California. Jacoby selected pro-life organizations at random but allowed the leaders of those organizations to handpick respondents to her questionnaire. Maxwell focused only on direct-action activists in a single city, not on the movement as a whole. Each of these studies is also now somewhat dated; the Granberg and Luker data are almost thirty years old, and even the more recent Maxwell and Jacoby data are from the early 1990s. A great deal has changed in the pro-life movement since then (Gorney 1998; Staggenborg 1991).[4] The data we have must therefore be interpreted with caution.

With these caveats in mind, some patterns do emerge from the four studies. Although the movement was almost certainly disproportionately female and Catholic in its earlier years (Maxwell 2002), this is no longer the case. These findings are consistent with the claims of many observers that pro-life activism saw an influx of evangelical Protestants, especially men, as the strategy of clinic rescues gained steam in the mid-1980s (Risen and Thomas 1998; Ginsburg 1989/1998). Nonetheless, Catholics remain disproportionately represented in the ranks of the pro-life movement, and activists are better off financially and better educated than the general population (like activists in many U.S. social movements). Both Granberg and Luker found average household incomes above the national mean, and college degree rates in all four studies are more than double the national average.[5] It also seems reasonable to infer from the available data that pro-life activists are more white, more often married, and have more children than the population as a whole.

Attributes Cannot Explain Mobilization

These basic statistics do help sketch an initial picture of activists. They do not, however, shed much light on the question of who becomes an activist and who does not. For one thing, none of these studies compare activists with nonactivists. Granberg and Luker compare only activists on one side of the debate with their counterparts on the other side, while Jacoby and Maxwell provide no comparisons at all. None of these studies tackle the boundary between those who are activists and those who merely express pro-life beliefs.

Attempts to explain pro-life activism based on the attributes of the people involved are plagued with other problems as well. Although previous studies have found conservative personal morality correlated with pro-life activism, the story is more complicated than the simple conclusion that pro-life activism is engendered by conservative beliefs. Beliefs and attitudes seldom line up in such tidy categories or allow lines to be drawn so easily. For example, the respondents in Jacoby's sample identified themselves as Republicans and held conservative ideas about sex, but most were also in favor of a national health insurance plan, increased federal funding for AIDS prevention, environmental protection, and affirmative action programs. Only 42 percent expressed support for the death penalty, compared to 71 percent of the general population.

My own findings on the larger moral worldviews of activists are similar. On the one hand, activists' beliefs seldom line up consistently as either conservative or liberal as defined by current American political divisions. On the other hand, activism itself changes the way activists look at other issues. For example, many in the pro-life movement have come to oppose the death penalty as part of their efforts to be "consistently pro-life." Carol, a fifty-two-year-old activist in Charleston, explains a common view among pro-life activists:[6] "I used to believe in capital punishment, but I had my whole heart changed on that; I converted from that. And I do not now believe in capital punishment; I haven't for years now, because I think that we've got a corrupt judicial system. And I think people are dying that are innocent. And if one innocent life is being lost, I just can't go for it. And I think we have the means in this day and time to be able to keep people in prison, you know, for life." Pro-life activists' moral universe is not easily mapped onto the standard conservative–liberal continuum or onto any existing categories of attitudes toward social and moral issues. As a result, it is difficult to account for activism on the basis of such preexisting beliefs.

A more theoretical difficulty lies in accounting for pro-life attitudes on the basis of other beliefs without reducing the explanation to tautology.[7] The problem is reflected in one study on abortion attitudes in which the authors conclude that "results indicated that the strongest influences on abortion attitude stemmed from belief that life begins at conception" (Tamney, Johnson, and Burton 1992, 32). Such findings

Table 2.2   Attributes of activists and nonactivists

	Activists	Nonactivists
Demographic measures		
White (%)	93	83
Male (%)	43	48
College degree (%)	71	76
Catholic (%)	66	45
Married (%)	65	62
Average number of children	2.4	1.6
Average age	48	37
Average household income ($)	72,143	61,364
Income as % of national mean	171	145
Attitudinal measures (% who favor)		
Police permits for guns	58	59
Cutting welfare spending	16	48
Sex education in public schools	23	41
Death penalty	28	34
Gay rights laws	13	7
Increased military spending	30	28

Note: $N = 82$ activists and 29 nonactivists.

should surprise no one and explain very little. Expressions of belief that life begins at conception are synonymous with a pro-life attitude; one is a measure of the other, not a cause. Moreover, studies that seek to understand pro-life activism by accounting for the pro-life attitudes of the activists assume—rather than test—the causal connection between beliefs and action.

An additional theoretical concern with the conventional approach to understanding activism is that it cannot differentiate between activists and the vastly larger group of people who have pro-life attitudes or attributes but never engage in sustained activism. Table 2.2 compares activists and nonactivists in my own sample on key attitudinal and demographic characteristics. The two groups are clearly similar in terms of their social attitudes. The table shows that support for gun regulation, gay rights, military spending, and the death penalty is much the same among nonactivists and activists. Activists are, however, much more likely to oppose sex education in the schools and further cuts in welfare spending.[8]

The two groups are also similar in terms of sex, race, education, income, and marital status. Activists are older and less affluent on average than nonactivists and are more likely to be Catholic. The larger average number of children among activists may be a function of their older average age. These data do not constitute a test of differences between the groups; the similarities between activists and nonactivists here are in part a function of the study design, as nonactivists were identified primarily through referrals from activists. Moreover, the research design does not provide a truly random sample of the two groups. The similarities between the two here do, however, demonstrate the need for an explanation of mobilization that goes beyond probabilistic statements based on differences in demographic or other kinds of characteristics. The problem is the same as that faced by scholars developing models of criminal behavior based on individual characteristics: no matter how many variables are specified and how precisely characteristics are measured, there will always be far more noncriminals than criminals who possess the given attributes of interest (Sampson and Laub 1993). In the context of the pro-life movement, far more people with high levels of education and religiosity do not become activists than become mobilized. How, then, can we account for their mobilization?

One alternative is to take seriously the idea that social movement mobilization is a process rather than a singular event. From this standpoint, we can look for the patterns in the biographies of activists and regularities in the dynamics of their becoming activists. Linda's story at the beginning of the chapter gives a taste of how one person got involved. I now turn to the stories of Ruth and Glen, two activists whose trajectory into the pro-life movement is also representative of the way many people become involved. Their stories show that the relationship between abortion beliefs and pro-life activism is often the opposite of what the conventional wisdom asserts: action frequently precedes the development of pro-life attitudes.

Two Stories of Mobilization

Ruth

Ruth is a tall, slender woman living in an upper-middle-class suburb of the Twin Cities. Now seventy-one, Ruth became a pediatric nurse after graduating from high school in Iowa. She then worked for several years before getting married and quitting her job to stay home with the first of her four children. She doesn't remember abortion being discussed at all when she was younger, even in her Catholic church. "It was just not a topic in that day and age that was really brought up much," she says. She did, however, have some direct experience with the issue; as a nurse trainee, she assisted with a patient who had come into the hospital after a botched illegal abortion. "I thought at that time, now even though our church was very much against it, . . . if it was legal, then this would be safer."

Nonetheless, Ruth did not get involved in the debate, neither then nor when the Supreme Court legalized abortion in 1973. She remembers her husband telling her about the Court's decision but did not think it was particularly important. Several years later, when her youngest children were teenagers, she decided she needed to spend some time outside of the home. She considered various volunteer opportunities for several months and ultimately decided to become a volunteer probation officer. Abortion, at that time, was not on her radar screen as a personal interest or an important social issue. Her concern then—as the mother of adolescents—was teenage drug abuse, and this led her to the probation officer work.

After Ruth had done this work for several years, her youngest child left home, an important transition point in her life. She describes it as a time when she was simply "freer" from family obligations than she had ever been before. Her old daily routines and personal relationships, once centered around her children, were changing. She continued her volunteer work but began to look for ways she could be even more involved. As a probation officer, she worked with a lot of troubled teenage girls and in some cases would refer pregnant girls to abortion clinics in the area. Referrals were handled by looking up agencies listed in a notebook maintained in the probation office. "This is how strangely you move from one place to another. In their research book, they had scratched out Birthright,[9] saying 'Only refer if they're carrying to term.' And I thought, what is this place?" She was curious why this one organization had been crossed out.

She asked her work partner, a professional officer who worked in the probation office full-time. He responded by showing her a row of baby pictures taped to the wall, all children of women he had referred to Birthright. He encouraged her to call Birthright and learn more about its work, which she did. This was her first contact with the pro-life movement. At this point, her concern was not the abortion issue at all—it was the quality of her referral network. "I had started, in referring to some of these clinics for help, . . . to want to see which ones were good and which weren't," she explains. "I saw the scratch-out, and I wanted to find out more about Birthright."

She did so by attending a training session run by the organization for how to counsel women with crisis pregnancies. Still, she continued to be most interested in improving her work as a probation officer. After the training, she felt her ability to communicate with youth and give them information was greatly improved. "My skills were much better. I still worked as a probation officer and dealt with kids, and still went into lockup, but I could speak to kids about relationships." She did, however, begin to keep in touch with Birthright and the people she met there.

Earlier in her life, Ruth's ideas about abortion were ambiguous. Although she knew the Catholic Church's position on the issue and had a sense that abortion was tragic, she had been open to the idea that legalized abortion would provide pregnant women with a better and safer option than the illegal abortions performed in unauthorized facilities. As a volunteer probation officer, she referred women to abortion clinics, often after only talking to them on the phone or meeting them briefly. Her growing involvement with Birthright guided her beliefs about the issue in a different direction, however. She now saw abortion as the destruction of life with great potential, children being lost, and women being scarred for the rest of their lives. "I have not really put all of this together right," she thought to herself as she got more information from Birthright activists. "And that's because I had none of these solid views on pro-life. You know, it wasn't there." As she got involved in Birthright, her pro-life beliefs began to develop. The group became her source of information, ideas, and claims about the issue. "That's where the change was," she says, "when I got with Birthright. I found out what they did, that they weren't in the political arena, and they didn't show pictures of aborted fetuses; they didn't get into the destruction, they got into the positive points."

After about a year, she decided to quit her work in the probation office and commit her volunteer time entirely to Birthright. She quickly became a counselor there as well as a local leader of the organization. Today she spends more than thirty hours a week on pro-life activity, much of it with Birthright, assisting a number of crisis pregnancy centers (CPCs) in the area. She has been involved in sustained activism in the movement for more than five years now, all focused on this specific kind of activity within the movement.

Ruth's story is typical of activist mobilization in a number of respects. Most important, moral opposition to abortion was not the immediate catalyst for her mobilization into the movement. Despite experience with abortion as a young woman and knowledge of the *Roe v. Wade* decision, she did not get involved with the movement out of moral outrage sparked by deep-seated (or even casual) prior beliefs about the issue. Indeed, if anything, she was disposed to the pro-choice perspective on the issue. Her trajectory into the movement began more by accident than by conscious design or recruitment. She initially chose a much different avenue for volunteerism—as a probation officer—and in the course of that work, she stumbled across a pro-life organization. It was only then that her pro-life beliefs began to develop. Her initial motivation for involvement was to improve her skills for probation work, not to learn about abortion.

Ultimately it was an organization and a relationship in which Ruth was already involved—the probation agency and the professional probation officer with whom she worked there—that connected her with Birthright and the pro-life movement, not preestablished beliefs about the issue. Like Linda, whose story introduced the chapter, Ruth did not seek out involvement in the abortion debate; she happened into it. The movement itself then helped form her beliefs about the issue. These same themes appear in the biographies of activists in each of the sites I visited, including activists who appear in many ways to be very different from Ruth.

Glen

I met Glen, a thirty-three-year-old political manager, in a Boston diner over a light dinner. Glen is the spitting image of Alex Keaton, the fictional character played by Michael J. Fox on the 1980s comedy show *Family Ties*. He is handsome, clean-cut, well-spoken, and has had an interest in politics since he was very young. Glen was born and raised just outside of Boston in a politically liberal and pro-choice family living in a largely pro-choice community. He always considered himself pro-choice as well but began to rethink his views after leaving home for college and becoming more politically active.

Glen attended a small liberal arts college in Ohio. The move marked an important change in Glen's life. He chose the college because of its "activist reputation." When he arrived, however, he felt there was too much liberal consensus on campus: "I think they sort of viewed themselves as a little holdout from the sixties. Like the final remnant, and they're going to bring it all back. It's one reason why I became conservative. I wasn't particularly conservative when I went there. But I reacted, I think, to that environment. I've always been somewhat of a rebel when it came to my political frame, and I suppose that's one thing I was affected in was politics." The effect on Glen was to push him to a variety of conservative causes and active involvement in campus student government. Glen helped found the first College Republicans group on campus and subsequently became active on the state level within the organization. He served on a variety of student government committees and organized campus rallies in support of U.S. intervention in Central America and the prodemocracy students in China's Tiananmen Square. He also helped in the campaigns of local conservative politicians.

Glen first came into contact with the pro-life movement in the context of this political activity. He was sometimes asked about his views on abortion in the course of doing conservative political work. "So I was asked if I was pro-life, and I remember saying yes and feeling it wasn't a very truthful answer." His colleagues must have sensed he wasn't being honest, as they began to give him a steady stream of pro-life materials—newsletters, brochures, and videos—mostly produced by the major political pro-life organization in the state. He began to question his pro-choice beliefs and decided that perhaps he was an "ally" of pro-lifers but was still not fully convinced of a basic tenet of the pro-life movement: "I'm not sure I bought the whole idea of making abortion illegal."

Between his junior and senior years in college, Glen returned to Boston for the summer looking for opportunities to continue his political involvement. He wanted to work with a political campaign, but there were none in the area at the time. He therefore began looking for other opportunities and ended up volunteering at Massachusetts Citizens for Life (MCFL), the state's largest pro-life political organization. Glen had heard of the group from the analogous organization in Ohio, but reflecting back, he has no explanation for why he actually got involved before he even believed himself to be pro-life: "I don't know why, I really don't. I think it was a hot issue. It was a big issue in Ohio; it was like the defining issue in Ohio. I think it was just, I still wouldn't call myself pro-life at that point. It probably wasn't until I actually started working at MCFL that I felt comfortable calling myself pro-life." Glen clearly indicates that his own mind wasn't made up about abortion until after he was involved with MCFL. He originally encountered the group by attending a monthly volunteer night at the invitation of a political friend. What drove him was politics, and he was interested in abortion because it was a "hot" political issue.

Since that time Glen has become a fully mobilized activist in the movement. He went from a part-time volunteer at MCFL to a full-time paid staff member for three and a half years. He continues his strong interest in politics, but the controversy around abortion has refocused his political involvement: "I've become single-issue. That's not a good way to term it because it's not really a single issue. I'd use the word *litmus test:* if someone is pro-life, that shows to my mind a whole worldview, a whole philosophy."

[margin handwritten note: pro-life is a worldview]

Glen comes from a much different background than Ruth. He belongs to a different generation, grew up in a different environment with a different socioeconomic background, has different political and moral views, and his activism has been as a member of different kinds of organizations doing different kinds of work within the movement. Nonetheless, both Ruth and Glen went through a similar process in becoming activists. Most important, both began their actual participation in movement activities before they had well-formulated beliefs about the issue. In Glen's case, he became a full-time volunteer in a pro-life group when he still wasn't sure he opposed abortion. It was only after his participation in the movement that he became "comfortable" calling himself pro-life. His initial participation with MCFL led him to learn more about the issue and meet other activists. He learned that the Supreme Court had legalized abortion in all three trimesters, for example, not just early on in a pregnancy, and he found that those he had previously regarded as "right-wing religious wackos" he now saw instead as "special, truly, deeply religious people." Today he is confident in his belief that abortion is a moral evil that should be illegal under all circumstances. "The pro-life position is fairly simple," he tells me. "It is that all human beings have human rights. An unborn child is a human being. The unborn child has human rights."

Action before Belief

Ruth and Glen are not exceptional in their road to pro-life activism. Although many interview participants expressed a primordial and timeless opposition to abortion in the initial telling of their mobilization stories, as the interview became longer and more specific, they admitted being ignorant about and indifferent to the issue prior to getting involved themselves.[10] Many reported ambivalence in their views on abortion before they got involved:

I didn't have a formed opinion. I mean, oh gosh . . . Isn't that . . . ? I really was kind of laissez-faire; I was happy. I was newly married, and I had a new baby. No, I wasn't newly married, I was married for two years and then I had my first baby, but you know, it wasn't something like, "Oh gosh, I got to stop that."
(PATRICIA, 55, TWIN CITIES)

I knew my parents were pro-life, but I certainly didn't feel one way or another about it when I was growing up.
(LISA, 38, TWIN CITIES)

And at this time, I really, when it came to things having to do with abortion, I never discussed it with anyone. I didn't really have an opinion, even as a Christian. It was one of those "I really don't want to think about this. And maybe if I don't think about it, then I won't have to do anything about it." So that was sort of my attitude.
(NICKY, 37, CHARLESTON)

And I really wasn't that opinionated about it. [Abortion] was just something that happened to me that I probably really didn't want anybody to know. And even if they did know and I had to talk about it, I couldn't even have talked about it. I mean I wouldn't even know what to say because I didn't have any information to go by.
(ALICIA, 49, OKLAHOMA CITY)

Each of these activists went through periods in their life where they were unsure where they stood on the abortion issue. They did not consider themselves pro-life and didn't articulate ideas about the issue until after they had already participated in at least some initial movement activity.

Even more surprising than this ambivalence is the fact that almost one in four activists (23 percent) are similar to Glen in that they consciously considered themselves pro-choice at some point in their life. "I was probably pro-choice by default," explains Glen. "Since my church was pro-choice, my family was pro-choice, my community was pro-choice, and I didn't want to be associated with religious right-wing wackos." Linda, whose path to becoming an activist was presented at the start of the chapter, saw a similar development of her beliefs. Linda was initially skeptical of pro-life ideas if only because she saw them in conflict with other values she felt were important, especially women's rights. Getting involved in pro-life activism changed her mind. For such activists, mobilization in the pro-life movement thus also entails a full transformation of their beliefs.[11]

Glen's and Linda's experiences are echoed by other activists who had previously considered themselves pro-choice. Josh, a direct-action activist in Oklahoma City whom we will learn more about in chapter 5, was pro-choice before his involvement with the pro-life movement. "Before that [a pro-life rally] I basically thought it sounded great that women had the right to choose what they do with their body and all that stuff," he says. Other activists expressed similar sentiments:

I would have been one of those people that said, "I don't think this is good, but you can't take a woman's choice away."
(NICKY, 37, CHARLESTON)

I just thought abortion was a small little issue. You just had an abortion, and it was just no big thing. You just scraped out some yolk and a little bit of an egg, and you went on about your life.
(MOLLY, 37, BOSTON)

Left to just kind of that gut-reaction thing, I probably would have . . . said, "Well, you know, it is a woman's body, and she has some rights to say what happens within it and to it."
(CRAIG, 45, OKLAHOMA CITY)

I was in the mind-set, you know, if the doctor said it [an abortion] should be done, it is evidently necessary.
(JOAN, 69, TWIN CITIES)

None of these people were pro-choice activists, undergoing spectacular conversions and making headline-grabbing defections to the other side in the fight over abortion.[12] They were, however, all people who were wary of or hostile to the movement when they first came in contact with it. Becoming involved in real pro-life activity is what made it possible for their pro-life beliefs to develop and their other ideas to be swept away.

Despite these surprising findings, there remain many activists who say they have always been pro-life. They are people who have grown up in pro-life families, attended pro-life churches and schools, and lived in neighborhoods and communities where it was simply assumed that everyone knew abortion was wrong. Even for these activists, however, the movement was critical in the development and crystallization of previously vague and fragmentary beliefs about the issue. For such people, activism transformed their opposition to abortion from a nebulous sense of abortion as being wrong, but with no knowledge or real understanding of the issue, to a strong position that the activists understand and relate to a larger moral universe.

Jason, a twenty-two-year-old activist in Boston, explains his beliefs before he got involved in the movement: "My family, my parents, they had never said, 'Don't do drugs,' 'Don't have sex before you're married,' 'Abortion is wrong.' It was almost as if we already understood that stuff; they never really laid those things out. And we did, we already did understand, but I never really thought about it as anything deeper than that." Jason has always understood abortion as being wrong, but it was wrong as a vague and general principle, not as an important and real moral issue. He believed abortion was wrong, but the belief was superficial, abstract, and unconnected to his life or other beliefs and values until his initial activism in the movement. Only then did he see the issue in any "deeper" way. Similarly, a Catholic priest in the Twin Cities admits that he didn't really know what abortion was before getting involved in the movement, that his opposition to abortion before that time was "pretty much an abstraction."

Those who believed abortion was wrong experienced a development of their pro-life beliefs similar to those who admit to being less sure at some point. Heather, a twenty-six-year-old in Oklahoma City, says she didn't really understand what it was all about until she was already involved in a Washington, D.C., rally: "I don't think I really realized until I was at the heart of it all in Washington, D.C., and hearing senators and congressmen who are pro-life talk. . . . I knew it existed, but I had never really witnessed very much of that up to that point." Tim, another activist in Oklahoma City, explained the crystallization of his pro-life ideas after he got involved in a CPC this way: "You're not thinking about things at the time you're [pause] I mean if you're like me, you go through something and you don't think about it, and then you reflect back. . . . Because we didn't have a lot of information about abortion. I guess there were certain entities at that time, ever since *Roe v. Wade* and probably before that, giving information, and we just weren't in the loop to have received that. I guess I just attribute it to God's timing. He wanted us to learn." Tim believes God is responsible for getting him involved in a pro-life organization so that he could learn about the issue and recognizes that it was involvement itself that really formed his pro-life beliefs, even though he had always considered himself pro-life.

The process by which all activists came into the movement exhibits a common pattern: people first get involved, and only then do their beliefs about abortion develop beyond simple labels used without much thought or understanding. This pattern is substantially at odds with the conventional wisdom that sees involvement as the acting out of existing preferences or attitudes toward the cause of a social movement. The movement is not a vehicle for the expression of preexisting feelings of moral shock (Jasper and Poulsen 1995; Jasper 1997) over the prevalence or legality of abortion in the United States. Individuals get involved in actual movement activity, and only then does such moral shock occur. Karl Weick (1979/1969; 1995) describes this as "sensemaking" of the situation in which individuals find themselves after participating in an organizational activity.

My data on the pro-life movement are in fact supported by previous studies that have demonstrated this same kind of relationship in other movements. Kathleen Blee's 2002 study of women in right-wing hate groups found that racist beliefs developed only after the women participated in actual hate group activity. Francesca Polletta (2002) found that the critique of racism developed by civil rights activists in the 1960s was the product of their involvement in movement organizations. Roy Pierce and Philip Converse (1990) have shown that participation in mass protests in France in 1968 transformed the beliefs of participants. Thus, from both the political left and right, in both the United States and Europe, there is evidence to suggest the pattern described here is not unique. Learning to care is an important part of the social movement mobilization process and one that does not occur before such mobilization begins.

Two Nonactivist Stories

Thus far, we have only looked at the biographies of pro-life activists. But the stories of nonactivists, the pro-life ideas they express, and their views about and relationship to the pro-life movement further demonstrate how the mobilization process works. Comparisons between activist and nonactivist experiences highlight the importance of the movement in shaping individual pro-life beliefs. They also show how initial organizational and relational contacts with the movement outside the immediate context of concern over abortion are critical in the mobilization process.

Jerome

Jerome is a nonactivist who was introduced in chapter 1. Forty-four years old, he lives with his wife and five children outside Charleston, where they are building their own home on some recently purchased land. We held our interview in the small trailer he uses as his base of operations for the building work. He was born and raised in Charleston, attended a large private university in the South, and married several years after he began his engineering career. Jerome is a member of an evangelical Presbyterian church in the area and is very involved in teaching Sunday school and participating in both domestic and international mission trips.

Unlike both Ruth and Glen, Jerome has always placed himself squarely in the pro-life camp. "It's about truth and what is right and wrong," he explains. "And killing a baby, killing anybody, is not right." Given his attitude toward the issue, he might be a likely activist. He has even had direct contact with at least one pro-life organization active in the area. The director of a local CPC spoke at his church seven years ago and asked him for financial support and help volunteering at the center. But despite his pro-life beliefs and a specific opportunity to become active, Jerome remains entirely uninvolved. What marks Jerome as different from those who, like Linda, Ruth, and Glen, have gotten involved?

A key difference between Jerome and the activists in the study is that Jerome's contact with the movement did not take place during any kind of turning point in his own life. Recall that both Ruth and Glen first came into contact with the movement when they were themselves going through major life transitions. Ruth had become an empty nester, and Glen had moved away from home and across the country for the first time. Jerome, by contrast, had already graduated from college, been married, held the same job, and attended the same church for many years when he was introduced to the CPC. This pattern is similar to that of many nonactivists: contact with the movement, if it has occurred, came at a time of relative stability and routine in their life. Among activists, the contact that led to mobilization occurred during an important period of personal transition in at least 89 percent of the cases. Although I discuss this issue in detail in the next chapter, for

no need to take a risk / try something new [handwritten margin note]

the present discussion it is sufficient to note that the coincidence of a personal turning point and direct contact with the movement is an important element in the mobilization process. Jerome's contact did not lead to activism in part because at that time he was neither looking for nor particularly open to the kinds of changes to his life that sustained activism would entail.

Jerome's lack of involvement is reflected in his ideas about the abortion issue. He considers himself "pro-life" but has never really thought out what this means. Consider, for example, his response when I asked him whether abortion should always be illegal:[13]

Now you're getting into definitions like a D & C. If a mother loses a child, she's pregnant, something happens, then they need to do the D & C. I mean, in that case, when the child is already dead in the womb, that's a medical procedure. The one question would be to me, would the delivery of the child truly threaten the life of the mother? . . . I'm not a doctor, so I have a hard time answering that. . . . That, you know, that would go into the realm I think of doing a medical procedure that maybe saves the mother's life. But you know it's going to be detrimental on the child. I don't know. I don't know. If that were [pause]. Well, it couldn't happen to us, but let's just say it happens to my daughter. My advice would be, I don't want [pause]. We'd need to pray about that one.

Jerome's answer is confused and rambling, even after being edited in the two places marked by ellipses. The question I asked was simple and clear, worded much like similar questions routinely asked in large attitudinal telephone surveys. Nonetheless, Jerome has clearly not thought through the issue for himself. He is thinking aloud in his response. He begins by suggesting there are abortions that aren't really abortions at all, when the fetus is dead. He then switches to the idea that an abortion to save the life of the mother would be acceptable but wonders aloud about the rights of the unborn child. He ends up saying he doesn't know how to answer the question, and he and his family would have to pray for an answer if they were faced with such a situation.

Ultimately Jerome understands "being pro-life" in very general terms: "And for us it's about being actively involved. Not jumping up and down and making speeches but actively, actively supporting with our lives and with our finances and our family, supporting that." For Jerome, "being pro-life" is a reflection of how he leads his life, raises his family, and makes a living. His claim to be pro-life is based on an identity, not a particular set of ideas about abortion or even a basic defining belief such as that abortion should be illegal or abortion is always wrong. Jerome is pro-life, but he is pro-life in the sense that he lays claim to membership in a particular community and general way of looking at the world, not in the sense that he has specific ideas and beliefs about the abortion issue. His fragmented ideas about the issue and his personal biography have never come together under the conditions necessary to make mobilization possible.

Cynthia

Cynthia is an energetic forty-three-year-old mother of three in Charleston who, like Jerome, claims a pro-life opinion about abortion but has never been mobilized as an activist in the movement. She grew up in a blue-collar neighborhood in Charleston, attended college for a year, then returned to Charleston, where she married a man in the air force. She has since gone back to college and now works full-time as a junior high school teacher. As with Jerome, religion has been an important part of her life. She was raised in a strict Lutheran home, repudiated Santa Claus and the Easter bunny because they were inconsistent with faith in God, and even considered a religious life for herself before first attending a Lutheran college.

Cynthia has had some direct experience with abortion. While in college, she accompanied a pregnant friend to a neighboring state to get an abortion. In fact, her trip to the abortion clinic with this friend is one of the defining experiences of her college life. Her detailed description is worth quoting at length:

I met this girl, and she was one of those cute little perky girls that just was, you know, my daddy would say she was like a fishing lure. I mean men were jumping out of ponds to get to this girl. And this guy that she was dating was, you know, kind of the typical northern guy from New York. He was very flashy and very different, and they began a relationship. And so she became pregnant. . . . And so then she and he decided that that [abortion] was the choice. She just did not want to tell her parents. I don't think she was really ashamed of what she'd done, or I really don't think she realized the repercussions. . . . She was upset, and she really felt like her dad would never understand, that she would be ostracized basically. So we all got together—the guy that was her boyfriend had a car, some kind of old, beat-up something or other—so we all piled in the car and went to Baltimore and went to the abortion clinic. And she was counseled. I felt like she got good counseling; I don't think it was a destruction mill or anything. I really feel like the people just said, "You're not ready, don't do this. If you're ready, we'll service you, but if you" . . . I really feel like it was an honorable, if honorable fits, you know. . . . So then after everything was over, she came out and she looked like a sheet. She was just so white and pale and grieved. I mean just grieved. . . . So then we got in the car and had some dinner and whatever, and went back to college. And on the way, . . . she started hemorrhaging, and we pulled over to the side of the road. And it was just blood, blood, blood everywhere. And I remember just sitting there thinking, what do we do? I mean I've seen all these movies about people with illegal abortions who like totally died, and I'm thinking, oh this is really good, she doesn't want to tell her parents that she was going to have a baby, and now she's going to die, and then they're going to come to us and we're going to have to explain all these things that she did not want to explain to her parents. But as I looked at her and I saw the pain that she was in, I saw the cramping, and I saw the hemorrhaging, I thought, I can never, ever, ever be privy to this again. It was just, it was just this absolutely heart-wrenching, just violent reaction. And, of course, you know me, I just sucked it in; southerner that I am, I would not speak my mind. And just, you know, I just said, "That's it." And I did have other friends that went for abortions that asked me to go with them, and I said no, I absolutely cannot.

Cynthia's story is one she has clearly thought about a lot and retells as an experience that was emotionally charged for her both at the time and now. Since then, she says, she has remained pro-life.

These experiences and the strong feelings about abortion they created, however, were not sufficient to lead to mobilization. Certainly they occurred at a turning point in her life. Moving away from home to attend college was a big change for Cynthia, as her description of her college experience indicates: "I went to a Lutheran college in Maryland, and I stayed there three semesters. And that was a shock because I was so sheltered. I found out there that just because you're Lutheran doesn't mean you do things right. It was quite a shock. Because, you know, I was just very sheltered. I mean my parents didn't keep beer in the refrigerator; they didn't drink. So I was kind of floored. It was like, whoa." She was far away from home, in an environment very different from what she was used to, and she was shocked at all the differences. Her daily routines were completely new, and she had to build new relationships with new friends who were very different from the people she had known when she was "sheltered" back home.

Why isn't Cynthia an activist? Part of the story behind Cynthia's lack of involvement is that she did not come into personal contact with the pro-life movement during this transformative period in her life. She doesn't remember the issue ever coming up outside of the experience of her college friend. She had never heard of any pro-life organizations in Charleston and didn't know of any pro-life groups on campus when she went to college. Cynthia had little chance of becoming an activist because she had no direct contact with the movement. The stories of both Ruth and Glen showed that direct, personalized ties to pro-life organizations were critical in the mobilization process. In the absence of such ties, Cynthia remains unmobilized.

As with Jerome, her views about the abortion issue are consequently undeveloped. When I asked her about situations in which abortion might be justified, she replied, "Well, I mean my mom always said, you know, the health of the mother. And yet when it came to her health, she took the option out. So I mean, [pause] I don't know. I think because I've had so much death, life is so precious. And I love children so much." Cynthia begins by answering the question with her mother's views rather than her own. She then thinks briefly and says she doesn't really know if there are justifications for abortion. Ultimately she doesn't resolve the issue in her mind even in the course of answering the question. She goes on to refer to a number of deaths in her family, then redirects the focus of the discussion to her love of children and (immediately after this quotation) to her philosophy as a schoolteacher that life is precious. Like Jerome, she calls herself pro-life but has thought so little about the abortion issue prior to discussing it with me that she cannot offer a clear response to even the most basic moral questions about the issue.

The Pro-life Beliefs of Nonactivists

By research design, all nonactivists I spoke to considered themselves to be pro-life. A close look at their actual beliefs about abortion, however, reveals that their commitment to pro-life ideas is extremely thin. Nonactivists make claims to a pro-life position—just as some activists do in describing their views before they became mobilized—but when faced with the need to explain what they mean by the term *pro-life*, they have difficulty responding, often providing stumbling responses, contradictory answers at different points in the interview, or, like Jerome, simply saying they don't know or they haven't really considered the issue. Rita, a twenty-one-year-old in Oklahoma City, is quite explicit about the fact that she hasn't thought through the issue when I asked the same question about when abortion might be justified: "I don't know. I've never really, I haven't thought about that. I think in talking,

[handwritten margin note:] don't have space that creates the identity ✓

especially with my mom, we see it on TV and then we talk about it. So the only justification we've ever talked about would be rape. I've never thought about a medical reason. I don't really have a view on that." Rita, like Jerome, is pro-life, but for her, the meaning is limited. Her beliefs about abortion do not extend even to the basic scenarios that are central to the public debate over the issue.

Nonactivists may have more difficulty responding to questions about their beliefs because in many cases they are formulating their opinions as the interview progresses. Doug, a thirty-two-year-old nonactivist in Oklahoma City, commented revealingly at the end of our interview, "Well, it's a pleasure to be able to think through what I believe as I explain it." In cases like Doug's, the occasion of the interview is itself the first time they have really sat down and formulated ideas about the issue.

Amanda, a twenty-two-year-old also from Oklahoma City, provides a more extended example. When I asked her whether abortion should be illegal, she replied:

Gosh, *I was just thinking about that.* That would mean like any medical procedures would be illegal. *If it was illegal, they couldn't do it, right?* As my father would say, he thinks that when it was made legal, that the respect for life in general, death penalty and things like that, went down. And so I think that legalizing it, they did I guess throw out a lot of that back-alley kind of stuff. But I don't think it's just, "Well, they're going to do it anyway, so let's just make it kind of safe." I don't think that's the answer either. *But I don't know. That's a tough question.* Because being so adamant about respecting life and not wanting those things to happen, would I want it to be illegal? Yes, I would want it to be illegal but also would want it to be like abolished. I would rather it not exist at all. It's kind of like dealing with the reality of it, you know what I mean? Because you want it to be illegal because you don't want it to happen. But it's going to happen, so *I don't know. Yes and no. That's not a good answer.* It's not a maybe; I would say yes. *Yes. I don't know.* [long pause] I would say yes. I really would. But that's just a hopeful part of me saying that if it's illegal, then it won't happen. *But I don't know.*

Amanda is clearly thinking out loud in her response, the highlights of which I have italicized in the quotation. She begins by suggesting she's not sure what making abortion illegal even means. She then expresses arguments on both sides, concluding that the question is a tough one and that she just isn't sure what she believes. After more comments, she says her answer is yes and no, then maybe, then yes, then she says she's not sure. These kinds of responses are characteristic of nonactivists: although they consider themselves pro-life in a general, abstract sense, their position is not sufficiently developed that they understand their own beliefs or even what being "pro-life" entails in the first place.

Nonactivists use the term *pro-life* very loosely, not as a label describing a particular set of beliefs about abortion. Albert, a fifty-year-old in Boston, considers himself pro-life but does not believe abortion should be illegal, only that it should not be used as a form of birth control. Paul, a thirty-four-year-old in Oklahoma City, believes both that abortion should never be available and that the government should not make it illegal. Another nonactivist in Boston says he is "personally" pro-life but would campaign and vote on a pro-choice platform if he were to enter politics. None of these opinions would be considered pro-life by the standards of the pro-life movement, yet they are all used by nonactivists to justify their claim to a pro-life label.

It is easy to claim to be "pro-life"—or any other clichéd label—when asked by a pollster. What beliefs such a label reflects, however, are unclear. Taeku Lee (1999) has shown that the social scientific community has come to see survey response data *as* public opinion rather than an indirect and imperfect measure of it. In this case, it is easy to mistake the claims to being pro-life for a commitment to a certain opinion about abortion. In a society and an age when everyone is normatively expected to have an opinion about every important issue and controversy, it is not surprising that the vast majority of people—more than 90 percent—say they are either pro-life or pro-choice.[14] In my data, however, individuals report believing they are pro-life but admitting that they don't really know what abortion is, what the legal status of abortion is, why abortion is wrong, or how abortion is related to other issues. To say that one is "pro-life" in these contexts seems more a statement of sociocultural identity than a reflection of an individual's beliefs or moral understanding about abortion. Saying one is "pro-life" is a statement about the kind of person one is, not necessarily a commitment to a certain set of beliefs.

Turning the Conventional Wisdom on Its Head

Many of the activists' stories discussed in this chapter demonstrate how the conventional wisdom is frequently wrong about the relationship between beliefs and action. Almost half of all activists in my sample did not hold pro-life beliefs prior to their involvement in the pro-life movement. Those who did consider themselves pro-life prior to mobization in fact held beliefs similar to those of the nonactivists in the udy: vague, incomplete, superficial, and inchoate. Activists come to heir understanding of abortion only after they have actually participated in the movement in some way. Comparisons with nonactivists confirm this view. Nonactivists exhibit thin pro-life beliefs, beliefs that are sometimes contradictory, composed only in the course of the interview, and in some cases inconsistent with common understanding of the beliefs to which the term *pro-life* refers.

Individuals stumble into contact with different pro-life organizations in the course of their daily lives. For Linda, a routine doctor's visit turned into a trip to the statehouse and ultimately transformed her adult life. Other activists introduced in this chapter demonstrated a pattern found among virtually every activist I spoke to: activism emerged not because they consciously sought it out to express their beliefs but as an unintended result of their ordinary lives. The organizations and relationships they have in their lives—and especially at times when their lives are dramatically changing—are the key to the mobilization process. Biographies of nonmobilized individuals notably lack such ties.

As this chapter has shown, social movements are spaces in which beliefs are formed and solidified, not simply reflections of preexisting beliefs, preferences, or grievances. This finding has implications for the "framing" activities that are so frequently a focus of social movement scholars (Benford and Snow 2000). The path to activism illustrated by the stories of Linda, Ruth, Glen, and others suggests that the key social movement framing processes are not those directed outward at potential conscience constituents or new sympathizers but instead those directed inward at people already involved in the movement. The belief work done within the movement is critical to solidifying the support of new activists, while the beliefs of those activists before they come to the movement are less relevant to the mobilization process. This pattern also suggests that a focus on how beliefs are produced, refined, debated, and disseminated within movements may be critical to understanding larger social movement dynamics. As Ron Eyerman and Andrew Jamison (1991) have suggested, social movements are public spaces—in the United States, one of increasingly few such spaces—in which new ideas are generated and discussed. Such public space has an effect on those who enter it, even briefly. Entering this space is critical in the process of learning to care about abortion.

This chapter has identified the central dynamic within the mobilization of activists into the pro-life movement. Yet the stories of Linda,

Ruth, Glen, Jerome, and Cynthia hint at larger commonalities in the process beyond simply the relationship between activism in the movement and the development of pro-life beliefs. The following chapter uses the insights developed here but situates them within the mobilization process as a whole and more fully fleshes out this common process of becoming an activist.

THREE

The Mobilization Process

Erin, a forty-seven-year-old activist in Charleston, is today a stay-at-home mother who homeschools her three children. People who knew her ten or fifteen years ago would not have guessed her life would take this direction. As a young woman, Erin was a workaholic who spent virtually every waking minute as a professional at the United Way. Her job left her with little time for a social life or even small things like watching television or reading the news. She burned out after almost ten years of this lifestyle and decided to move and take another job. "I came down not knowing a soul, which is a little scary," Erin explains. "But," she continues, "I was young enough. . . . Young enough that I could still make some friends." The move separated her from her church, her longtime workplace, and virtually all the people she knew.

Erin began to reevaluate her life and her priorities soon after this move. She had always been a regular Lutheran churchgoer—even in college—but had never given her religious faith much time or thought. Church was "just a rote thing that you would do and not put too much thought behind it." After the move, however, she immediately began to take an increasing interest in her faith and decided to participate in a pilgrimage to Israel being sponsored by a local church. "You know, I was single and I was making good money, and I thought, 'Well, why not go?'" she says. The trip opened Erin's eyes to the importance of her faith life, which she now believed she had been ignoring for years. She decided to join this new, "more spirit-filled" Lutheran church.

There she met her future husband as well as a woman who was active in the pro-life movement. Erin explains how they first began discussing the abortion issue: "Well, she can play the piano like nobody else. She can! And on Wednesday nights, they would have a piano and guitar–type thing back then, and she would play the piano. And she could do ragtag, ragtime, I guess that's what it is. But she wouldn't do that during the service. But I could tell that she could, and I just went up to talk to her about her piano playing because I took piano. And how good she played. And then we just got talking, and that [pro-life activism] was what she was doing at the time." This initial contact led to an invitation to help out at a local crisis pregnancy center (CPC), which Erin accepted. Soon she became as focused on pro-life activism as she had been on her work, becoming the leader of a local group, editing a regular pro-life newsletter, and getting actively involved in political organizing for pro-life candidates.

The preceding chapter showed that an individual's first steps into activism are seldom rooted in a long-standing or deep-seated moral opposition to abortion. The analysis here examines the next steps in the mobilization process, a process illustrated in many respects by this short summary of how Erin became involved in the movement. The model highlights the dynamic, contingent nature of becoming an activist. The mobilization process is characterized by a number of specific steps that can be found in each of the activist biographies. I will briefly outline the entire process, then show how the model helps illuminate Erin's journey into the movement as well as that of all the other activists.

The Mobilization Process

The mobilization process in the pro-life movement takes place in a series of analytically distinct steps, summarized in figure 3.1: contact with the movement at a turning point in one's life, initial activism, the development of pro-life beliefs, and finally sustained activism. Previous steps do not cause later steps but are necessary prerequisites for them. Learning important new information about the abortion issue, for example, will not lead to mobilization unless the individual has also experienced a turning point and had some contact with the movement. The model of mobilization presented here is thus more than simply a collection of "factors" that must "come together" to produce mobilization but instead specifies a clear set of stages through which each activ-

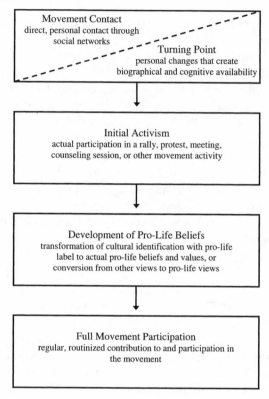

Movement Contact
direct, personal contact through
social networks

Turning Point
personal changes that create
biographical and cognitive availability

Initial Activism
actual participation in a rally, protest, meeting,
counseling session, or other movement activity

Development of Pro-Life Beliefs
transformation of cultural identification with pro-life
label to actual pro-life beliefs and values, or
conversion from other views to pro-life views

Full Movement Participation
regular, routinized contribution to and participation in
the movement

3.1 The mobilization process

ist passes in the overall process. These steps highlight the high degree
of contingency in the process, a contingency that helps explain why
very few people actually become activists despite pro-life identity's being commonplace in the United States. Even more important, the steps
show how mobilization into activism is a dynamic process, not a singular event.

Movement Contact

Contact with the movement is the first step of an activist's mobilization. I define this contact as a point at which an individual has direct experience with a pro-life social movement organization (SMO). In
Erin's case, this contact came in chats with the piano player at church
who was also the director of a CPC. Other examples of such contact
include a neighbor who is active in a pro-life group talking about the

organization's work, a presentation about alternatives to abortion conducted in a student's high school class by a local CPC, a friend badgering someone to come to a group's fund-raising banquet, or an individual simply calling up a local pro-life group and asking about the issue. "Another nurse told me about it," says Molly, a fifty-one-year-old emergency room nurse in Boston, in explaining how she first heard about pro-life CPCs. "I was with this patient, a high school student, who came in looking for an abortion. . . . That was the first time I ever heard even an inkling of a crisis pregnancy center." Molly subsequently visited the CPC personally to find out what services it might offer future patients. In Molly's case, simple talk among colleagues at work about the best way to help a pregnant girl led to contact with the movement.

The kind of movement contact that can lead to mobilization has two defining characteristics. First, the experience must be a personalized one. Simply driving by a billboard sponsored by a pro-life group or hearing about movement activity on the news doesn't constitute contact in this sense. Second, the abortion issue must be made an express part of the experience. Simply meeting someone at a prayer breakfast is obviously not enough unless the person's affiliation with the movement is raised or discussed in some way.

Individuals come into contact with the movement through connections they have forged in the different arenas of their everyday lives, whether it be in church, at school, at home, or in the workplace. In the previous chapter, Linda's first contact came through a visit to the doctor, Ruth's through her work as a volunteer probation officer, Glen's through his political activities. As each of these examples illustrates, the motivation behind such contact is seldom concern over abortion; contact occurs through the ordinary experiences of one's life. The likelihood of movement contact in the sense I am pointing to here is thus not heavily dependent on active advertising or consciousness-raising efforts on the part of pro-life SMOs.

One of the most consistent findings in studies of social movement mobilization is that social networks play a key role in bringing people into social movements.[1] The pro-life movement is no different. Table 3.1 identifies the avenues through which the activists in my sample came into contact with the movement and shows that social networks were critical to the mobilization process in more than 80 percent of the cases. The most important such relationships were developed through religious, familial, and friendship ties.

Table 3.1 Routes to movement contact

	Activists	
Route to movement contact	Number	%
Social network routes		
Religious network	33	40
Family or friendship network	20	24
Professional network	11	13
Political network	3	4
Total	67	81*
Other routes		
Self-starter	11	13
Random contact	3	4
Unidentified route	1	1
Total	15	18*

*Percentages do not add to 100 due to rounding error.

RELIGIOUS NETWORKS Churches have long been identified as important sites of social movement mobilization (Morris 1984; Smith 1996; Wood 2002).[2] Churches and related activities such as prayer groups, Bible study meetings, and religious ministries offer channels through which individuals come into personalized contact with the pro-life movement. Among the pro-lifers in my study, fully 40 percent of all activists encountered the movement through a religious network. This contact occurs through existing religious ties, volunteer opportunities made available through their churches, and deliberate pro-life recruitment efforts permitted by church and other religious leaders.

In many cases, churches or other religious organizations serve as the institutional matrix in which people come into contact with one another, even when religious faith is not the central motivation for such contact. This was certainly true for Erin: the initial impetus for her relationship with a local pro-life leader was a common interest in the piano, not concern over either her religious faith or abortion. Erin's story is not unique. Indeed, the initial contact with the pro-life movement experienced by most other activists has similarly little to do with religious activities per se; such activities merely provide the opportunity

for nonactivists to get to know those already involved in the movement. Ron, a fifty-four-year-old in Boston, went to a pro-life prayer vigil
for the first time after repeated requests from a longtime friend in his
church. Stephanie, another Boston resident, aged twenty-six, attended
a small Catholic college where many in her dormitory regularly participated in pro-life protests; after several weeks, she went along as part of
the crowd.

These people stumbled into contact with the movement in the
course of different kinds of religious activities. In other cases, people
were consciously seeking out opportunities to volunteer or "get involved" through their church, although here, too, the initial impetus is
seldom related to the abortion issue. Consider the way in which Frank,
a fifty-eight-year-old in Boston, explains his first contact with the
movement: "There was an ad in my parish paper. There was a group
meeting in Dorchester. So I don't bowl and I had a free night, and I
thought, 'Well, I'll go up and check that out.' The people were very
personable. There were different ages. There were men, women, different ages. And I thought, 'Well, this is something I can find out more
about.' So that was it." Frank felt he should get involved; after all, he
was not bowling or doing anything else with his time. When he saw
a notice in the church newspaper about a pro-life group, he decided it
might be worth considering more carefully, not because of the importance of the issue but because the people he met were personable, diverse, and interesting. Frank was looking for an opportunity to get involved in something, and his religious network led him to the pro-life
movement. In Oklahoma City, twenty-six-year-old Heather first joined
a pro-life group in high school because she was interested in religious
ecumenism, and the group was the only explicitly ecumenical group
at her school. In Boston, forty-three-year-old Beatrice had wanted to
be sure she got involved in extracurricular activities when she first left
home for college. During her freshman year, she signed up to participate in a number of student groups, including a pro-life group, through
the campus Catholic Union.

Although religious networks are important conduits for contact
with the movement, there is no evidence that churches are institutions in which movement organizations recruit entire congregations
at one time—the so-called bloc recruitment of churches (Oberschall
1973; Smith 1996)—because even sympathetic congregations are wary
of and resistant to such attempts. Pro-life organizations are seldom
able to work through churches directly, an issue discussed in detail in
chapter 7. Religious networks are an important source of contact with

the movement, but churches and other institutions act as the milieu in which such contact occurs—they do not themselves consciously or explicitly create such contact.

FAMILY AND FRIENDSHIP NETWORKS One-quarter of my activist respondents came into contact with the movement through family or friendship networks outside of a church or some other kind of religious activity. People who are involved in the pro-life movement often ask their family, friends, and acquaintances to accompany them to different kinds of movement activities. Personal ties are critical to the movement, because they create contacts with new potential activists through people they already know and respect.

Family is certainly one very strong form of personal tie. Marcia, a forty-year-old in Oklahoma City, first came into contact with the movement through her mother-in-law: "I think I was a freshman in college. I had to write a paper, and I chose the subject of abortion because my mother-in-law was one of the first volunteers at BirthChoice in Oklahoma City, then called Birthright. And she had a lot of information, you know, easy access; I can get in and get all the information I want, free. You know, this is great! I mean, I don't have to spend hours at the library for this paper." Marcia saw her mother-in-law as a resource she could use to help her write a course paper quickly and easily. Her mother-in-law, of course, was happy to share her perspective on Birth-Choice and encouraged Marcia to get involved. A family tie initially used to help with schoolwork ultimately led to contact with the pro-life movement.

Close friends form another critical network. Friends might invite friends to attend an informational meeting, a rally, or a vigil with them. The rationale is sometimes to learn more about an important moral issue and sometimes simply to spend time together as friends and "have fun." Josh, a forty-five-year-old in Oklahoma City, came into contact with the movement when he tagged along with his longtime roommate to a pro-life rally. In other cases, the contact can be motivated much more explicitly by the desire of friends to mobilize others into the movement. Daniel, a seventeen-year-old in Charleston, was first exposed to a pro-life organization after a number of his friends got involved and urged him to attend their weekly vigils.

THE IMPORTANCE OF RELATIONAL TIES, NOT PREEXISTING DESIRE TO STOP ABORTION Contact with the movement through the other kinds of networks identified in table 3.1—professional and political—look much the same as the contacts through church and personal networks. In each case, individuals came into personal contact with the movement through people they knew at work or from political activities. Once again, abortion is generally not the motivation behind the contact in these situations. For example, Molly, the Boston nurse quoted earlier, phoned a CPC on the recommendation of a colleague when trying to help a patient. Another Boston activist came into contact with a pro-life group in the course of helping with a political campaign. The pattern is thus exactly the same as in the cases of religious, familial, and relationship ties; only the context of the network differs.

The findings here are consistent with the long-standing axiom in social movement scholarship that "networks matter," but they also challenge past work in an important way. Although network connections are critical to pro-life movement contact, the activation of such networks is seldom part of an explicit campaign by pro-life SMOs. The pro-life movement, or even the abortion issue, is not the raison d'être for the contact between the individual and the movement. Nor is such contact generally the result of active mobilization efforts on the part of pro-life organizations, although groups routinely encourage members to bring in others. Instead, contact with the pro-life movement can most frequently be described as haphazard and accidental. This suggests that the most important role of networks is "structurally connecting potential participants with an opportunity to participate" (Passy and Giugni 2001, 123) rather than acting as the net through which SMOs actively seek out new sympathizers. It is also consistent with the findings of Verba, Schlozman, and Brady (1995) that one of the most important predictors of activism is an invitation to participate.

People happen across pro-life organizations in the course of their everyday lives, with the motives behind such contact lying elsewhere. This has been true for all the activists we've met thus far, and the experiences of other activists are similar. Elizabeth, a twenty-one-year-old in Boston, first came into contact with the movement by going with a friend to the annual March for Life in Washington, D.C.: "She invited me to come back early from Christmas break to go and drive down to Washington, D.C., and I was like 'Oh, that will be fun.' I mean I really wasn't thinking too much like this is a pro-life event. I'm like, 'Oh, it will be fun. This'll be like a nice little trip.' So I just went." Elizabeth's motivation for joining the trip was friendship, travel, and fun. She says quite explicitly that getting involved in the March for Life was not about abortion but about her social life in college. Brenda, a fifty-three-year-old activist in Oklahoma City, says she came into contact with the movement simply because she couldn't say no to an old friend: "A former teacher of mine called me on the phone. We had always kept in touch; she was one of the ones I called after I had my first child, and she was like a grandma, you know. She called me and said there was gonna be this talk at my old high school about abortion and she wanted me to go. And my response was, I don't wanna go! I would never have an abortion, you know, but I don't wanna know anything about it. You know, I've got this baby, I'm too busy. I gave her every excuse I could think of, but I didn't know how to really say no to her." Brenda ended up attending the meeting with her former teacher, a personalized contact that started her down the road to activism. Although the claim that social networks are important to mobilization is neither controversial nor novel, the key finding here is that the motivation behind the activation of network ties is often idiosyncratic and unrelated to the abortion issue.

The analysis here also makes explicit that just as potential activists do not get involved because of preformed beliefs about abortion, their contact with the movement occurs for reasons unrelated to the abortion issue. "Many of the things we care most about in life are the result of accident," explains Kwame Anthony Appiah in his recent work on identity. "By accident I acquire a family; by accident I acquire a profound commitment to this or that social or political agenda. By accident, I am who I am" (2004, 243). Accidental, however, does not mean random. Different patterns of life are obviously more or less likely to lead to contact with existing pro-life organizations and activists. People come into contact with the movement as part of the unfolding of friendships, careers, and relationships to church and family.

 SELF-STARTERS The focus on relational ties to explain pro-life involvement—and especially the claim that contact occurs for reasons other than concern over abortion—differs substantially from previous work on the movement. One of Luker's chief arguments about the mobilization process of pro-lifers is that first contact with the movement is instigated by the individuals themselves who want to get involved in the movement: "Two-thirds of the pro-life activists we interviewed were what might be described as self-recruits to the anti-abortion cause. That is, they encountered on their own information about the abortion situation that distressed them, and then they actively sought out an organized political group that shared their values" (1984, 147).[3] Jacoby (1998, 115) suggests that this kind of self-initiated involvement has defined pro-life recruitment throughout the history of the movement.

As table 3.1 shows, several pro-life activists in my sample might be described as the self-starters envisioned by Luker and Jacoby—individuals who made a conscious decision to contact a pro-life organization on their own. Dorothy, a single sixty-seven-year-old in the Twin Cities, herself contacted a local CPC in response to an ad for volunteers in her church bulletin. Jason, a college student in Boston, had sought out a direct-action group while writing a report on abortion in high school. These kinds of contact experiences, however, are rare in my data. Even with the most generous possible interpretation of self-recruitment,[4] only 13 percent (eleven) of the activists could be considered self-starters.

Moreover, the image of individuals encountering information about abortion on their own and initiating contact with the movement out of a resulting moral outrage leaves out much of the story. In Dorothy's case, the issue had come to her in the form of an ad in the church newspaper. When I asked her what made her respond to this particular ad, she replied, "Well it was because it was so close. . . . And I just thought, well, you know, I'm not doing anything. And so because it was close, then that's when I started there." She clearly did not hear something about abortion and rush to do her part for the movement; she got involved because the practicalities of her time and the organization's proximity allowed her to do so. Jason, another so-called self-starter, was assigned the task of looking at the abortion issue in school; he did not seek it out on his own. Although I have classified both of these activists as self-starters, neither got involved entirely on his or her own initiative.

Turning Points

Personalized contact with the movement is the critical first step in the mobilization process but only when it occurs in the context of a turning point in an individual's life. Turning points are those periods when people are required to make significant changes in their everyday life and, as a result, must also reorient their way of looking at and understanding the world. They are periods of practical and ideational change, "unsettled times" (Swidler 1986) in their lives.

Many turning points are regular features of a person's life course: moving away from home, marriage, birth of a child, divorce, death of a parent, retirement, and so on. Life course studies have consistently identified such moments as particularly important in an individual's biography (Elder 1985). My understanding of turning points follows

Victor Turner's (1969) discussion of liminal states: they are points at which an individual is "betwixt and between" different roles, expectations, relationships, and understandings. Turning points are transitional periods that mark moments when individuals are open to the substantial changes in activity and outlook required of social movement activism. After the birth of a first child, for example, a new mother's daily schedule changes dramatically. Her old routines are no longer possible, so she must settle into new routines and new relationships. She also looks at the world through new eyes, not simply because she is watching out for her newborn but also because her life is now different from what she had been used to.

Turning points are important to mobilization for two reasons. First, they represent times at which people become biographically available for activism. McAdam (1986, 70) coined the term *biographical availability* to refer to "the absence of personal constraints that may increase the costs and risks of movement participation such as full-time employment, marriage, and family responsibilities." Although the romantic notion of social movements holds that people seized by a moral cause will drop what they're doing to participate in a movement, the reality is that people seldom become mobilized except at moments in their lives when they are relatively free of other commitments and demands on their time. This is the reason many people become activists in high school and college: these are periods when they have few responsibilities and a great deal of control over their free time. Having one's children leave home and changing one's workforce participation are other key moments in which the mobilization process can proceed. These, too, are points in a person's biography at which he or she is more "available" for social movement activities than at other times.

The second reason turning points are important is because they are moments when a person is cognitively and emotionally available for activism. Commitment to a social movement requires changes in an individual's understanding of the world and his or her place in it (as chapter 2 demonstrated). It requires a rethinking of the relationship between beliefs and action. It necessitates that a person change his or her daily or weekly habits for something other than job, family, or recreation. Such changes are difficult and therefore resisted by most people most of the time. At turning points, however, individuals are already making adjustments. Moving to a new city and joining a new church as Erin did, for example, requires an openness to new ideas and a rethinking of old ones. It introduces individuals to new social relationships and new ways of doing things. It also frees people from old emotional attachments and social pressures that previously helped to maintain the status quo in their lives. These moments, important turning points in an individual's life, make potential activists cognitively and emotionally available. They are open to considerably new ideas. Experience thus changes both everyday routines and cognitive maps in ways that matter a great deal for becoming an activist.

In the previous chapter, Linda, Ruth, and Glen all came into contact with the movement at turning points in their own lives. Linda had her doctor's appointment soon after the birth of her first child; all four of Ruth's children had left home after she had spent almost thirty years as a full-time mother and homemaker; Glen had just moved across the country to attend college and live on his own for the first time. Their stories mirror Erin's from the beginning of this chapter: she came in contact with the movement soon after moving to a new city and joining a new church. Such turning points occur regularly but infrequently in every individual's life. Table 3.2 summarizes the turning points experienced by activists at the time they came into contact with the movement. Unfortunately, I was not sensitive to the issue of turning points when actually collecting the data and thus didn't ask about them specifically. The fact that they can nonetheless be clearly identified for seventy-two of the eighty-two activists (88 percent) suggests their central role in the process.[5] Moreover, such turning points can all be classified into one of five specific categories: changes in educational, labor, family, or religious status or physical relocation to another part of the country (often in conjunction with multiple changes in education, labor, and family status).

More than a quarter of pro-life activists began the mobilization process like Glen—during college or, less frequently, in high school. College is a time in which many people are biographically available. Perhaps more important, however, it also represents the first time many individuals have lived on their own, outside the direct supervision and influence of their parents. Colleges deliberately expose students to new ideas and new ways of thinking. Students are often challenged to question their beliefs and come into contact with a more diverse set of people than most have encountered previously.[6] College is thus also a period of cognitive availability (McAdam 1988).

Debbie, a Catholic forty-six-year-old activist in the Twin Cities, describes college this way: "I said I was looking for how the rest of the world thought, and I kind of ran into more of that than I expected to, you know. I thought I was going to, like, meet Protestants. Not people who are going, 'Is there reality?' And it was very challenging. It

Table 3.2 Turning points leading to activism

Kind of turning point	Activists	
	Number	%
Change in education status		
College	15	
High school	5	
Total	20	28
Change in family status		
Birth of first child	7	
Children leaving home	5	
Marriage	2	
Other*	4	
Total	18	25
Change in labor status		
Career change	7	
Retirement	4	
Dropping out of labor force	4	
First job	3	
Total	18	25
Change in religious status		
Religious awakening	7	
Religious conversion	4	
Total	11	15
Change in location	5	7
No turning point	10	

*Includes death of husband, a failure to adopt, a divorce, and reuniting with a child given up for adoption.

was a wonderful place to go for me, because no matter what you were interested in, there was someone else on that campus who was, too. And I think just the people that I got to know and the conversations that we had in the dorms, all that stuff was probably even better than the classes." Like Debbie, many activists found college to be both an eye-opening experience and a period when they could discover their own niche for the very first time. An openness to new activities and new ideas during college is a hallmark of those activists for whom college was the transition point during which their mobilization began. Several spent their college years examining their religious faith and trying out different churches and different religious traditions. Many attended college far from their hometowns in much larger cities. College thus changed their daily experiences, gave them the time and the resources to examine their beliefs about the world, and provided exposure to others with very different ideas and interests.

Changes in family status, such as that experienced by Ruth, are a second kind of turning point common among activists. Parents whose children recently left home described having more time on their hands and actively seeking out volunteer opportunities once their children were off to college or "out of the nest." Besides simple biographical availability, however, an empty nest also signals a major change in family relationships and patterns of interaction.

The birth of a first child was an even more frequent turning point that led to mobilization. The arrival of children marks an important transition in an individual's life and gives many the opportunity to reevaluate their priorities, goals, and ideas about the world. Julie, a thirty-two-year-old activist in Oklahoma City, explains: "Well, I had just gone through having our first, Samantha, and it was just a real eye-opener for me. It's just truly, it was one of those things where it was amazing. I just found everything about the pregnancy and things that I felt, truly to me it was amazing." Her first birth left Julie in awe of the process and led her to focus on new ideas, which left her open to pro-life involvement. Soon after her daughter was born, she became involved in a CPC.

Significantly, it is only the birth of a first child that serves as a turning point among activists in my sample, as it is at this point that a new parent's worldview as well as his or her daily lifestyle are altered most drastically. No activist began the mobilization process immediately after the birth of subsequent children, probably because such events, while important, do not have the same kind of life-changing quality.

A significant change in occupation is yet another kind of turning point. Routine changes in one's job—salary raises, promotions, demotions, transfers, and the like—are not significant enough to be relevant here. One activist in Oklahoma City owned a deli for fifteen years before selling it and becoming an Episcopal priest. Another activist was an insurance salesman for many years before inheriting land and devoting himself full-time to real estate management. A woman in Boston taught in public schools for almost twenty years before returning to college and becoming a nurse. Retirement and dropping out of the labor force also represent a life turning point. It is a time in which opportunities open up, daily routines change, and an individual's ideas and beliefs need to be recalibrated to a new period in his or her life. Theresa, a sixty-seven-year-old in Charleston, laughed as I pressed her about what was going on in her life just before she first got involved. After retirement, she explained, "I just had the time, and my husband was agreeable for me to do it."

Religious change was the turning point for 15 percent (eleven) of the activists. In some cases, mobilization into the pro-life movement followed on the heels of a full religious conversion experience. In Boston, for example, a woman rejected the "New Age philosophy" she had embraced for several decades in order to become a conservative Episcopalian. In Oklahoma City, a woman's conversion from being a Muslim to being a Christian in a Baptist church marked the turning point that led to her mobilization. More frequently, however, a major religious awakening rather than an outright conversion signals a turning point in a person's life. As with other turning points, significant religious changes lead individuals to change their lifestyles and rethink their ideas about the world. Mark, a forty-three-year-old in the Twin Cities, explains his experience this way:

I discovered God. And I don't say it lightly, and I know that there's a lot of things that have been said and written about the whole coming into conversion, and there's a lot of stuff talked about in the fundamentalist-type, born-again experience. And in reality it was that type of experience, yet it led me directly back into the church I'd been neglecting since I was probably in early high school. And it was the Catholic Church. I realized that a very important part of life, and in particular my life, needed to be God. It needed to be religious truth. And, as I came to that, it was the very core and the very center of life for me, and so I questioned what I was doing. I questioned everything at that time.

The questioning of existing beliefs and ways of doing things is a hallmark of the cognitive availability made possible by turning points.

Several people experienced a major geographic relocation as a turning point in their life, although it may be that such a change is simply a proxy for a number of the previously discussed turning points put together—such moves also entailed changes such as beginning college, getting a divorce, or changing careers. Nicky, for example, a thirty-seven-year-old in Charleston, describes her initial move to the area this way: "We were making a major change. We were moving to another city. My husband was pursuing his career, an academic career, and I put my theatrical career pretty much on hold. And I knew I was going someplace that was fairly dry theatrically. And I really didn't know what I was going to do careerwise. So I was really exploring what am I going to do careerwise." Nicky was in a new environment with few social connections, searching for a new job, when she came into contact with a CPC. In Nicky's case and every other instance when such a change led to pro-life mobilization, activists made a geographic move to a distant place where they had no family or other connections. In one case, an activist retired in Boston after having lived in Germany for fifteen years. Another activist was born and raised in upstate New York and attended college there, then moved to Oklahoma City and got involved in the movement.

These five different kinds of turning points—changes in educational, family, labor, religious, and geographic status—all share two important characteristics. First, they constitute change in a person's daily activities and routines, creating biographical and cognitive availability. Second, each of the five turning points represents a moment in which the individuals' social networks change dramatically. Retirement, for example, signals the end of active participation in some social networks; religious conversion helps establish new networks. The process opens up the possibility of being introduced to new networks of people with very different ideas and values while at the same time becoming free of the pressures to maintain old worldviews from old social ties.

Turning points are thus extremely important in the mobilization process. They create "windows of opportunity" (Maxwell 2002, 91) in which an individual's material, social, and emotional circumstances allow him or her to be mobilized. Recall that one of the things that distinguished Jerome's nonactivist biography in the previous chapter was that his contact with the movement occurred outside of a personal turning point. As a result, he was neither biographically nor cognitively available for mobilization. Turning points create the possibility for such movement contact to grow into sustained activism.

Initial Activism

After an individual experiences personalized contact with the pro-life movement at an important turning point in his or her life, initial activism is the next step in the mobilization process. Initial activism represents the first time the person actually participates in pro-life movement activity. The kind of activism in which someone first participates flows from his or her contact with the movement. I saw no evidence of the overly rationalized model of individual recruitment: people with particular preferences toward abortion weighing the range of possible activity before choosing a particular type of involvement. Instead, a person's first activism experience is determined by the organization with which he or she has come into contact. This process thus involves a great deal of path dependency and the "lock-in" of activists. The precise manner in which individuals begin their activism has a strong influence on their subsequent trajectory.

The mobilization of both Ruth and Glen described in chapter 2 exhibits this pattern. Ruth's first contact with the movement was through the CPC Birthright, and this contact led directly to her initial activism with the same group. Glen came into contact with political groups within the movement. Although his initial activism was not with the same organizations, it did remain within the political stream of the movement; he never considered getting involved in direct protest in front of abortion clinics or working with individual pregnant women. His trajectory into the movement thus had an important impact on his subsequent activism.

Like Ruth, initial activism for many activists occurs with exactly the same organization with which they experienced their first contact. The movement contact and initial activism stages of the process in such cases often occur at one and the same event. An activist in Oklahoma City, for example, helped out some of her friends in a Rose Day campaign. Rose Day is an annual event in which local pro-life activists deliver roses to state political leaders. Her participation was both her first contact with the movement and her first actual pro-life activism. Similarly, a young activist in Charleston was urged by his best friend in high school to attend a prayer vigil with him outside the area abortion clinic one Saturday morning. His participation in the vigil simultaneously put him into contact with the movement and served as his first experience with pro-life activism.

Most activists do not get involved for the first time because they care about the abortion issue. An individual often initially becomes active with some vague idea that he or she is doing good, saving babies, or fighting for the rights of those who can't help themselves. "You know, I don't know why I did it," says thirty-eight-year-old Twin Cities activist Tom in explaining how he first started attending prayer vigils outside a clinic. "I don't remember. It just seemed like the right thing to do. I said, 'I'll go down and help my brother out,' you know." Tom was not unsympathetic to the movement at the time, but his real motivation was to help out his brother.

Activists bring a whole variety of idiosyncratic motives to their initial activism. Twenty-six-year-old Twin Cities activist Michelle's primary interest as a teenager was the party scene. When she left for college, however, she found herself living in a dormitory in which virtually everyone regularly participated in weekly pro-life rallies outside a local abortion clinic. Having little interest in either the abortion issue or the predawn hours at which the rallies began, she nonetheless participated in order to "fit in," "make friends," and learn more about the issue. Mike, a forty-two-year-old activist in Boston, first became involved as a favor to his father, who was once a major financial contributor to local pro-life groups. When his father was unable to attend a meeting or follow through with a project, Mike would help the movement on his father's behalf. Although both of these activists have always been sympathetic to the movement, the abortion issue was not the underlying motivation for their initial involvement.

Initial activism is important because it is not about abstract ideas regarding abortion or pro-life values; it is about social involvement. Individuals get involved in the pro-life movement by participating in pro-life events, not necessarily because they are thinking pro-life thoughts. For those being mobilized, this participation can be meaningful in myriad ways—a favor for a cousin, an interesting thing to do with a roommate, a duty to a friend, an attempt to get more involved in the community, burnout in their regular career, a desire to help out in church ministry, a wish to meet new friends. Individuals need not be convinced of a pro-life set of values and beliefs or even fully understand what the event in which they are participating is really about. The mobilization process is first about doing things with others; only after individuals dip their feet in pro-life activism do they develop a full pro-life understanding and worldview.

Development of Pro-life Beliefs

The development of pro-life beliefs is the third step in the mobilization process. As chapter 2 demonstrated, concrete beliefs about abortion develop *after* some initial involvement. Before becoming activists, some in the movement would have described themselves as "pro-life" in a public opinion poll or survey but in fact knew little about the abortion issue or what the pro-life label represents in political, legal, or even moral terms. In these cases, the mobilization process crystallizes their beliefs, leading them to a particular understanding of what it means to be pro-life. In other cases, people were either ambivalent or confused about the issue and would have been hesitant to label themselves pro-life before their initial activism. Finally, a significant number of activists—23 percent—considered themselves pro-choice before getting involved; they were, at least tacitly, supporters of legalized abortion. For these individuals, the mobilization process is also a full conversion process with respect to this issue.

Regardless of their prior beliefs, new activists are exposed to a rich set of ideas about the issue when they first start getting involved. In previous steps of the mobilization process, we saw how individuals are drawn into the movement through relational ties and how their initial activism typically occurs through the group with which they first happen to come into contact, not necessarily a group they have sought out or chosen based on preformed preferences. The development of their beliefs about abortion in the present step of the mobilization process works the same way. Activists seldom come into their initial activism with a clear understanding of why abortion is wrong or what can be done to end it. Instead, their beliefs develop as the result of learning about the issue from those with whom they first become active in the movement. This process leads to very different understandings of abortion among activists, as they are socialized into the particularistic abortion beliefs that characterize the different segments of the movement.

With her first activism taking place in a CPC, Erin was exposed to the beliefs of the other women working at the center and in particular their ideas about abortion that focus on how the procedure further harms women who have often been through difficult or traumatic experiences already. In the context of getting to know and work with these other volunteers, Erin's beliefs developed in a similar vein: she has come to an understanding of abortion in which all abortions are wrong. In describing how her initial activism has affected her beliefs about the issue, she explains that "I've become convinced that abortion in the cases of rape and incest should not be exceptions." Erin believes abortion simply compounds the pain of the victims of such crimes.

Other activists who work in CPCs similarly focus on abortion's negative effects on women. "The biggest thing for me is I see what it does to people. It is gut-wrenching," explains Brenda, a fifty-three-year-old in Oklahoma City, "I think of some of the cases I've had. A woman came in a year after her nineteen-year-old son was killed in a car accident. The only other child she had was aborted twenty-five years before." Brenda's focus is on the woman, not the fetus. "I've counseled girls and women that have had abortions and their life is never the same again," says thirty-four-year-old Sandra, another Oklahoma City activist who works with a CPC. "They didn't become happy or fulfilled or less burdened or have any one good thing come from having an abortion, not a one."

Those whose beliefs about abortion are developed in the context of direct action have a different understanding of the issue. Ron, a fifty-four-year-old in a direct-action group in Boston, explains his beliefs about abortion this way: "I think there are other very serious issues and everything, but I think this [abortion] is life and death. Let's take civil rights. It's usually considered to be, you know, a priority case. It usually involved something that is an injustice. But they're not dying. Maybe they'll overcome the injustice, maybe they won't. But it doesn't compare. . . . There are people that are here that are not going to be here. There's not going to be a second chance. It's definitive. Tomorrow if we feel like we discriminated against a man, we can let him into college or we can give him a higher raise or appoint him to that appointment. But once they're dead, they're dead." Ron believes abortion is a more important issue than civil rights because it represents the death of a life that can never be brought back. The comparison he makes between the two issues reveals how his beliefs are rooted in the direct-action approach to the abortion issue. Ron sees abortion as an immediate threat to a life. He thinks about it not in terms of its negative effects on women but in terms of the direct life-or-death decision about a fetus that is being made in individual cases. His beliefs are rooted in concerns over what happens "today" and "tomorrow," expressed in terms of how abortion or discrimination differentially affects individuals. This core understanding of the issue comes from the direct-action stream of the movement, where the focus is on the immediacy of abortion and the need to save the lives of individual babies.

Those in the political arena develop an understanding of abortion that is primarily concerned with the legal status of the procedure, not the immediacy of abortion or the effects on individual women. Bill, a sixty-eight-year-old longtime activist in Boston, sees only political options for dealing with the abortion issue. "Well, there are really, if you think about it [eliminating abortion], only two ways you can do it. One is with the constitutional amendment, and the other is with a reversal by a majority of the Court," he explains. A Twin Cities activist tells me, "The law has an immensely important role to play in educating people. And I would value a law primarily for its educational function, far more than for its enforcement provisions." Glen, introduced in the last

chapter, sees the only avenue for the movement as being "through politics, through effective spokesmen and passing legislation." Although
not unsympathetic to other types of activism in the movement, Glen
has never been involved in anything besides institutional politics, and
not surprisingly he regards that kind of work as the most effective and
important.

An interesting contrast can be drawn between the development
of pro-life beliefs among activists and the ideas about abortion expressed by nonactivists. Most important, nonactivists are unable to
express their ideas in the same concrete way that activists do. After I
asked one nonactivist in Charleston what he thought about the commonly discussed cases of abortion after rape, incest, or when the life of
a mother is in jeopardy, he simply replied, "Well, I've never heard that
one!" Another nonactivist in Oklahoma City—who identified himself
as pro-life—describes what it means to be pro-life as "probably about
the death penalty. Then maybe euthanasia." Only after I suggested the
abortion issue did he agree that perhaps the term referred to that as
well. This kind of evidence from nonactivists suggests that ideas about
abortion are developed as part of the mobilization process.[7]

Participation in pro-life activity puts people in groups with homogeneous and deeply committed beliefs about abortion. A large proportion
of what pro-life organizations actually do is provide repeated situations
in which a pro-life message can be delivered to activists themselves.
Sidewalk counselors, for example, spend far more time talking to and
interacting with one another than they do with women entering abortion clinics. These are the kinds of contexts in which movement organizations educate their members about the issue and offer a narrative
understanding of moral opposition to abortion. Pro-life organizations
thus act as crucibles in which abortion beliefs are formed.

Full Movement Participation

The development of pro-life beliefs establishes the basis for the fourth
and final step in the mobilization process, that of regularized, sustained participation in the movement. Individuals can stay involved
in the pro-life movement in various ways, ranging from continued
episodic participation in rallies, protests, or specific campaigns to full-
time commitment to activism. People settle into routines of particular
kinds of activism: "In some ways, pro-life can become very comfortable
after a while," explains thirty-four-year-old Twin Cities activist Jeff.
"You know the people. The only time you debate is when you're deal-

ing with people who are on the borderline or who may be challenging you." Activists frequently talk about the camaraderie of activism, the time spent with friends, and the other social aspects of the movement. It is the "fellowship that we have with other pro-lifers" that helps define the regular activism of Mildred, an eighty-year-old Boston activist. "They are the nicest bunch of people you could ever want to know."

Other activists put it in much stronger terms. After the development of their beliefs about abortion, they see activism as the only possible course. Incredulity at the ideas and actions of pro-choice forces is what Beatrice, a forty-three-year-old Boston activist, credits with her continued involvement: "And you're just like, 'WHAT!?' You see how abusive they are with people, and not only just [of] the children but of people in general. And so then I'm like, how could I not come? Because I know I have this knowledge. I have the ability to speak out. I have the vernacular. How could I not be a person that does work like this?" Activists feel pulled into the movement as they learn more and more about the issue from pro-life organizations and other activists.

The only thing that I can tell you that happened in that year and a half [of involvement], I guess every year as I moved forward, is that I think the more you know, the more you value human life, and then the more you put aside everything and just act the way you'd act if you heard that a lady was getting ready to kill her husband across the street. . . . I can't turn around and walk away and feel like a decent human being. I can't; I feel selfish. I go to my sister and brother-in-law's house, and they live normal lives. Like, let's buy a car, let's buy a house, you know, let's go to the movies on Saturday. And there's nothing wrong with that; that's how it should be. But I can't, I can't do that. There's something that keeps me here, and it's well worth the fight.

This explanation by Dana, a twenty-eight-year-old in Charleston, reflects the feeling of many who have gone through the mobilization process. She got involved in the pro-life movement and learned more and more as she continued her participation. As her pro-life beliefs deepened, she increasingly came to regard her activism as more than just an interesting activity—it became an obligation.

It is thus at this last stage in the process where moral shock is both common and important. Individuals feel outrage, disbelief, and amazement after they have gone through each stage of mobilization, and it helps sustain their continued involvement. These emotions reflect the culmination of the mobilization process. Here is where the framing activities so well identified in other work on social movements matter the most (Snow et al. 1986; Benford and Snow 2000). As individuals continue to participate in particular movement organizations, their beliefs about abortion become further developed and refined through the pro-life frames they learn in the course of that participation. Beliefs and action at this stage reinforce each other.

The Overall Mobilization Process

Figure 3.1 summarizes the entire mobilization process. It begins when an individual comes into personal contact with the movement, usually inadvertently through participation in religious, familial, and friendship networks. Such contact leads to mobilization, however, only when experienced during a turning point in a person's life, a major change in which his or her activities and relationships are in a state of flux. Contact with the movement can lead to initial participation in a pro-life event or activity, often soon after the first contact. Both of these steps, movement contact and initial activism, take place before an individual has a well-formed understanding of or strong beliefs about the abortion issue. Only after a person has actually participated in movement activity do his or her pro-life beliefs and understanding of the issue deepen, the fourth step in the mobilization process. Finally, initial experience with the movement and its activists, combined with a more developed understanding of the issue, leads people to regularized participation. At this point in the process, many regard mobilization as not just a choice but a compulsion—something that the situation requires of them.

Few activists would themselves understand the mobilization process in the way I have analyzed it here. Activists would not accept that their contact with the movement was almost accidental nor in many cases that their beliefs about abortion have not always been at the core of their values and beliefs. "I know instinctively that abortion is wrong," says fifty-nine-year-old Diane, an activist in Charleston. "As a woman, it is just part of my nature to know that a growing human life is precious. I think I can know that on a natural level." I found little evidence that movement leaders have any more practical understanding of the underlying process of becoming an activist. Leaders of organizations in all four cities I visited operate with a theory of recruitment that understands the abortion debate as a battle over information, ideas, beliefs, and policies. They see their job as one of conversion; they believe that people will get involved in the movement only when they care enough or their conscience is pricked in the right way. Nonetheless, this model of the mobilization process maps onto all of the biographies of pro-life activists in the study.

Activist Biographies

Table 3.3 summarizes the mobilization trajectory of three activists into the movement whom I have not yet discussed in detail. All three experienced a mobilization process consisting of the same four steps in the same order. All three were going through a turning point in their life when they first came into contact with the movement. All three were drawn into initial pro-life activity for reasons other than deep concern over abortion.

KEVIN Kevin, the first activist profiled in table 3.3, is a married father of four living in suburban Charleston. Kevin attended law school soon after graduating from a local college, then married and opened his own private law practice. Soon after the birth of his first child (a turning point), his parents asked him to attend the banquet of a local CPC with them. Not really wanting to take the time out of his schedule and not even knowing what a CPC was, Kevin nonetheless agreed to go (contact with the movement), justifying it to himself as a good opportunity to meet potential clients for his new practice. Before the banquet, Kevin would have described himself as pro-life. "Probably if you had asked me, I would have said, 'Yeah, I'm pro-life.' But not really thought through it and not had any good arguments for it. It was just the right thing to do in my culture," he says.

After participating in the banquet (initial activism), Kevin's beliefs about the issue began to crystallize. Although having previously given little thought to the issue, and admitting he would have supported abortion under some circumstances, he now began to understand abortion as an evil, one that is always morally wrong. "It was very moving hearing the testimonies of the girls whose lives had been changed because they opted to keep their babies," he explains. "That kind of clicked" (development of pro-life beliefs). After his experience at the banquet, he learned more about the issue. He began to help out the CPC, first with financial contributions and later as an active member of its board of directors (full movement participation). He has also offered his legal services pro bono to other pro-life activists who have been arrested for movement activity in front of the area's abortion clinic.

Table 3.3 Activist biographies in the mobilization process

	Kevin	Mary	Elizabeth
Basic information	Married, father of 4, 37 years old, attorney, Baptist, white, Charleston	Married, mother of 3, 37 years old, homemaker, Baptist, white, Oklahoma City	Single, 21 years old, college student, Catholic, white, Boston
Turning point	Birth of first child	Being newly married and pregnant with first child; having just left the workforce for the first time	Having moved across the country to attend college
Contact	Attended banquet of a CPC at request of parents to get contacts for law practice; didn't know what a CPC was at the time	Attended presentation given by a CPC at church; thought previous abortion gave her special insight for talking to pregnant girls	Asked by a friend in local Feminists for Life to go to Washington, D.C., march; went along for social reasons: "Oh, that'll be fun!"
Initial activism	Donated money and joined board of directors after banquet	Was trained and began counseling at CPC	Participated in Washington, D.C., pro-life march
Development of beliefs	Called himself pro-life before banquet because it was "the right thing to do in my culture" but could be convinced abortion was acceptable; at banquet, "It was very moving hearing the testimonies of girls whose lives had been changed because they opted to keep their babies. That kind of clicked." Experience led to conviction abortion is always wrong	Not sure abortion was wrong at first but wanted girls to know what they were getting into; began to see abortion as wrong after discussing her volunteer experiences with husband. Pro-life beliefs result of "I think just that time with him [husband] and learning more about it and just maturing enough to understand what it all meant"	Always considered herself pro-life but neither cared nor knew anything about the issue until after the march, which deeply moved her; she then learned more: "Now reading some of the literature about what they do exactly to abort the baby and especially like when it's in the third trimester. . . . So that's why I'm convinced, I think"
Full participation	Serving on board of directors of CPC; acting as chairman of the board; becoming involved in several abstinence education groups; providing legal defense for pro-lifers	Weekly work at CPC; participation in Rose Day and Life Chain, both local pro-life events	Holding officer positions in local and regional pro-life groups

MARY Mary is a married mother of three living in Oklahoma City. Unlike Kevin, she has not always had even a vague sense that she was pro-life or that abortion was wrong. In fact, she became pregnant soon after graduating from high school and chose to get an abortion herself. She never really considered any other options; at the time, she believed it was simply what a woman did in such a situation. Although she twice attended college, she never graduated and worked as a hospital orderly for a number of years before meeting her husband and getting married. She and her husband made two important decisions when she became pregnant with their first child: they would start attending church, and she would quit her job to stay at home full-time (a turning point). In church, she heard about a center that counsels pregnant women about their pregnancies. Thinking back to the abortion she herself had had, Mary felt she should get involved and spoke to a woman in her church who was already a volunteer at the CPC (movement contact).

Although still not sure abortion was wrong, Mary wanted girls to know what they were getting into, and she saw it as a volunteer opportunity where she could meet new people. She therefore agreed to be trained and begin counseling at the CPC (initial activism). Even after regular weekly counseling at the center, her mind was still not 100 percent made up about the abortion issue. Her pro-life beliefs came later, after discussing her volunteer experiences with her husband (development of beliefs). She now does weekly counseling at the CPC and has participated in a number of other pro-life events in the area (full movement participation).

ELIZABETH Elizabeth, the last activist profiled in table 3.3, hadn't thought much about the issue at all when she left the home in which she grew up in Montana and moved to the Boston area for college (turning point). Among the new friends she met at school was a fellow student who was active in a local chapter of Feminists for Life (movement contact). This new friend invited her to come back to school early after the holiday break to attend a pro-life march in Washington, D.C. Elizabeth agreed to go because she wanted to meet new people and thought it would be fun, not because she was committed to pro-life beliefs. In fact, she says quite explicitly she wasn't convinced of the pro-life position until she began reading the material she gathered while attending the rally (initial activism): "Now reading some of the literature about what they do exactly to abort the baby and especially like when it's in the third trimester. . . . That's why I'm convinced" (development of pro-life beliefs). She invested herself in the movement after the rally, getting involved in Feminists for Life and becoming the editor of a regional pro-life newsletter for young people (full movement participation).

Nonactivist Biographies

Comparisons with nonactivists can also help to show the utility of this model in explaining the difference between who becomes an activist and who does not. Nonactivists' biographies are very different and demonstrate that stages in the model here represent necessary, yet contingent, conditions for mobilization. Table 3.4 summarizes the biographies of three nonactivists. Although some of them have experienced some of the steps in the mobilization process, none exhibit all four steps.

SHAWN Shawn is a single thirty-one-year-old in Boston who was introduced earlier. He has had personalized contact with the movement. In fact, the office where he works is directly across the hall from the pro-life office of the Catholic archdiocese, and he frequently interacts with the office staff. He has not, however, gone through a transition period of his own while this contact has existed, and, therefore, it has had little chance of developing into activism. Consistent with the argument in chapter 2, Shawn's pro-life beliefs remain undeveloped. He considers himself pro-life but cannot explain why he is pro-life aside from the abstract idea that God provides life and therefore "we need to love it." He is a deeply religious man who holds a full-time position in the Catholic Church, yet he is unsure of basic facts around the issue, including the Church's position on permissible abortions. He also doesn't believe that voting for pro-life candidates is particularly important or related to overall support of the pro-life movement.

ALLEN Allen is a married father of two living in Charleston. He was recently laid off from the company where he worked for almost twenty years. As a result, he and his wife have relocated to South Carolina after decades living in Arizona. Allen is clearly experiencing a turning point in his life. He has not become an activist, however, because none of the organizations and relationships in which he is involved have put him into direct contact with the movement. He has never even heard of the largest pro-life organization in the country, the National Right to Life Committee (NRLC).

Table 3.4 Nonactivist biographies in the mobilization process

	Shawn	Allen	Evelyn
Basic information	Single, 31 years old, public service coordinator, Catholic, white, Oklahoma City	Married, father of 2, 58 years old, substitute teacher, Catholic, white, Charleston	Married, mother of 2, 50 years old, nurse, independent church, white, Charleston
Turning point	None	Laid off from corporation after 20 years; moved to new part of country	Moved to new part of country
Contact	Holds job in archdiocese in same office as archdiocesan pro-life office; frequently interacts with office staff	None; can name only 1 (obscure) pro-life group; has never even heard of largest organization, NRLC	Leader of local pro-life group is a parishioner in her husband's congregation
Initial activism	None	Has given money several times to national pro-life group through church	Helped pro-life group with fund-raising event
Development of beliefs	Calls himself pro-life but can provide no rationale for this position other than because God provides life and therefore "we need to love it." Deeply religious, with a full-time position in a Catholic church, he nonetheless does not know his church's position on when abortion is permissible; doesn't even believe voting for pro-life candidates is particularly important	Believes that Catholic church's pro-life teaching is important but its teaching on capital punishment is flawed; believes issue of Vatican II's corrupting Catholic Church to be more important and pressing than abortion	Holds contradictory beliefs about issue. Works out position in course of interview: says abortion is wrong in all circumstances, later says there are allowable exceptions; says pro-lifers shouldn't compromise on issue in political realm, later says compromise is necessary to enact legislation and elect pro-life politicians. In several places, says she doesn't know or hasn't thought about issue enough
Full participation	None, other than helping to move boxes in office where he shares space	None	None

Note: Shaded portions of the table indicate steps in the mobilization process not experienced by the nonactivists.

EVELYN In contrast to Shawn and Allen, Evelyn has experienced several of the steps in the mobilization process. A married mother of two, Evelyn has recently moved to a new part of the country (a turning point) and has had personal contact with the movement through a local pro-life leader who is also a parishioner in the congregation of her husband (a minister). She even once participated in some initial activism, helping the pro-life leader with a fund-raising event.

This initial activism, however, never led to sustained activism in the movement or the crystallization of her pro-life beliefs. Instead, her beliefs on the issue are contradictory, and she seemingly tries to work out her ideas about abortion in the course of the interview. She initially says that abortion is wrong in all circumstances but later says there may be cases when it is acceptable. At one point, she says that the pro-life movement should never compromise on the issue but later says compromise is necessary in order to defend life wherever possible. She repeatedly admits she doesn't know or hasn't thought about the issue enough to answer basic probes about her feelings and ideas regarding the issue. As with the other nonactivists, Evelyn's biography is missing important stages in the process.

———

Figure 3.1 summarizes a general process that can be seen in the more specific trajectories profiled in table 3.3. At an analytic level, the path all these activists took to their involvement in the pro-life movement looks similar to that of Erin, whose story began this chapter. Erin's turning point was her move to a new city and a new church after years of focusing almost exclusively on her career. Her initial contact with the movement came in the form of a new friendship with a piano player who also happened to be a local pro-life leader. She began her activism by agreeing to help out at a CPC run by this leader. Her understanding of abortion and commitment to the pro-life movement blossomed at this point, and she began to devote herself almost exclusively to the movement.

Although the specific details differ among activists, sometimes substantially, the basic underlying process looks the same. Nonactivists, by contrast, have organizational and relational networks that do not put them in contact with the movement at the right moments in their lives or are unable to support continued activism even when such contact occurs. As a result, their beliefs about abortion differ from those of activists in both depth and breadth—even as they are similar to the initial views activists held before they became involved. Becoming an activist is a process, an important part of which is learning to care and developing the "right" beliefs about abortion and orientation toward the movement.

The process of becoming an activist also does not occur in a vacuum. Both the range of activities in which new participants engage and the range of ideas about abortion to which they are exposed are the products of the historical development of the movement. As activists are mobilized, they are faced with a social movement terrain created by several decades of the movement's prior history. In order to understand how people become pro-life activists, it is therefore necessary to look next at the development of the movement as a whole and how it has shaped the organizations in which people now become involved.

FOUR

The Birth of a Movement

Bill, a sixty-eight-year-old activist in Boston, has a lot to say about the 1973 members of the Supreme Court and their *Roe v. Wade* decision: "Think of the monumental arrogance of those seven people. This has been a pro-life country. A pro-life attitude has been the public policy of the country since before there was a Congress! . . . Over all these years, from 1607 on. I mean, seriously! All these pro-life views and the attitudes of the public, which was 80 percent opposed, but we seven say, 'This is the constitutional interpretation that prevails.'" Bill's opinion reflects a fairly common view of the origins of the abortion debate, both within the pro-life movement and among the general public. The abortion controversy is seen as having begun with the *Roe v. Wade* Supreme Court ruling. The pro-life movement is then understood as a reaction to this watershed event: a mobilization of organizations and people to reverse what they view as an outrageous and flawed decision that flies in the face of decades of jurisprudence and centuries of moral standards. In the terminology of social movement theory, *Roe v. Wade* represents a suddenly imposed grievance, a dramatic change in the status quo that motivates activism (Walsh 1981).

Pro-life activists themselves certainly view *Roe v. Wade* as such a grievance—a shock requiring a response and a bright line demarcating the beginning of the movement. "I was startled and surprised and appalled by that decision," says Sidney, a seventy-two-year-old activist in Oklahoma City, "just like many people were." Robert, a fifty-four-year-old activist in the Twin Cities, explains it this way: "Before *Roe v. Wade* came down, [abortion] was something outside of human decency. I mean, I thought about it the same way I thought about cannibalism. It just wasn't something that happens." For the many activists such as Bill, Sidney, and Robert, discussion of abortion is almost inconceivable before this Supreme Court decision. In fact, Luker (1984) found that many pro-life activists became involved as a direct response to the *Roe v. Wade* decision.

These activists understand the movement in classic Tocquevillian terms; that is, they see the movement as a group of people who have come together and organized themselves in order to address a common concern. The moral outrage expressed over abortion today, however, is not timeless and was not widespread prior to the emergence of the movement itself. Continuing to look at the mobilization process through the activists' eyes thus requires that we now turn our attention to the historical development of the movement that individuals enter when they become activists.

This chapter traces the history of the abortion debate in the United States in order to establish the context in which individuals today become activists. Abortion was not in fact rare or even illegal through all of American history up until the Supreme Court decisions in 1973. Abortion became illegal only in the nineteenth century, as a result of discussions limited to elite physicians, attorneys, and some politicians. Moreover, abortion has only been a public, moral concern since the late 1960s. Before that time, abortion was debated by medical and legal professionals but was not an issue about which most Americans had formed a meaningful opinion. Only after the establishment of pro-life and pro-choice social movement organizations, which started in earnest in the 1970s, did abortion become a grassroots concern in the country. Although Bill and other activists sometimes trace the beginning of the controversy to a single Supreme Court decision in 1973, the reality is that the abortion debate has its origins in a much longer historical process. This history differs from the understanding of most activists on both sides of the debate.

Before the Grassroots Movement

Despite the common belief that the abortion debate began with the *Roe v. Wade* decision, the historical beginning of the controversy occurred long before 1973. Indeed, scholars, theologians, physicians, and politicians have debated the morality of abortion for literally centuries.

Nor is it true that abortion was universally considered murder before *Roe v. Wade*, another common misunderstanding of the controversy's history. In fact, until the nineteenth century, abortions were permitted in the United States (and elsewhere) if performed before the "quickening," the point at which a pregnant woman can feel fetal movement. Because such a standard relies on the testimony of the woman herself and in any case generally doesn't occur until between the sixteenth and twenty-fourth weeks of pregnancy, in practice many abortions were permissible, both morally and legally. In 1800, no U.S. state even had a statute governing abortion procedures (Luker 1984).

Over the course of the next century, however, abortion was made illegal everywhere in the United States, at all stages of pregnancy, except when deemed medically necessary to save the life of the mother. Abortion went from being largely unregulated to being completely banned by law. Medical doctors were the primary force behind this sea change in the acceptance and legality of abortion. Physicians did not hold the same social status in nineteenth-century America that they enjoy today. Instead, they competed with faith healers, patent medicine salesmen, and other entrepreneurs who claimed the ability to improve people's health. Physicians needed a way to raise their status above that of their competitors, to show that medical expertise came from scientific knowledge and training not available to others, and they saw in abortion a way to professionalize. Doctors made abortion an issue during the nineteenth century as a platform for asserting their monopoly on scientific medical knowledge.

The medical community made a simple argument: it asserted that medical science could show definitively that abortion constitutes the murder of a human being. Abortion ought to be permissible, they argued, only when a properly trained physician determined it was necessary to save a mother's life. Abortion was thus made an issue for the first time in the United States not by churches or moral activists but by physicians who used abortion to make a symbolic claim to medical expertise (Luker 1984). Abortion became a vehicle for physicians to assert their professional qualifications in the eyes of the law and the public.

Their calls for criminalizing abortion were heeded. By 1900, every state had banned abortion except in cases when a mother's life was endangered by continuing a pregnancy (Mohr 1978). For the first time in American history, abortion was illegal throughout the country. Abortion's new legal status went unchanged throughout the nineteenth century. By legal statute, abortion was considered a form of murder. It is this era to which Bill and other activists refer nostalgically as the period when abortion was both illegal and seldom discussed. But far from being a timeless truth, the situation was in fact a relatively recent innovation in history, brought about because of changes in medical science and the social and political status of physicians.

These new laws did not eliminate the availability of abortion services in the United States, however. Indeed, during much of this period, abortions were available to many women who could afford them. Hundreds of thousands of abortions—perhaps more than a million—were performed annually by the early 1940s (Gold 2003). Some were legal, "therapeutic" abortions performed by doctors who deemed them medically necessary for the mother. The list of medical problems used as rationales for therapeutic abortions was continually expanded until World War II, making it increasingly easy for physicians to justify performing abortions under medical necessity exceptions to the law (Solinger 1998). At the same time, illegal abortion providers operated openly in many communities with little or no interference from authorities (Solinger 1994). These two factors made abortion widely, if not universally, available despite its remaining technically illegal in the late nineteenth and early decades of the twentieth centuries.

This status quo was challenged beginning in the late 1940s and early 1950s. The medical community was again at the forefront of the change. Many doctors began to raise concerns over the number of abortions being performed and express doubts about the medical rationales given for them. Technological innovation created the basis for this renewed concern. Advances in medical knowledge and the ability to treat medical problems during pregnancy had drastically reduced the number of conditions that represented a true threat to a pregnant woman's life. By the 1950s, the rationale for most abortions—even legal ones—involved the pregnant woman's psychological or emotional health, not the immediate need to save her life. The expanding rationales for abortion made increasing numbers of physicians uneasy in a legal context in which such abortions remained technically against the law.

The medical community responded by creating a new procedure for handling abortions. Beginning in 1939, hospitals established "therapeutic abortion committees" to make decisions regarding abortion procedures—effectively cutting family physicians out of the decision-making process. These committees became the new gatekeepers for access to abortion services by the early 1950s, both setting the medical standards for a legal abortion and judging each individual case to determine whether an abortion was warranted.

The establishment of therapeutic abortion committees dramatically

[handwritten marginal note: medical not social community for G]

reduced the number of legal abortions performed in the United States. The individual family doctors who had been responsible for making abortion decisions over the last century often knew their patients well and were sympathetic to their overall personal situations. The hospital-appointed obstetric and gynecological specialists who staffed the new abortion committees, by contrast, were primarily concerned with the overall reputation of the hospital and knew few particulars about the patients on whose cases they ruled. Far fewer abortions were therefore authorized when the committees took over, and increasingly the permissions that were granted went to women from affluent, well-connected families who could influence hospital committee members.

At the same time as the availability of legal abortions was tightening around the country, the tacit acceptance of illegal abortion providers was also ending. Police began to shut down abortion clinics, and illegal abortion providers were prosecuted with greater frequency starting in the early 1950s. One result was an increase in the number of abortions being performed in unsafe conditions by unqualified providers, often with fatal consequences. In New York City, for example, the mortality rate of women receiving abortions almost doubled between 1951 and 1962, even as the total number of abortions performed actually decreased (Reagan 1997, 211).

The seeds of a crisis had been sown: advances in medical technology, the creation of hospital abortion committees to replace the judgment of individual physicians, varying interpretations of what constituted a danger to the life of a pregnant woman, and the increasing danger of and inequality in abortion services led some physicians, lawyers, and lawmakers to again argue for changes in the legal status of abortion in the late 1950s and early 1960s. This time these elites called for a liberalization of abortion law, making legal abortions available under a broader range of circumstances. They argued that such changes would only grant legal sanction to the way abortion was already being handled by the medical community. Moreover, they believed more liberalized laws would save women's lives, decreasing the danger of abortion by taking it out of the hands of untrained and sometimes disreputable illegal providers.

Like the physicians who first sought to criminalize abortion a century ago, these new reformers were largely successful in their efforts— at least at first. In 1959, the widely respected American Law Institute (ALI) adopted a model abortion law as part of a campaign to standardize American legal statutes more generally. The new law explicitly permitted licensed physicians to perform abortions for either physical or mental health reasons as well as in cases of fetal defects or pregnancies resulting from rape or incest (Tribe 1990). Over the next decade, twelve states adopted abortion reform measures based on the ALI model (Reagan 1997, 222). During this same time, the American Medical Association, American Academy of Pediatrics, American Psychiatric Association, American Bar Association, American Baptist Convention, United Methodist Church, Sierra Club, and dozens of other medical, professional, and religious organizations all supported liberalized reform of abortion law (Tatalovich and Daynes 1981, 64–65).

Physicians, attorneys, and some politicians continued to be the primary audience for debates over abortion well into the 1960s.[1] Few, if any, grassroots organizations were devoted to advocacy around the abortion issue, and few Americans had formed explicit opinions about it. Many regarded abortion as a medical procedure best left to the technical judgment of trained physicians. As Luker (1984) notes, most people had no more opinion about abortion than they do about coronary bypass surgery today; abortion was a medical concern rather than a moral or political one.

Beginning in the late 1950s and throughout the 1960s, however, the growing controversy over abortion began to seep into the public consciousness for the first time. Certainly the legal changes surrounding abortion throughout this period brought the issue to the public's attention. So, too, did an increasing concern over the country's sexual mores. Newspapers, magazines, and other media began to discuss abortion and the new liberalized laws. Between 1950 and 1955, for example, there were only 24 citations to articles about the abortion debate in the *Readers' Guide to Periodical Literature;* between 1965 and 1970, there were 191 (Tatalovich and Daynes 1981, 41).

Two health scares in the United States greatly increased the public debate over abortion in the 1960s. The first was the case of Sherri Finkbine, a married mother of four and local television personality in Phoenix, Arizona. Finkbine was pregnant with her fifth child when she found out in 1962 that tranquilizers she had been taking contained thalidomide, a drug that was linked to severe birth defects. Her doctor recommended a therapeutic abortion and had the procedure approved by the local hospital abortion committee. Finkbine was relieved but also concerned that there might be other women who were unaware of the dangers thalidomide posed. She therefore contacted an acquaintance at the local newspaper and asked him to run a story about thalidomide and pregnancy. The resulting article appeared on the front page of the *Arizona Republic* and created a firestorm of controversy that neither Finkbine nor the newspaper editors had anticipated (DeVries 1962). Although the story did not identify Finkbine by name, the hospital was uncomfortable with the publicity and canceled the approval for her abortion. After failing to get a court order compelling the hospital to allow the procedure, Finkbine and her husband eventually traveled to Sweden to obtain an abortion.

The Finkbine case made headlines across the country and brought widespread public attention to the moral dimension of the abortion debate. The Finkbines were swamped with reporters and received both hate mail and death threats after their situation was publicized. A Gallup poll conducted a month later, however, found that 50 percent of Americans felt Finkbine had made the right choice, and only 32 percent felt she had made the wrong one (Risen and Thomas 1998). The Finkbine case was soon followed by an outbreak of rubella in which thousands of women who contracted it between 1964 and 1966 bore children with birth defects. This health scare, coupled with the Finkbine publicity several years earlier, put the abortion issue firmly in the public spotlight (Staggenborg 1991; Tatalovich 1997). Abortion was beginning to emerge as a public, moral issue.

The Catholic Church played an important role in the development of pro-life ideas and pro-life organizations in the 1960s and 1970s. Beginning in 1966, the Family Life Division of the National Council of Catholic Bishops (NCCB)—originally established to oppose the legalized sale of contraceptives—turned its focus to opposing the abortion reform efforts in California, New York, and seventeen other states considering liberalized abortion laws. It did so through a combination of lobbying, public education campaigns, and support for the fledgling grassroots organizations that were beginning to appear around the country (Blanchard 1994; Segers 1995).

Minnesota Citizens Concerned for Life (MCCL) was just this kind of grassroots organization and was the first pro-life organization to be founded in any of the four cities in which I collected data. A small group of people began meeting in Minnesota in 1967 to discuss their opposition to a bill that would relax the state's ban on abortion. This group formally incorporated MCCL in 1968. A similar group began meeting in Massachusetts in 1972, also in response to a liberalized abortion law then working its way through the state legislature. Several other groups were being formed elsewhere, but such groups were still uncommon; despite the growing publicity around abortion, most Americans did not yet see it as an important issue. Early organizations such as MCCL, however, were key to the grassroots mobilization that occurred after the Supreme Court decisions in 1973.

Lighting the Fuse

The *Roe v. Wade* case had its origins in Texas in 1969. Sarah Weddington and Linda Coffee, two young, feminist attorneys in the state, decided to challenge the state's abortion ban (Craig and O'Brien 1993). After finding a pregnant woman, Norma McCorvey, willing to sign on as an anonymous plaintiff, they filed a federal class-action lawsuit against the Dallas district attorney, Henry Wade, arguing that the state law banning abortion was unconstitutional. Their goal was to force Texas to liberalize its abortion statutes along the lines of what had already occurred in several other states. The federal court that had jurisdiction over Texas produced a mixed ruling on June 17, 1970, and Weddington and Coffee appealed to the U.S. Supreme Court, which agreed to take the case. Oral arguments were held in 1971, and on January 22, 1973, the Supreme Court issued a decision that astonished even the strongest abortion rights supporters at the time.

The *Roe v. Wade* decision invalidated the abortion statutes in forty-six states. It declared that any law regulating abortion in the first trimester was unconstitutional, that laws regulating abortion in the second trimester were constitutional only if they were designed to protect the health of the woman, and that laws regulating abortion in the third trimester must allow for abortion in cases in which they are necessary to protect the health of the woman (Hull and Hoffer 2001). In *Doe v. Bolton,* a companion case based on a challenge to Georgia's abortion ban and decided at the same time as *Roe,* the justices spelled out explicitly that by "health of the mother," they meant her psychological, emotional, and familial health as well as her physical health.

Roe v. Wade and *Doe v. Bolton* did not mark the start of the abortion debate. In fact, in many ways they marked the culmination of a debate that had come full circle since it first began in the United States more than a century earlier. The 1973 Supreme Court decisions, however, do mark the beginning of grassroots social movement mobilization on both sides of the abortion issue. For the first time, large numbers of Americans became activists in newly formed pro-life and pro-choice organizations.

Many pro-life activists today remember being shocked, angry, disappointed, or saddened when they first heard of the decisions. Diane, a fifty-nine-year-old in Charleston, sums up the experiences of many when she describes the time she first became interested in the abortion issue: "It was right after the Supreme Court decision, probably right after. I mean, when that happened, I went WHOA! what a change." Previous scholars have found that _Roe v. Wade_ was a critical catalyst that led people into activism (Luker 1984; Staggenborg 1991). They argue that people such as Diane flocked to the pro-life movement, driven by the shock the Supreme Court decision gave to their moral views and understanding of the world.

Only a handful of the activists I spoke with, however, actually became mobilized immediately after the Supreme Court rulings. While the _Roe v. Wade_ decision remains important symbolically as the target of political and legal campaigns within the movement, for most activists today it does not mark the moment they first became involved in pro-life activism. In part, this is a reflection of the fact that a new generation of pro-life activists has entered the movement: some of them were not even born in 1973; many others were only small children. Fifty-four percent of my sample were not even eighteen years old when _Roe v. Wade_ and _Doe v. Bolton_ were decided.

Still, even those of today's activists who were adults in 1973 didn't necessarily become mobilized right away. Diane didn't get involved for almost twenty years. In this respect, Sidney and Diane are no different from many of today's activists who did not join the movement right away in 1973. "I was busy, in a busy, growing pastorate and finishing a doctor's degree and all kinds of things," explains Tony, a fifty-one-year-old Baptist minister who is now a pro-life activist in Oklahoma City. "I don't know that I really thought things out then." Max, a forty-nine-year-old in Boston who was a college student at the time of the _Roe v. Wade_ decision, thinks there were just too many other issues being raised at the time. "The big, big political topic on campus when I was there was Vietnam," says Max. "So that was the big topic on campus. And abortion was not a big thing."

As I explained in chapter 2, becoming an activist involves much more than simply a moral shock, perceived wrong, or suddenly imposed grievance, as the Supreme Court decisions were to many Americans in 1973. It is a process that occurs in several steps that bring together personal biography with social dynamics and the activities of social movements. _Roe v. Wade_ was thus not the cause or even the immediate catalyst that brought most of today's activists to the movement. The decision does, however, mark the beginning of the modern abortion debate in the United States. The debate has since seen hundreds of thousands of people drawn into grassroots activism, the expenditure of hundreds of millions of dollars to influence public opinion and impact elections, and an increasing polarization of views and strident moralizing on both sides.

Organizing a National Movement: Mobilizing after *Roe*

In 1973, the pro-life movement was very small, confined mostly to an elite group of lawyers, politicians, and physicians. Activists were almost exclusively Catholic. Before the *Roe v. Wade* decision, the only coordinated national effort to oppose abortion came from the Catholic Church (through the Family Life Bureau of the National Council of Catholic Bishops). The few local organizations that had emerged by this time had an almost entirely Catholic membership and were supported nationally by the Catholic Family Life Bureau. In describing the reaction of abortion opponents to the Supreme Court decision, the *New York Times* could not cite a single pro-life organization or national spokesman for the movement; it referred only to the shock of Catholic cardinals (Van Gelder 1973). The Catholic Church was so important at this time, in fact, that Connie Paige (1983, 51) declared, "The Roman Catholic Church created the right-to-life movement. Without the church, the movement would not exist as such today."

Large-scale mobilization of opposition to abortion began immediately after the Supreme Court handed down its *Roe v. Wade* and *Doe v. Bolton* decisions. The various fledgling organizations that existed in some states to oppose abortion liberalization, nurtured and funded by the Catholic Church, began immediately to forge a national movement. Five months after the Supreme Court decisions, pro-life activists from around the country met in Detroit to organize and plan a response. The result was the formation of the National Right to Life Committee (NRLC), an organization that inherited much of the original movement infrastructure and personnel of the Family Life Bureau of the National Council of Catholic Bishops but was now explicitly and consciously separate from the Catholic Church.[2] Organizers felt that the movement had to expand beyond the hierarchy of the Church if it was to generate broad public support and political power. In order to underscore the separation of the movement from the Catholic hierarchy, the NRLC chose a Methodist—Marjory Mecklenburg—as its first leader.

The pro-life movement consciously chose to distance itself from its

Catholic roots because those already active in 1973 believed (probably correctly) that an entirely Catholic movement would not be able to generate widespread support throughout the country. Linda, a fifty-three-year-old activist in the Twin Cities, recalls that Mecklenburg's Methodist background was important to her when she was first getting involved during this period, even though she herself had been raised Catholic. "It made a big difference to me, because I was seeing the Catholic Church as being kind of stodgy," she explains. "I didn't want to be associated with anything that was—in those days—stodgy. The Methodists just seemed so much more broad-minded to me." The formal separation from the Church helped the NRLC gain the confidence of activists such as Linda, but it nonetheless remained a largely Catholic organization. In a 1980 study of NRLC membership, for example, Granberg found that 70 percent of the members were Catholic (Granberg 1981).

The organizational infrastructure of the nascent pro-life movement exploded after 1973. The NRLC founded independent state affiliates in every state in the country within eighteen months. Oklahomans for Life, Massachusetts Citizens for Life, and South Carolina Citizens for Life were all founded within a year of the creation of the NRLC. MCCL, the Minnesota pro-life organization, worked with the newly minted NRLC to help found offices in other states. Other organizations not affiliated with the NRLC were also created. In the Twin Cities, Human Life Alliance, New Life Family Services, and Total Life Care Centers are all contemporary pro-life organizations originally founded in the wake of *Roe v. Wade*. At the national level, groups such as the American Citizens Concerned for Life and March for Life were founded in 1973 or early 1974 (Encyclopedia of Associations 1978).

The first grassroots activists who came into the movement through these new organizations regarded the issue as one that would be quickly settled. "In those days, we didn't consider ourselves a movement," explains Linda. "We thought we were going to go home in a year." Activists such as Linda saw the Supreme Court decisions as an aberration—a mistake that would be quickly corrected once enough people knew about it. Early activists were surprised when this didn't happen. Carol, a fifty-two-year-old in Charleston, explains: "I think all of us wondered where the outrage was. Because I think that we thought that it would be overturned immediately. And when it didn't happen, we were stunned, you know."

The partisan valence of the abortion issue had not yet developed in these early years of the pro-life movement. Today pro-life political views are strongly tied to the Republican Party, while pro-choice views are tied to the Democrats. This has not always been true. The Republicans first adopted a pro-life position in their national party platform in 1980. At the same time, longtime Democrat Jesse Jackson spoke out consistently against abortion rights throughout the late 1970s and early 1980s. In a 1977 article written for the NRLC newsletter, Jackson explained that "human beings cannot give or create life by themselves, it really is a gift from God. Therefore, one does not have the right to take away (through abortion) that which he does not have the ability to give." Prominent pro-life leaders have also been committed Democrats. Jackie Schweitz, who led MCCL for eighteen years until 2001, was active in the Democratic Party through the 1980s. Rank-and-file members, too, have not always felt naturally drawn to the Republicans. Max, a forty-nine-year-old in Boston, says that "it actually took me a little while to switch parties, but I was just turned off by the Democrats and their position on abortion." Although the political lines are clear today, the conflict over abortion has not always aligned with the divisions between the major parties.

Evolution of the Abortion Debate

Although the contours of the conflict looked different in the first fifteen years of the movement, the political and legal story of abortion since 1973 has shown a consistent pattern of slow but steady erosion of the rights granted to women by the landmark Supreme Court decisions. At the same time, the basic finding of those decisions—that women have a legal right to abortion, at least under some circumstances—has been consistently and repeatedly confirmed. State legislatures, the U.S. Congress, and the courts were the primary venues in the battle over abortion beginning in 1973. Both the legislative and judicial systems have faced an avalanche of abortion-related bills and cases since that time. Legislatures in all fifty states review hundreds of new pieces of legislation annually that affect abortion services.[3]

The pro-life movement secured its first major victory in 1976 with congressional passage of the Hyde Amendment. This rider to spending legislation prohibits Medicaid coverage of abortions for low-income women.[4] Congress has renewed it in various forms every year since 1976. There have also been periodic efforts in Congress to pass a constitutional amendment prohibiting abortion,[5] though no proposal has ever passed and these efforts have largely been abandoned since the mid-1980s.

The Supreme Court has also weighed in on the abortion issue literally dozens of times since its landmark 1973 rulings. Most of these rulings involve the constitutionality of various state efforts to regulate or restrict abortion services. A number of these cases stand out as particularly important in defining the direction of the abortion debate. In 1980, the Court upheld Congress's right to restrict federal funding for abortion, declaring the Hyde Amendment constitutional in *Harris v. McRae*. In 1989, the Court ruled in *Webster v. Reproductive Health Services* that states could bar public employees from performing abortions as well as prohibit abortion in state-owned hospitals and other facilities.

In 1992, the Court declared (in *Planned Parenthood v. Casey*) that states could ban abortion anytime after fetal viability as well as impose requirements for abortions such as counseling, parental notification, and twenty-four-hour waiting periods. Requirements that constitute an "undue burden," such as mandating the notification of a husband, were ruled unconstitutional. *Casey* is considered a landmark case, however, less for the new restrictions it allowed states to impose on legalized abortion than for the fact that it explicitly reaffirmed the Supreme Court's commitment to the *Roe v. Wade* decision and women's legal right—at least under many circumstances—to choose to terminate a pregnancy.

The 1990s also witnessed a sharp rise in the amount of violence associated with the pro-life movement. Between 1991 and 1998, there were twenty-three murders or attempted murders of physicians who perform abortions or staff members at clinics that provide abortion services. At the same time, the incidence of bombings, vandalism, death threats, acid attacks, and other forms of violence increased dramatically. For example, in the thirteen-year period between 1977 and 1989, there were 70 reported death threats against abortion providers; in just the following six years, 1990 to 1995, there were 196 (National Abortion Federation 2005).

Such violence accompanied a rise in the amount of street protest done in the name of the pro-life movement. Pro-life protests and blockades of clinics occurred regularly throughout the late 1970s and early 1980s, with activists comparing themselves to nineteenth-century abolitionists and more recent civil rights workers. Such events, however, were sporadic and localized. They were eventually organized into a nationally coordinated strategy, however, in the fall of 1986 under the leadership of New York native Randall Terry.[6] Terry founded Operation Rescue in 1987 for the purpose of using civil disobedience to shut down abortion clinics nationwide. Although such tactics had been employed before, they increased in frequency, size, and media coverage beginning with the establishment of Operation Rescue (Lawler 1992). Terry staged his first clinic blockade in 1987 in Cherry Hill, New Jersey (Jacoby 1998). Since that time, more than thirty-three thousand pro-life activists have been arrested for participating in direct-action activities against abortion providers.[7]

The rise of Operation Rescue also heralded a change in the composition of the pro-life movement. Street protest generated a younger and more male activist pool. Several scholars and commentators have also noted that the rise of the organization also marked the entry of evangelical Protestants into the movement in large numbers (Connors 1989; Ginsburg 1998; Gorney 1998; Maxwell 2002). The national Operation Rescue once had a staff of twenty-three and almost a million dollars in annual donations (Shepard 1991). It collapsed, however, in the face of disintegrating leadership, lawsuits, and harsh jail terms for rescue activity. Its name, organizational structure, and leadership have changed several times since 1991, and today it is no longer a nationwide group. What remains are a variety of different local and regional organizations that existed before Operation Rescue's rise to prominence. Protest continues in front of abortion clinics, but it occurs on a much smaller scale and is coordinated by these more local groups.

Abortion in the United States Today

Abortion is one of the most common medical procedures in the United States. More than one pregnancy in five is ended by abortion, a total of 1.29 million abortions in 2002 and more than 42 million since the procedure was legalized in 1973 (Finer et al. 2005). Before the age of forty-five, fully a third of all U.S. women will have one or more abortions (Henshaw 1998). The ubiquity of abortion in American life has done little to reduce the controversy that continues to surround it. Survey evidence suggests that abortion is one of the only morally charged social issues about which American opinion has become more polarized over the last three decades (DiMaggio, Evans, and Bryson 1996; Hout 1999; Evans 2003). The battle over the issue is evident in the political realm: state legislatures considered more than 1,120 pieces of legislation related to abortion in 2006 alone (NARAL 2007). Abortion was the central focus of the debates over the confirmation of Supreme Court justices John Roberts and Samuel Alito in 2005 and 2006. The 2007 Supreme Court decision overturning the constitutional requirement for a health exception in any state abortion ban has once again put the issue squarely at the top of the national agenda.

The absolute number of abortions as well as the abortion rate grew steadily after 1973. The highest recorded number of reported abortions (1.61 million) occurred in 1990; the highest abortion rate (29.3 per one thousand women of childbearing age) occurred in 1981 (Jones et al. 2008). Since that time, both the number of abortions and the abortion rate have steadily declined. In 2005, there were an estimated 1.21 million abortions and an abortion rate of only 19.4 per one thousand women (Jones et al. 2008). The causes of this decline are hotly debated and include changes in ideas about abortion, couples' contraceptive habits, and young women's demographic situations. It may also be affected by the availability of abortion services in different parts of the country, a factor that has been influenced by the political and social debates over legalized abortion.

There are in fact substantial obstacles to obtaining a legal abortion today, in comparison to the availability of other gynecological/ obstetric services. The vast majority of counties in the United States—87 percent—have no abortion provider at all. Almost a quarter of women who have an abortion travel more than fifty miles to obtain one, and the costs of abortion—which start at about four hundred dollars—have risen 9 percent in recent years (Finer and Henshaw 2003). Clinics are also subject to increasing pressure by pro-life protesters. Although the incidence of violence against abortion clinics has declined in recent years, the amount of pro-life picketing has steadily increased. There were more than ten thousand cases of picketing in front of clinics in 2007 (National Abortion Federation 2008).

Despite these changes, public opinion about abortion has remained remarkably stable. Since 1972, the number of Americans who believe abortion should be legal in cases where there is a high chance of fetal defects has remained between 78.5 percent and 85.5 percent (see figure 4.1). Since 1977, the number of Americans who support legalized abortion for any reason has stayed consistently between 33.3 percent and 43.5 percent. Results are similar for other variations on polling questions. Despite all their efforts over the last three decades, neither the pro-choice movement nor the pro-life movement has succeeded in shifting the weight of public opinion on abortion even as the social, political, legal, economic, and medical contexts of legalized abortion in the United States have all changed over the same period.

Abortion today is a public, moral issue. The pro-life movement, in turn, is well entrenched in the United States, embedded in everything from politics to the media, academia, law, and civil society. Most im-

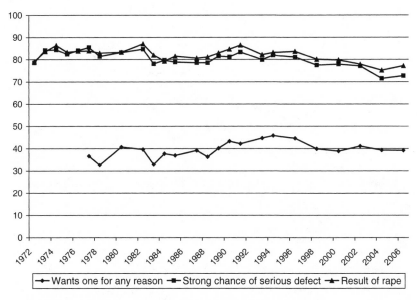

4.1 Consistency of public opinion on legalized abortion over time

portant, a vast array of pro-life movement organizations exist at the local, state, regional, and national levels. Such groups serve as abeyance structures (Taylor 1989), allowing the movement to survive through setbacks and periods of low activity. They also play a key role in the mobilization of activists, as the vast literature on resource mobilization has documented and analyzed (McAdam 1988; Zald 1992; Caniglia and Carmin 2005). Movement organizations provide money, leadership, ideological continuity, bureaucratic capacity, institutional ties, and a whole range of other resources that play a role in mobilizing activists.

In 1973, many individuals getting involved in pro-life activism had to start from scratch. There were few established organizations that focused on grassroots mobilization around the abortion issue, and most people did not have ready access to information on strategies and pro-life ideas. Today, a potential pro-life activist faces a much different landscape. Those who become involved need not found and organize an entirely new group. Most activists get involved through an existing organization, participating in that group's actions and adopting that group's ideas about the issue. The NRLC is the largest national pro-life group. It has an annual budget of nearly $14 million and has several hundred thousand individual members.[8] Other large national organizations that focus exclusively on the abortion issue include the Amer-

Table 4.1 Local pro-life movement organizations, by city

	Founded	Affiliate	Annual budget ($)	Paid employees	Mailing list	Newsletter
Twin Cities						
Human Life Alliance	1977	N	386,000	5	5,000	Y
Minnesota Physicians for Life	ca. 1980	N	< 25,000	0	n.a.	Y
Prolife Minnesota	1989	N	611,000	5	10,000	Y
Respect Life Office (Catholic Church)	1973	Y	n.a.	3	n.a.	N
Christian Coalition of Minnesota	ca. 1994	Y	n.a.	n.a.	n.a.	n.a.
Minnesota Citizens Concerned for Life (MCCL)	1968	Y	1,418,000	22	50,000	Y
Minnesota Family Council/Institute	1983	Y	879,000	10	25,000	Y
Minnesota Lawyers for Life	1991	N	< 25,000	0	300	N
Minnesota Taxpayers Party	1995	Y	n.a.	3	200	N
Pro-life Action Ministries (PLAM)	1981	N	406,000	8	9,500	Y
Birthright of Minnesota	ca. 1975	Y	6,300	1	n.a.	n.a.
New Life Family Services	1973	Y	758,000	30	n.a.	n.a.
Total Life-Care Centers	1974	N	168,000	2	8,000	Y
Oklahoma City						
Life Issues	1988	N	< 25,000	1	n.a.	n.a.
Social Ministry Office (Catholic Church)	ca. 1985	Y	n.a.	2	n.a.	n.a.
Christian Coalition of Oklahoma	1994	Y	n.a.	1	3,500	N
Oklahoma Family Policy Council	1989	Y	250,000	4	7,000	Y
Oklahomans for Life	1973	Y	50,000	1	50,000	Y
Birth Choice of Oklahoma	1972	N	251,000	8	n.a.	Y

ican Life League, Human Life International, and Life Dynamics.[9] All three of these groups have thousands of members and annual budgets in excess of $1 million.[10]

Although the national organizations are an important part of the pro-life movement, local groups are far more consequential for the mobilization process of individual activists. These groups define the paths to activism available to potential new activists and organize the range

Table 4.1 (*Continued*)

	Founded	Affiliate	Annual budget ($)	Paid employees	Mailing list	Newsletter
Crisis Pregnancy Center	1985	N	n.a.	2	0	N
WomenCare Ministries	1982	Y	200,000	3	n.a.	Y
Boston						
Pro-life Office (Catholic Church)	1985	Y	n.a.	5	n.a.	n.a.
Women Affirming Life	1990	N	49,000	1	2,500	Y
Christian Coalition of Massachusetts	ca. 1992	Y	n.a.	n.a.	n.a.	n.a.
Massachusetts Citizens for Life (MCFL)	ca. 1973	Y	453,000	11	160,000	n.a.
Operation Rescue Boston	1985	N	n.a.	2	800	Y
A Woman's Concern	1993	N	267,000	4	n.a.	Y
Charleston						
African Americans for Life, Save the Seed	1991	N	< 25,000	1	200	Y
Social Ministry Office (Catholic Church)	ca. 1985	Y	n.a.	n.a.	n.a.	n.a.
South Carolina Citizens for Life (SCCL)	1974	Y	140,000	3	72,000	N
Birthright of Charleston	1976	Y	< 25,000	0	0	N
Low Country Crisis Pregnancy Center	1985	Y	247,000	6	3,000	N

Sources: Financial information from Internal Revenue Service filings; all other data from organizational literature and personal interviews with group directors and/or presidents, 1999–2001.
Note: n.a. = not available.

of ideological beliefs and identities possible within the movement. This is not to say, however, that local groups are disconnected from state or national organizations; many of the most successful are local affiliates of national groups.[11] There are thirty-two legally recognized local and statewide pro-life organizations across the four cities on which this study focuses, including some groups affiliated with national organizations such as the NRLC, the Christian Coalition, and Care-Net (see table 4.1). In addition to these groups, many more smaller, less formal groups of activists exist in each metro area, but their activity tends to be more fleeting than that of the officially established organizations.

As table 4.1 shows, there is considerable variation in the number and type of organizations across the different cities. The Twin Cities area, which played a key role in the early mobilization of the movement nationally, currently has thirteen organizations with a range of foci, budgets, and members. These groups continue to be national movement leaders in terms of funding and developing new pro-life materials and campaigns. Charleston, by contrast, has only five local organizations, three of which are affiliated with larger national groups. Based on the model of mobilization I have outlined in previous chapters, I suspect these differences affect the likelihood of individuals' being mobilized into the movement. Compared to the Twin Cities, for example, Charleston has fewer organizations with which potential activists might stumble into contact and thus a lower likelihood of people's becoming mobilized.

These groups are also involved in much different strategies to end abortion in the United States. Some, such as the NRLC affiliates (for example, Oklahomans for Life), focus on the political and legal fronts. Many more activists, however, are involved in organizations that pursue different strategies—including efforts to convince women to carry their pregnancies to term; direct protest (and sometimes harassment and violence) outside of facilities that perform abortions; and efforts to change public opinion regarding abortion through public relations campaigns and outreach efforts in schools, churches, and other institutions. These differences have an impact on the development of activists' pro-life beliefs, a subject I examine in some detail in the next chapter.

Today's pro-life activists are thus part of a long-standing, mature social movement. A few were active even before the 1973 Supreme Court decisions, and some have been involved since the movement exploded in the wake of those decisions. The majority of activists today, however, came to the movement years (and, increasingly, decades) after 1973, when many pro-life organizations were already established, the ideological focus of the movement was set, and the structure of the movement was well defined. It is this structure that is the focus of the next chapter.

———

Like Bill, whose remarks introduced this chapter, many pro-life activists have created a historical mythology in which the *Roe v. Wade* and

Doe v. Bolton decisions were lightning bolts from the dark, completely upsetting centuries of consensus that abortion was a form of murder. John, a sixty-eight-year-old in the Twin Cities, reflects this common view as he expresses his outrage at the Supreme Court decisions: "And the basis of it—privacy rights—are a dreamed-up constitutional right. Dreamed up! You know, there was no basis in history before, no precedent at all, in regard to it [the Court decision]." Despite the prevalence of such views, the history of the abortion debate proves to be much older—and more complicated—than John's perspective allows for. The contours of the abortion debate began in the mid-nineteenth century, before abortion was illegal anywhere in the United States.

For the purposes of understanding how individuals become activists, this history is important primarily because it shows that the movement did not simply emerge in response to the demands of a preexisting constituency of people with deep moral concerns about abortion. The moral concern about abortion has been constructed in bits and pieces over the course of American history by different sets of people and organizations.[12] It is this moral concern, developed and nurtured by the movement itself, rather than latent grievances in the population, that forms the backdrop to becoming an activist.

The legal status of abortion following *Roe v. Wade* and *Doe v. Bolton* was the most permissive since the first statutes outlawing abortion were passed in the early 1800s. Since that time, new federal and state laws, along with a whole series of Supreme Court rulings that support them, have generally imposed new limits on the availability of legal abortions. The pro-life movement that has mobilized and pushed for these restrictions is today a well-institutionalized and heterogeneous phenomenon. It includes a whole range of organizations both nationally and in cities and towns across the country. How this movement is structured is the subject to which I turn next.

FIVE

Together but Not One: The Pro-life Movement Structure

I met Josh, a forty-five-year-old computer technician, in the small Oklahoma City apartment he shares with a long-time friend. Josh is originally from Missouri and came to Oklahoma City almost two decades ago after graduating from college. His apartment is crowded with piles of books, computer equipment, old mail, and boxes of dolls, model trains, and other collectibles. Nothing in the apartment reveals his involvement in pro-life protest and civil disobedience or the strong conservative religious beliefs he has developed since becoming involved in pro-life activism.

Josh's first experience with the movement was participation in a Life Chain, an annual pro-life street demonstration in which hundreds (and sometimes thousands) of activists form a human chain along public streets by holding hands and pro-life signs. Through this event, Josh discovered a group called Oklahoma Repentance and Rescue that focused on high-profile protest at abortion clinics.[1] Soon after, he was arrested for blocking a clinic door. Since then he has participated in similar civil disobedience campaigns in Oklahoma City as well as in Wichita, Kansas, where he took part in several nationally coordinated campaigns to shut down a women's clinic there. He has also regularly been involved in more standard protest in front of area clinics on Saturday mornings with other local activists.

Josh has never been involved in any kind of activism except this form of direct protest activity against abortion. Indeed, he views virtually everything about the world through the prism of his pro-life activity. He has dropped out of the Republican Party due to his disgust over what he sees as a wavering position on abortion. "We were fed up with their stands," he explains of himself and his roommate. "We felt like they didn't represent pro-life at all. They're wishy-washy people." He believes those who actively protest in front of the clinics are the "backbone" of the movement: "I guess you'd call them the hard-core pro-lifers. The people who do the rescuing. The people who stand out and picket. The people who sit there and risk their lives in rescuing and so forth." It is not simply that protesters are the most dedicated activists; in Josh's view, they are the only authentic activists: "I get perturbed with people who do politics stuff. There's a lot of them, and we call them 'pro-life buts.' In other words, they're willing to give in to this or give in to that to get this. Well the hard-core pro-lifers, we don't go for that. A loss of a life is a loss of life. Whenever you have politicians talking, they're always talking about their own agendas. They don't really care about the child's life. . . . They don't really care about the pro-lifers." Josh regards those who engage in the political process as sell-outs, pretenders, pro-lifers in name but not in deed. Direct action in front of abortion clinics, he believes, is the only true pro-life activity.

Glen, a thirty-three-year-old political manager in Boston, has had a completely different experience in the pro-life movement. Recall from chapter 2 that Glen is a young, clean-cut activist who grew up in a pro-choice family and has been interested in politics since adolescence. He developed his pro-life beliefs only after moving to Ohio to attend college. He began working for a pro-life advocacy group one summer even before he was willing to call himself pro-life, and it was there that he finally became a committed activist.

Today Glen works in political campaigns and political organizations full-time, so it is not surprising that he doesn't share Josh's rejection of the political process. His pro-life activism stems from his political activism, and he has never been involved in any other kind of pro-life activity besides political efforts to change the legal status of abortion. He has worked for the election campaigns of pro-life political candidates, pro-life groups of students and young professionals trying to become more politically active, and Massachusetts Citizens for Life (MCFL).

Far from seeing political compromise as selling out his principles, he views it as the only effective way to end abortion in the United States. "I believe you should save children as you can save children. If you can save a child here, two children there, fine," Glen explains. "You've got to fight your battles where you can." He doesn't believe civil disobedience in front of clinics—such as what Josh does—is an effective form of activism. In fact, he suggests that those involved are more interested in the media spotlight than they are in the abortion issue. His views are echoed by many in the movement, including Suzanne, a fifty-year-old activist in Charleston. She worries that street protest might be not only ineffective but also outright harmful to the movement. "So many people are pro-life and self-righteous about it. And they don't have a clue about what the real issues are and how to get involved and make a difference. . . . They don't understand or don't want to understand."

At first glance, the contrast between Josh and Glen might be chalked up to a simple difference of opinion regarding strategy. Such conflicts are common in all social movements, and some activists see the internal differences in precisely these terms. "The pro-life movement as a whole needs a lot of work in unity," says Mariah, a twenty-four-year-old in Boston. "They kind of self-destruct in their little pettiness." Claire, a fellow Boston activist, agrees, explaining that the pro-life movement "uses up a lot of energy fussing about" how to implement its goals.

On closer examination, however, the differences between Josh and Glen run deeper than a simple contrast between their tactical preferences. Both men understand the movement and their own activism in terms of what activists ought to be doing to end abortion. Both of them believe the most appropriate kind of activism is the kind in which they personally are engaged. Both also question the motives of those involved in other kinds of activism. Such differences are far from petty. In fact, the structure of the movement in the United States today is largely defined by exactly these kinds of differences. There is only minimal cooperation among pro-life groups pursuing different strategies, and surprisingly few activists cross the ideological boundaries that define the structure of the movement over the lifetime of their activism.

This chapter continues an examination of the mobilization process by looking at the particular constellations of ideas and organizations that individuals confront as they become activists. It shows how pro-life organizations and activists are tied together by a shared goal of eliminating abortion. Beyond this ultimate goal, however, the movement is structured into a number of different and mutually exclusive camps that I call *social movement streams*. Streams are collections of organizations and activists that share an understanding of the best means to achieve the goal of ending abortion. In other words, differences in beliefs about action constitute the different streams, and the streams, in turn, define the structure of the movement.

A focus on social movement streams helps us better understand the pro-life movement and how individuals become involved. In particular, understanding how streams structure activism reveals how activists become locked in to particular types of activity and—as with Josh and Glen—particular ways of understanding the issue. Streams also offer a useful starting point for greatly expanding our thinking about the role of ideas in social movements more generally. The ideational component of social movements is typically analyzed using some version of the concept of movement frames (Snow et al. 1986; Tarrow 1994; Benford and Snow 2000). Frames are "interpretive schemata" that give meaning and provide an interpretive framework for experiences and events. The framing concept has proved helpful in a variety of studies, but it has also constrained our thinking about the role of ideas in social movements (Oliver and Johnston 2000; Steinberg 1999). The streams of the pro-life movement demonstrate that ideas and beliefs play a much larger role in movement activity than the framing concept allows. Ideas (about abortion, politics, strategies, and so forth) are in fact integral to understanding the very structure of the movement and ultimately play a role in how people become mobilized into the movement as well as what form their activism takes once they are involved. My analysis thus joins a growing body of literature that breaks down the analytic barriers among strategy, identity, and organization that have long existed in social movement theory (Clemens 1997; Polletta 2002; Armstrong 2002).

The Common Goal of the Pro-life Movement

Before delving into the real differences reflected in the contrast between Josh and Glen, it is important to understand that the movement is completely united in its pursuit of a single, ultimate goal: an end to all abortions in the United States. There is universal consensus regarding this goal among pro-life organizations and activists, even if they disagree on everything else about the abortion debate. Pro-life activists categorically reject all abortion as morally wrong, including abortion in cases of rape, incest, or medical/genetic problems with the fetus. They hold this view even when their own activism is aimed at stopping only some cases of abortion or when politically they are willing to accept laws that allow for some exceptions.

Sandra, a thirty-four-year-old in Oklahoma City, reflects this view in her explanation of why even the rape of a ten-year-old does not justify abortion:

A good friend of mine's little sister was . . . Her mother was ten years old. Ten years old! Which is a horrible thing to even think about. A ten-year-old child getting pregnant and carrying a baby for nine months and laboring to give birth to a child at ten years old. But I can't imagine not ever knowing her. And if the woman is raped and then has to go through an abortion also, how is that [pause] . . . I think it would be very hard to go through a nine-month pregnancy if it was rape. But I don't think it's in any way healing to abort it either. Every person is their own person in their own right, in their own merit, and if a life is conceived, it was meant to be conceived, because it has a reason and a purpose on this earth.

Sandra's explanation sums up many pro-life understandings of why abortion must be stopped in all cases: every person is unique regardless of the circumstances of his or her conception; abortion only compounds the pain of a crime such as rape; and pregnancy is a unique gift of God, not to be judged as wanted or unwanted.[2] They thus do not see abortion as a matter of personal choice. Their understanding of the issue is rooted in a universal moral commitment. It is not enough simply to avoid having abortions in their own lives (as their pro-choice counterparts suggest) or even to persuade others of their views. The only final goal of the movement must be to eliminate abortion on behalf of society as a whole.

Activists believe that eliminating abortion means ending all abortions. They do not see "exceptions" or special circumstances as making any particular abortion less abhorrent. "A life is a life is a life. Rape, incest, life of the mother—is that baby any less a human life?" asks Stan, a forty-one-year-old in Oklahoma City. Similarly, a fifty-year-old in Charleston asks, "In the case of rape, why should the child suffer for the sin of the father?" Claire, quoted earlier, agrees: "You can't take a life because of something that the father did." Nor is incest a justification, no matter how hard the decision might be at the time. A number of activists point out that abortions after incest simply cover up a crime and compound the pain victims are already experiencing.

Abortion in cases of genetic disorders—supported by 73 percent of the general public[3]—are particularly abhorrent to pro-life activists. Those in the movement regard abortion motivated by genetic defects

as a kind of genocide that weeds out people with undesirable characteristics. "They were talking about abortion in cases of rape, incest, life of
the mother, psychiatric health of the mother, and defective child. And
it was the defective child one that really upset me the most," explains
Linda, introduced in chapter 2. "That was a eugenics thing!" Many also
worry about a slippery slope in abortion mentality. A gay activist in
Boston put it this way: "If they ever isolate a gene for sexual preference, parents are going to say, 'Well, we live in Marblehead [an affluent
suburb]. And I'm for gay rights, but I don't want to subject my infant,
my child who has this gene and is going to come out gay, to that. So
I'm going to abort to save him. . . . I don't want to bring a gay person
into this world because it's going to be hurtful.' So genetics—that's just
misguided." Even those active in the political arena who work to ban
abortion legally except in cases of rape, incest, or genetic defect see
such legislation as an "incremental" milestone toward the final goal of
eliminating abortion altogether. As Angela, a thirty-year-old in Boston,
explains, "Sometimes you just kind of win things a little at a time, and
you make whatever strides you can." I did not speak to a single pro-life
activist in any of the four cities who believes abortion is justified even
in these difficult situations.

The only cases over which there is some disagreement are those in
which the life of the mother is jeopardized by continued pregnancy.
Most activists largely dismiss these cases as being a red herring in the
debate because of their rarity.[4] When pressed, however, about two-
thirds say that abortion decisions in such cases should ultimately belong to the woman involved—especially if she already has other dependent children. They always point out, however, that "life" for them
refers only to life-and-death situations, not to broader physical or psychological health. Michael, a forty-two-year-old in Boston, says abortion might be justified "if it can be proved that the mother's life, her
life—not health, her *life*—is in jeopardy." Such a woman who continues
her pregnancy at risk to her life is heroic. The other third say abortion is wrong even in these cases. We can't judge whose life is more
important, the mother's or the unborn baby's, and therefore, abortion
is never morally appropriate. Some say that the baby's life is actually
more important; the mother has lived her life, but the unborn baby has
not yet had that chance. "If you understand that that is another life,"
says Jeff, a thirty-five-year-old in the Twin Cities, "even at the peril of
your own life, you always try to do your absolute best to save that child,
to save that other life."[5]

Streams of the Pro-life Movement

Within a common commitment to ending all abortions, the movement is structured by the kinds of dramatic differences in outlook high-lighted by Josh and Glen at the beginning of the chapter. These dif-ferences have created several separate *social movement streams*. Streams are subsets of individuals and organizations that approach social move-ment action in a way that is distinct from others that are part of the movement. Beliefs about how to end abortion in the United States are the defining characteristic that separates the different streams in the case of the pro-life movement.

The stream metaphor is helpful, as it highlights the fact that such subsets of the movement are not fixed, static entities. Instead, their composition can change as the individuals and organizations that compose them, and the environment around them, change. The pro-life movement consists of four movement streams, which I will refer to as (1) politics, (2) direct action, (3) individual outreach, and (4) public outreach. The politics and direct-action streams are perhaps the best known; in the popular imagination, these streams alone compose the pro-life movement. The others have received less media and scholarly attention but are nonetheless equally important in understanding the movement as a whole.

Politics Stream

The political arm of the movement consists of those individuals and organizations whose primary concern is the legislative and legal are-nas. The fight over abortion—and in this stream, it is largely thought of as a fight, battle, or war—is waged through involvement in political campaigns, lobbying, and litigation. Like Glen, activists in the politics stream believe the way to end abortion is to fight the laws and court decisions that make abortion legal. Much of the day-to-day work in this stream of the movement involves standard, institutionalized po-litical and legal activity. Activists try to influence the political process through the use of phone trees, petitions, postcard and letter-writing drives, statehouse rallies, lawsuits, political campaign contributions, and lobbying.

Those in the politics stream understand the abortion issue in politi-cal terms; they see abortion as a political or legal problem that can be most effectively solved through political involvement. What is the most effective way to end abortion? "Through politics. Effective spokesmen and passing legislation and through having debates," says Glen. Many other activists agree:

You're going to have to end it on a legislative and legal front and in court.
(CLAIRE, 59, BOSTON)

It's definitely going to have to come with our legislators.
(MELISSA, 37, CHARLESTON)

I think ultimately, of course, it's going to require some act of government.
(HEATHER, 26, OKLAHOMA CITY)

Joe, a seventy-one-year-old in the Twin Cities, is even more unequivocal: "Abortion will go on and on. It will never stop until something happens. Either the end of the world or get enough Republicans in there that they will pass a [constitutional] amendment." All these activists regard politics as the key arena in which the abortion debate is being fought. In Joe's case, a political solution is the only alternative short of the "end of the world" that might put a stop to abortion.

From the perspective of the politics stream, the immediate tasks of the movement are (1) passage of a "human life amendment" to the Constitution and (2) overturning of the Supreme Court's *Roe v. Wade* and *Doe v. Bolton* decisions.[6] "I don't know another way other than a human life amendment," says fifty-five-year-old Twin Cities activist David in describing how he believes abortion might be ended. Mark, a forty-three-year-old fellow Twin Cities activist, explains further that a "constitutional amendment is the ultimate that would give the law absolute clarity on the issue." Activists in the political stream are distrustful of the courts—which they feel are responsible for making abortion legal against the will of most Americans—and thus see a constitutional amendment as the best kind of victory for the movement. The next best thing would be to overturn the existing Supreme Court rulings that permit abortion. "I think that we have to get *Roe v. Wade* overturned. I think that's an important first step," says Michael, a forty-two-year-old in Boston.

These aims are only sometimes central political issues nationally—the last time Congress voted on a human life amendment, for example, was 1983. The potential for overturning *Roe v. Wade* and *Doe v. Bolton* was raised more recently in the 2005 and 2006 confirmation hearings for Supreme Court nominees John Roberts and Samuel Alito. Before this time, however, the issue had not been significant nationally for at least a decade.

Because both a constitutional amendment and the possibility of overturning *Roe v. Wade* are only partially and episodically in the eye of the larger public, the everyday efforts of the politics stream of the pro-life movement are more frequently devoted to fighting for smaller political objectives, such as passing laws that reduce the accessibility of abortion or the ease of obtaining one. These efforts call for the barring of government support or payment for abortion services; restrictions on particular abortion procedures (especially intact dilation and extraction—commonly referred to as "partial-birth" abortion);[7] restrictions on who can perform abortions and where they can be performed; changes in how abortion facilities are regulated; requirements for spousal notification, parental notification, and/or consent for minors to undergo abortion procedures; mandatory "cooling-off" or waiting periods before abortions can be performed; and requirements for counseling on fetal development or abortion alternatives such as adoption.

Many within the politics stream see these smaller legislative and legal goals as building to larger objectives. Bill, a sixty-eight-year-old pro-life leader in Boston, describes the approach this way: "It's possible to achieve a consensus on some of these areas where the polls say people are not satisfied with the status quo. Straighten those out state by state by state. You know, if you can't do it by a constitutional amendment, it really becomes in a sense a state's rights issue. I think if we could get parental consent—the state legislatures are positive about that—get a twenty-four-hour waiting period so people aren't rushed into it, get critical need-to-know information provided to every woman who is considering abortion, that kind of thing." The idea is the same as what Glen expressed at the beginning of this chapter: take whatever steps are possible to further restrict the availability and incidence of abortion, even if you cannot ban it altogether. Faith in this "incremental" approach is common within the politics stream of the movement.

The politics stream contains many movement organizations. The National Right to Life Committee (NRLC) is the best known and best financed. Other notable national pro-life organizations in the politics stream, such as Americans United for Life and Feminists for Life, have substantially fewer resources and less influence. State affiliates of the NRLC lead the politics stream of the movement at the state and local levels, although there also exist local politics stream organizations—such as Minnesota Lawyers for Life in the Twin Cities—that are not related to the NRLC.

What unites organizations and activists within the politics stream of the pro-life movement is a common understanding of abortion in political terms and a vision of the movement's strategies as rooted in legislative and legal change. "The ultimate goal of the National Right to Life Committee," says its introductory literature, "is to restore legal protection to innocent human life" (National Right to Life Committee 2000). The opening presidential letter in its 1999 handbook is an extended defense of the NRLC's political focus: "Changing public policy is one of the essential components of any strategy to change and subvert the 'culture of death.'" The organization was heavily involved in all stages of the 2000 U.S. presidential campaign, including helping George W. Bush secure victories in the Republican primaries and filing its own lawsuit in Florida to stop manual recounting of votes that could have changed the outcome of the general election (Morris 2000).

More generally, both the NRLC and its state affiliates in the cities I visited publish their own voter guides, endorse pro-life candidates, and make donations to pro-life politicians. The NRLC's chief activity is lobbying, and the group is considered to be one of the most effective lobbyists in Washington, D.C. (Birnbaum 1999). Although the NRLC and the state affiliates do sometimes support nonpolitical programs and activities, their central focus and the bulk of their resources and effort are devoted to politics. "I believe it's important to be involved in politics," says Sidney, a seventy-two-year-old in Oklahoma City, summarizing his pro-life experience, "and I suppose the main way I've been involved is writing letters and also supporting with modest amounts of money legislators and congressmen who are running for election or reelection." Sidney, Claire, Mark, Heather, Bill, Joe, Melissa, Michael, Glen, and all the other activists in the politics stream of the movement agree: abortion is a political problem that requires a political solution.

Direct-Action Stream

The atmosphere outside the Charleston Women's Medical Center early on most Saturday mornings is tense. Although protest in front of this abortion clinic can happen on any day of the week, the bulk of the pro-life activists come at this time. A large, bearded security guard in a bright yellow T-shirt glowers at the small groups of people from near the door of the clinic. The first time I pulled up and parked in the public lot across the street, next to the cars of the pro-life activists, the guard crossed the street with a video camera and made a show of filming both me and the license plate on my car.

The Charleston clinic had ten to thirty activists in front of it on any given Saturday morning during the period I observed their activity; my interviews suggest this number was typical at other times as well. Some activists pray silently, their heads bowed, for the entire time they are there. Others attempt to talk to women arriving at the clinic, calling to them in the parking lot and offering them pamphlets. Still others hold pro-life signs ("Choose Life"; "Abortion Is Murder"; "Human Garbage") and yell out slogans and accusations ("Abortion is murder"; "Baby killer"; "Mothers are meant to protect their children"). I never witnessed any violence or arrests at the Charleston clinic, nor were the police ever summoned, but those possibilities always seemed very real.

Attending pro-life protests in front of the clinics is the hardest part of conducting research on the movement, largely because emotions among the participants are always so high and the conflict between pro-life and pro-choice forces is so palpable. The intensity, anger, and sadness of pro-life activists is frequently combined with crying young women (or their crying mothers) entering the clinic; shouting matches between activists and those using the clinic; honking and yelled-out insults from drivers of passing cars; and grim-faced, determined pro-choice volunteers who are sometimes present at the clinics to escort clients into the centers. "It's kind of like going to another country and learning how things are done," explains Suzanne, a fifty-year-old in Charleston, in describing what it is like to spend time in front of the Charleston clinic. "I don't think people can really understand the issue unless they've been there some, just to see what is going on." Clinic protest is a world unto itself, populated by a distinct group of activists who understand abortion and their involvement in terms much different from those in the politics stream of the movement.

Pro-life activists who focus on protest and other activities at abortion clinics are part of the direct-action stream of the pro-life movement. The stream is composed of those individuals and organizations that emphasize the immediacy of abortion and focus on "saving" individual babies by intervening directly to stop women from having abortions. This is the thoroughly noninstitutional side of the movement. Their actions consist of protests, picketing, demonstrations, vigils, and civil disobedience. They believe that only by directly and personally intervening in the provision of abortion services is one really "doing something" about the problem.

Pro-life direct action has led to the innovation of two new tactics unique to the pro-life movement: rescues and sidewalk counseling. The goal of both techniques is to stop abortion on the level of each individual occurrence; sometimes through persuasion and sometimes through force, activists seek to prevent imminent abortions from occurring. Dana, a twenty-eight-year-old in Charleston, describes her feelings at a pro-life meeting when she realized she had to get involved more directly: "These children that are dying don't need people to sit around and talk about them. They don't need people to rally. I mean you have pep rallies, that's fine. But I'll tell you what, it does strike a chord in me—we have to do something further." For direct-action activists such as Dana, the immediacy of the danger posed by abortion calls for an immediate and direct response, something "further" than trying to work out an agreement through meetings and discussion.

The first civil disobedience to oppose abortion actually occurred several years before the *Roe v. Wade* and *Doe v. Bolton* decisions: a march that turned into a sit-in at George Washington University Hospital in Washington, D.C., on June 6, 1970. The event looked like many of the antiwar protests of the period, and participants did not intend to be arrested (Boldt and Hobald 1970). The first sit-in of any size took place five years later, just outside of Washington, D.C., and a series of sit-ins then occurred in a number of states over the course of the late 1970s (Maxwell 2002). The term *rescue* to refer to saving babies by shutting down abortion clinics was first used in Philadelphia in 1985 (Shepard 1991). Rescues bring hundreds or even thousands of protesters to a single abortion clinic and shut it down by physically blockading the building and preventing both clinic staff and clients from entering. Rescuers sit or lock arms in front of clinic entrances to bar access and are often trained in passive resistance to arrest. Efforts to keep clinics closed became increasingly elaborate in the 1980s as the police became more efficient at arresting protesters and clearing entranceways to clinics. Ron, a fifty-four-year-old in Boston, describes one such incident: "There were people who had outfitted a van so that it was well locked. You'd almost need to have equipment to get into it. . . . You'd block the [clinic] door with the van. It was all set up so there would be a hole in the van and we would be sitting on the ground, but up above, we would be locked into the floor of the van. So it would be a very sticky thing to get everybody out. And there were special locks and everything." Ron was "honored to be asked" to be one of the activists locked to the van in front of the clinic entrance. Police eventually extricated him and the other activists after several hours. Ron was arrested, convicted, and spent three months in jail for his rescue activities. Activists used similarly elaborate schemes at many clinics in the late 1980s.

Rescues can last from a few hours to several days, and participants generally chant, pray, and sing songs throughout the protest. Those actually blockading the clinic are supported by others who bring them food and water but do not risk arrest. Jail sentences and the conditions of incarceration stiffened in the early 1990s, however. Direct campaigns to close clinics are now a thing of the past, due in large part to the Freedom of Access to Clinic Entrances (FACE) law passed by Congress in 1994 and the National Organization for Women's success in having the RICO (Racketeer Influenced and Corrupt Organizations Act) antiracketeering statutes applied to protesters. FACE and RICO impose draconian penalties for civil disobedience in front of abortion clinics, and long jail sentences coupled with massive monetary fines have all but eliminated the tactic.[8]

The direct-action stream of the movement has not been eliminated; it has simply changed its tactics. Today, direct action looks like the scene I described in front of the clinic in Charleston; individuals and organizations hold regular demonstrations and prayer vigils in front of abortion clinics, picket clinics and prominent public locations (such as schools, hospitals, courthouses, and statehouses) with large posters displaying pro-life slogans, and even distribute leaflets in the neighborhoods of physicians who perform abortions. Activists such as Josh, introduced at the beginning of the chapter, no longer participate in rescues, but they remain in front of clinics around the country.

The direct-action stream has also developed a second innovative movement tactic: sidewalk counseling. Sidewalk counseling is the term activists use to describe attempts to contact pregnant women as they enter a clinic and persuade them to carry their pregnancies to term. Individuals who participate in sidewalk counseling run the gamut from quiet and passive to vocal and aggressive. Some sidewalk counselors I observed would approach women and ask them if they were interested in learning more about their baby. Others would try to give women literature without saying anything at all. At the other extreme are activists who yell at pregnant women, screaming "Don't kill your baby" or calling them "murderers."[9]

Sidewalk counselors see themselves as the central front in the battle over abortion. "I think it's the thing that really steps you over the line into the pro-life movement," says Charles, a sixty-four-year-old in the Twin Cities, "If you've gone and done sidewalk counseling, there's no question that you're pro-life, you know." The telling of success stories—the "saves," in the parlance of sidewalk counseling—is an important element in reinforcing this sense that sidewalk counseling is central. Consider the following narrative given by Josh:

See, we save children at the clinic. We do it in more of a quiet way; we do it through the sidewalk counselors. We saved one lady, and she and her husband came to be Christians. She was pregnant with what I believe was her fourth child, and they couldn't afford it. They just couldn't afford it. But they knew that killing a child was wrong. So our sidewalk counselors . . . sat there, and they were going to abort it, and we sat there and we talked to them about it. And they finally decided to save it. . . . So later on, about eight months later, before the child was born, we called. We were constantly in contact with them. If we can find a name and stuff, these ladies are with them all the time. And we called them, and the father talked with us, and he said, "Hey, Mom went for a checkup. Mom is doing great. And babies are doing great." And we said, "Babies!?" He says, "Oh yeah. They didn't pick up one heartbeat, they picked up three heartbeats." That day she was going to abort triplets. . . . And I guess they're about three or four [years old] now. But we saved those kids.

Gary, a forty-seven-year-old in Charleston, provides another example:

We did save a baby two weeks ago. There was a black man that was out there with a little one-year-old or two-year-old baby, holding it, and his girlfriend went in. And he was outside, so I called him over, and I said, "Oh, is that your girlfriend?" And he said, "Yeah. Man, you don't know." He said, "We can't afford it." You know, blah, blah, blah. So we talked, and I told him a little bit about my story. And I said, "Here, let me hold your baby; you go in there and stop her." He said, "You'd do that?" I said, "Yeah." I said, "I'm a white man." I said, "If I was a racist . . . you know, I wouldn't be out here standing. Let me hold your little boy while you go in and stop her. I know all these people, like the NAACP, they see this and they wouldn't believe it. Because they've stereotyped us as being, you know, that we want to keep the [Confederate] flag flying for racist reasons. That we want to be superior. And that has nothing to do with it." I said, "Here I am; I just want justice and stuff." So he went in, and he came back, and he said, "They kicked me out." And I said, "Well, try again.' So he went back in, so he came out, and he said, "I can't change her mind." So, anyway, I left, but some of my people stayed behind. He came out later, and she came out. She had changed her mind, saved the baby, a little boy. A little baby is living today. So there are some good stories.

Success stories like these validate direct-action activists' efforts; they are offered as proof both that they make a difference and that they are right in their beliefs about strategy. These narratives dramatize the fact that actual babies are saved by sidewalk counseling. They also articulate other moral lessons beyond the "saves." Josh's story highlights the concern of many activists that pregnant women don't have all the information they need when they choose abortion. In Gary's case, his telling of the success story centers on how sidewalk counseling transcends racism. Regardless of whether sidewalk counseling actually leads to fewer abortions,[10] these stories play an important role in the activists' own self-understanding.

Sidewalk counselors hand out literature on fetal development, the possible medical complications of abortion procedures, and potential psychological effects of having an abortion. Figures 5.1 and 5.2 show examples of the kind of material used in sidewalk counseling efforts. The first, entitled "What They Won't Tell You at the Abortion Clinic," is produced by Pro-life Action Ministries in the Twin Cities and focuses on the inhumanity of abortion and the danger of the procedure. The second, entitled "It's Your Turn," is produced by a national sidewalk counseling organization in Atlanta and lists more than thirty-five negative physical and emotional effects of abortion on women. Such brochures do not try to encapsulate the entire set of pro-life arguments but instead focus on immediate concerns that a pregnant woman might have and that might persuade her to continue her pregnancy. Counselors also have brochures specialized to particular audiences; thus there are brochures with titles such as "For Men Only" and "Abortion: The Black Woman's Voice."

The most violent elements of the direct-action stream receive the bulk of both media and academic attention (for example, Jenkins 1999; Reiter 2000; Bader and Baird-Windle 2001). Harassment and abuse certainly occur in front of abortion clinics, but the activists involved in such attacks are a distinct minority even in this stream of the movement. Direct action is distinctive because it consists of noninstitutionalized behavior carried out in the street and usually right in front of freestanding abortion clinics.[11] The focus on the most confrontational elements of the movement leads to an image of direct action as violent and episodic, an image that overlooks most of the activity that actually takes place in the direct-action stream. Hundreds of pro-life activists are involved in direct action every day in just the four cities I visited. Their regular presence in front of clinics, daily conversations with clinic staff, and never-ceasing attempts to stop women from entering clinics almost certainly have had a stronger effect on the accessibility

What They Won't

Tell You

at the

ABORTION

CLINIC . . .

This is a tough decision you have to make, but please be mature. Only an immature person thinks of herself alone. This brochure was not written by a militant, pro-life male, nor a 50-year-old grandmother who has never been faced with a problem pregnancy. It was written by a woman who was eighteen and pregnant once. A woman who was scared, like you are, and chose abortion. After nine years I know what the right choice was, and is, and I just want you to know
What They Didn't Tell Me . . .

This brochure was written by a Pro-Life Action Ministries member who experienced abortion personally.

To order copies of this brochure, please write:

PRO-LIFE ACTION MINISTRIES
P.O. BOX 75368
ST. PAUL, MN 55175-0368
(612) 771-1500

They Won't Tell You . . .

1. Abortion is not safe.
Contrary to the belief that abortion is as simple as removing a wart, it is actually a very serious procedure that can have very serious results. The clinic personnel will lead you to believe that complications rarely arise, but that is not the case. Many women have been damaged for life as a result of their *legal* abortion.
Your cervical muscle may be damaged in an abortion because the cervix is forcefully dilated. This means that any future pregnancies have a greater chance of resulting in miscarriage or premature delivery. Damage to the uterine wall is another concern. Perforation (puncturing) of the uterus, infection, hemorrhage, and blood clots are only a few of the complications that you could end up with. If you do have a "successful" abortion, scar tissue may still form which can cause infertility, miscarriages or tubal pregnancies.
Some women are able to become pregnant only once in their lives. **This may be the only child you'll ever have. An abortion can increase your chance of not being able to become pregnant again when you desire a child.** Do you want to take that kind of risk?

They Won't Tell You . . .

2. Abortion leaves emotional scars.
Most often a woman will feel the consequences of her decision within days of her abortion. If they don't appear immediately, they will appear as she gets older. Emotional scars include unexplained depression, a loss of the ability to get close to others, repressed emotions, a hardening of the spirit, thwarted maternal instincts (which may lead to child abuse or neglect later in life), intense feelings of guilt and thoughts of suicide.[2] Don't be fooled — every abortion leaves emotional scars.
[1] Questions & Answers on Abortion, Minnesota Citizens Concerned for Life.
[2] "Before You Make the Decision . . ." Women Exploited by Abortion.

They Won't Tell You . . .

3. Abortion kills a baby.
Before you even know you're pregnant, your baby's heart begins to beat. At six weeks brain waves are measurable and your baby moves and responds to touch. At eight weeks she is perfectly developed, with fingers and toes, even her own set of fingerprints. By ten weeks she can squint, swallow and suck her thumb. If you tickled her nose she would move her head away. By 11-12 weeks, all body systems are present and working.[3] All she needs to become a healthy newborn is time and nourishment. Nothing new develops after 12 weeks! What would you name her? Rebecca? Stephanie?

They Won't Tell You . . .

4. Abortion is violent.
The most common method of abortion used in early pregnancy is suction aspiration.[1] The cervix is forced open. A vacuum device 29 times more powerful than a home vacuum cleaner is used to suction out the "contents of the uterus."[4]
A D & E is performed after 16 weeks. As in the suction method, your baby is torn to pieces, but this time the abortionist uses a special instrument to tear the arms and legs from the body. He punctures her soft spot, suctions out the brain and crushes the skull, then removes the remaining body parts.
Another method done after 16 weeks is the saline abortion. A salt solution is injected into your baby's bag of waters. It poisons the baby and burns off the outer layer of skin. She actually convulses in pain for the hour or so that it takes for the solution to do its deadly job. You then go into labor and give birth to a dead baby.[5]
A hysterotomy abortion (last trimester) is done by making an incision in the mother's abdomen. The child is lifted out and left to die.
[3] "Handbook on Abortion," Dr. and Mrs. J.C. Willke.
[4] Ibid.
[5] Ibid.

They Won't Tell You . . .

5. Abortion exploits women.
The counselors at an abortion clinic will use obscure terms such as "product of conception," "contents of the uterus," and "fetal tissue" to refer to your baby. They will rarely advise you to carry your baby to term because they are operating for profit and they don't want to lose your business. Essentially, they are making money off of your problem! The abortionist can make more money in 30 minutes doing an abortion than a regular physician will caring for a woman through a nine-month pregnancy. Are you going to be the poor woman who finances his next trip to Europe?

They Won't Tell You . . .

6. There *are* alternatives to abortion.
There are many organizations that can offer you practical support such as maternity and baby clothes, a place to live, pre-natal care, and financial aid. Counseling is also available to help you through this traumatic time.
Please think carefully about your future. The decision you make in the next few weeks will affect you for the rest of your life. If you're unsure about having an abortion, take just one more day to think about it — don't let anyone pressure you into a decision you're not ready to make yet.
Please call us — we want to help . . . and we'll give you the truth.

[handwritten note: ← use "her" to get more sympathy]

5.1 Sidewalk counseling brochure from Pro-life Action Ministries

of abortion services than the more violent tactics that certain activists have sometimes used.

Individual Outreach Stream

Carol, a fifty-two-year-old in Charleston, explains why she liked to provide pro-life advice to individual pregnant women: "They were alone, had nowhere else to turn. They were scared, they were trying to do the

It's Your Turn
Please Think of Yourself

Don't let anyone deprive you of your health or the love of your child.

Abortion can never solve any problem. It will only create new ones, and open the door to physical, mental and emotional pain that can scar you for a lifetime.

You will not *"become a mother."* You are a mother right now. Let us help you protect yourself and your child.

* *Do what many other women before you have done.*
* *Simply get up and walk out!*
* *There are many people waiting to help you through your entire pregnancy.*

**FOR HELP WITH AN
UNPLANNED PREGNANCY,
CALL TOLL-FREE:
1-800-542-4453
OR LOCALLY:**

Lowcountry Crisis Pregnancy Center
553-3505
Alpha Outreach Ministries
845-5623

When you have a chubby little baby with its arms wrapped around your neck saying, "I love you, Mommy," you will know you have made the right decision to leave this place and give you and your child life.

If you have already had an abortion and now know it was a mistake, please get the help you need.

Contact a pregnancy help center in your area and they will direct you to someone who understands and cares.

OR

If you need any kind of medical, legal, or emotional help after an abortion, call:

1-800-634-2224

Written by Karen Black
(770) 232-1991
Women 4 Women
"Speaking the Truth in Love"

It's
Your
Turn

It's Your Turn
To Protect Yourself
Physically

Possible Effects

* Intense Pain
* Excessive Bleeding
* Infections
* Shock
* Coma
* Death
* Loss of Other Organs
* Breast Cancer
* Peritonitis
* Future Menstrual Problems
* Stillbirths
* Tubal Pregnancies
* Sterility
* Insomnia
* Vomiting
* Gastro-intestinal Problems
* Frigidity
* Weight Loss/Gain

ABORTION IS
NOT SAFE

Hundreds of women have died from legal abortions and thousands more have been injured. Continuing your pregnancy is safer than having an abortion.

Laminaria CAN be successfully removed by a competent doctor, preventing infection and allowing your pregnancy to continue normally.

It's Your Turn
To Protect Yourself
Mentally/Emotionally

Possible Effects

* Depression
* Anger
* Feelings of Hopelessness
* Mourning
* Regret and Remorse
* Intense Feeling of Loss
* Guilt
* Self-Hatred
* Self-Destructive Tendencies
* Suicide
* Inability to Forget Baby
* Nightmares
* Inability to Forgive Yourself
* Can't Forget Baby's Due Date
* Loss of Sexual Interest
* Drug/Alcohol Abuse
* Child Abuse
* Troubled Relationships
* Flashbacks of the Abortion
* Repeat Abortions

You, as a woman, have strong maternal instincts made to protect your child at any cost.

If you violate those instincts and actually pay someone to harm your child, you will bring great emotional damage to yourself.

Listen to a woman who did NOT protect herself:

I wish I could be there in person to tell you all that I went through as a result of choosing abortion.

I thought that after my abortion all my problems were over. They had only begun. During the next six years I experienced so much guilt, shame and disgust for myself. I began a course of self-destruction with alcohol, cocaine and men. This course only led me back to where I began--pregnant again, which led to another abortion.

After the second abortion, I hit an all-time low. I was in serious financial trouble, couldn't stand men anymore, and drank all the time.

It wasn't until I saw a picture of an unborn child that I realized my guilt and self-destructive behavior were due to the fact that I let someone harm my children.

I hope that as you read this you will not make the same mistake I made. -- Carol W.

Listen to a woman who DID protect herself:

In March 1990 I was 4 1/2 months pregnant, living alone, and barely making ends meet. I did not have a way to pay for the expense of having a baby and I was very confused about what would be the right thing to do. I felt that I wouldn't be able to provide a good life for my unborn child, but I also knew in my heart that harming my baby was wrong and that it would haunt me for the rest of my life.

I had already made the appointment and arrived at the place where the abortion would be performed when I changed my mind. I realized that giving my child life, whether it was filled with worldly possessions or not, was better than never giving my baby a chance at all.

I didn't realize all the help that is available for women in my position. I gave birth to my daughter in August 1990. There is no greater joy than holding your own child. To look into her eyes and know that I almost killed her overwhelms me, and I thank the Lord every day that I changed my mind in time. The love that we share could never be replaced by anything money can buy. -- Karen O.

5.2 Sidewalk counseling brochure from Women 4 Women

right thing, or they just accidentally called Birthright thinking that they were going to have an abortion. And then you had the opportunity to give your best, in the hopes that you could reach her to help her understand that there is help, there are people willing to help, and she is not out there by herself. She doesn't have to go through this by herself. And that's the biggest message." Carol's description sums up the feelings of many within the third stream of the pro-life movement—the individual outreach stream. The people and organizations that comprise this stream concentrate on individual relationships—away from both the abortion clinic and the political realm—as the key to addressing the abortion issue. Their focus is rooted in a belief that women with unplanned, crisis, or problem pregnancies need to be reached and helped psychologically, emotionally, and materially. In Carol's words, they don't have to go through such pregnancies by themselves. Activists in the individual outreach stream believe that such women, with the proper support and guidance, will naturally choose to forgo abortion, carry their pregnancies to term, and either keep their baby or give him or her up for adoption.

Individual outreach is perhaps the least publicized and least understood stream of the movement. Ironically, it is also the stream to which the majority of all volunteer hours in the pro-life movement is devoted. More individuals are involved in volunteering more time in the individual outreach stream than in any other movement activity. The number of organizations involved in individual outreach is greater than the number involved in all the other streams combined, in large part because one-on-one counseling is very labor-intensive.

The activism of this stream is carried out primarily in what are called crisis pregnancy centers (CPCs).[12] CPCs vary from single rented rooms or empty storefronts to large freestanding clinics with space devoted to records, administration, counseling, clothing and baby supplies, and even medical care. In all, there are between 2,500 and 4,000 CPCs nationwide (Lin and Dailard 2002; O'Bannon 2000), a staggering number considering that there are only 447 abortion clinics and a total of fewer than 2,000 abortion providers (Finer and Henshaw 2003). In some cases, CPCs are established next door to or directly across the street from abortion clinics. Although many people remain unaware of this network of pro-life centers and the tens of thousands of volunteers who work at them, CPCs first appeared in the late 1960s, years before the *Roe v. Wade* and *Doe v. Bolton* decisions.

The primary goals of all CPCs are first to convince women who are considering abortion to come into their centers and then to convince those who do come in to continue their pregnancies to term. All clinics offer free pregnancy testing.[13] They also try to counsel women, especially those with positive pregnancy tests. The form and content of such counseling vary from center to center. Counselors range from untrained volunteers in some organizations (for example, Birthright of Charleston) to professionally trained, government-licensed, paid social workers in others (for example, New Life Family Services in the Twin Cities). Some offer a religious message (for example, Crisis Pregnancy Center in Oklahoma City) and evangelize openly with all the women they counsel, while others advocate against abortion on entirely secular grounds (for example, A Woman's Concern in Boston). Some centers include abstinence, birth control, and other related issues in their counseling, while others consciously avoid such topics.

CPCs also offer an array of services beyond basic pregnancy tests and one-on-one pro-life counseling. Centers provide ongoing classes on labor, parenting, and relationships; financial management and job search education; referrals for discounted or free medical care and homes for unwed mothers; new and used baby clothes, cribs, baby seats, and diapers; and direct financial assistance for food, rent, and other expenses. In some cases, CPCs offer a range of medical care beyond pregnancy tests by volunteer physicians and licensed midwives, including prenatal care, routine checkups, immunizations, tests for STDs, and other non-emergency services. Centers also hold baby showers, birthday parties, and other celebrations for women who go through their programs.

Women come to CPCs for a variety of reasons. CPCs are listed as "abortion alternative" clinics in most yellow pages listings, and their advertising is often deliberately ambiguous. Figure 5.3 reproduces the first two pages of the main yellow pages in Oklahoma City. "Abortion Alternatives" is the second entry in the entire phone book and comes before "Abortion Providers." Every paid advertisement on these two pages is for a crisis pregnancy center, even though the ads use phrases such as "Considering Abortion?" and "Abortion Information." Every one of the ads offers free pregnancy tests and counseling. "A lot of times we deal with people calling on the phone and they think we're an abortion clinic," says Jean, a forty-six-year-old CPC volunteer in Oklahoma City. "We're not, but at least that voice is on there, and we try to give them as much as we can on the phone to try to direct them and have them come in to see us so they can have all the facts." Volunteers and staff in most of the clinics say that these yellow pages ads are important in generating such phone calls and bringing women to their organizations. Many come solely because of the offer of free pregnancy tests. Others come under the mistaken belief that the CPC provides abortion services or referrals.

Most CPCs are independently organized, funded, and staffed. In some cases, such as Total Life Care centers in the Twin Cities, an organization will run a network of several centers in one area. There are also several national crisis pregnancy organizations with which many local organizations choose to affiliate. Three of the largest today are Birthright, the National Institute of Family and Life Advocates (NIFLA), and Care-Net.[14] The federations facilitate communication among CPCs, provide legal help and liability insurance, set standards for counseling and the operation of member CPCs, and conduct some national advertising and fund-raising.

Although the bulk of individual outreach in CPCs consists of prolife advocacy to pregnant women, activists in this stream of the movement have also been developing outreach to women who they believe have suffered psychological trauma as a result of abortion and former abortion providers who have renounced pro-choice views. Activists talk about "postabortion trauma" as a documented medical condition brought on by the experience of having an abortion,[15] comparable to posttraumatic stress disorder. Such women are sometimes called abortion survivors, and CPCs have begun to expand their counseling to them. The Catholic Church has also been active in developing such outreach; the Catholic dioceses in all four cities I visited have begun "Project Rachel" programs designed to offer religious reconciliation and emotional healing for such women.

Activists in the individual outreach stream understand abortion in terms that are much different from those used in the politics and direct-action streams. They are more likely to express sadness than anger over abortion and are more likely to talk about the problem in terms of relationships rather than individual choices. Erin, whose story was introduced in chapter 3, describes the volunteers at CPCs this way: "They don't judge the young ladies that come in or the young men that come with them. They help them. They love them. And even if they have an abortion, they are still welcome to come back. They'll still love them and help them. Because most women that I know that have had abortions really struggle with that afterwards, too." Erin reflects the views of many in her focus on love, help, and other relational resources as the key tools in the fight against abortion.

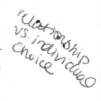
relationship vs. individual Choice

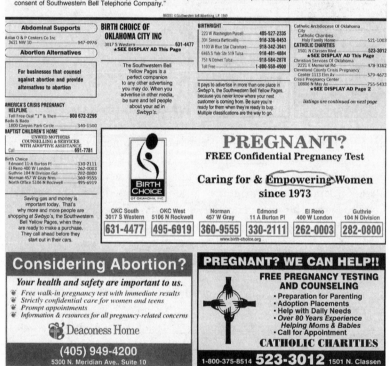

5.3 Crisis pregnancy center yellow pages ads, Oklahoma City

Public Outreach Stream

The fourth stream of the movement is the public outreach stream. Activists and organizations in this stream seek to end abortion by educating the wider public about what they see as the horrors of abortion and the lies of the pro-choice movement. By doing so, activists hope to create a "culture of life" in the United States in which individuals will vote for pro-life candidates, publicly associate themselves with a pro-

listings are continued on page 4

life worldview, and refuse to consider abortion for themselves or advocate abortion for others. "First and foremost, you have to get people to understand that an unborn baby is a human being and that all human beings, the very first and foremost fundamental human right of everyone is to not be murdered," explains Tom, a thirty-eight-year-old in the Twin Cities. Public outreach activists believe that if they could just "get people to understand," abortion would no longer be tolerated.

In contrast to individual outreach, this stream focuses on reaching the maximum number of people as frequently as possible. Public outreach generally takes one of two forms: advertising or specialized educational programs. Pro-life organizations use a variety of ads just as any other advocacy group or for-profit business does. Pro-life messages appear on billboards and bus banners as well as in radio spots, television commercials, and newspaper ads (see figure 5.4). To educate the public, the movement produces pamphlets, handouts, newspaper inserts, speakers programs, and even school curricula. Education is seen as crucial because this stream understands public support for abortion not as a reasoned difference of opinion but as a result of ignorance about the issue. Brian, a thirty-year-old physician in Charleston, expresses faith that Americans would be overwhelmingly pro-life if they just had the scientific facts: "I think if the average American understood the development of a fetus, you know, organ systems intact by what, week seven or eight and can process pain by week fifteen or whatever, I think they would—with that in conjunction with actually viewing what happened in one [an abortion]—I think a lot of misinformation would be dispelled and the average American who now claims to be pro-choice wouldn't be." Misinformation is thus the source of the problem. The solution is to concentrate on educating the public about the facts rather than persuade people of a particular point of view, as twenty-four-year-old Boston activist Mariah explains: "I mean we do have the scientific information [on fetal development] available to us. . . . And it irks me to no end when you read all this stuff saying, well, they 'believe,' and it's all religious, encased in the lingo and whatever. And that those Roman Catholic right-wing extremist conservatives believe that it's a baby. Well, it is scientific fact!" For Brian, Mariah, and other activists in the public outreach stream, the pro-life voice is not being heard. Education is needed to inform the public.

Direct public advertising—and especially paid newspaper supplements—is the way this stream most commonly brings its viewpoint to the public. Human Life Alliance in the Twin Cities, for example, focuses entirely on the production and distribution of newspaper inserts on abortion and, more recently, euthanasia. Founded in 1977, Human Life Alliance first placed its inserts in Minnesota daily newspapers; now it places inserts in college campus papers nationwide. More than twenty million copies of its pro-life "She's a Child, Not a Choice" insert have been distributed in the last fifteen years. In Oklahoma City, Life Issues places a variety of similar inserts in local city and college newspapers.

The educational focus of organizations in this stream of the movement is evident in their self-descriptions. The short mission statement

5.4 Prolife Minnesota/Prolife across America billboard in the Twin Cities. Source: Photograph courtesy of Bruce Munson.

of Prolife Minnesota, which sponsors pro-life billboards across the state, uses the word *educational* in every sentence: "Since 1989, Prolife Minnesota's educational mission is to reach out through media ads to people who may not be reached in any other way. Totally educational in its approach, Prolife Minnesota is the only group bringing life-saving informational messages on a state-wide, continuing basis through: Billboards, TV Ads, Radio, Newspaper Ads, Poster Projects, 800# Hotline Link to Prolife Crisis Pregnancy and Post-abortion services, Providing literature. Totally educational, tax-deductible and non-political." Life Issues in Oklahoma City describes its purpose as "to educate the general public on the issues of abortion, euthanasia and infanticide." Such groups limit their pro-life activities to the production of pamphlets, handouts, and inserts that explain various aspects of the pro-life movement or controversies in the abortion debate. This literature is tailored to its intended mode of distribution, so materials destined for state institutions (especially schools) are doggedly secular, while pamphlets to be laid out on church tables make God the central focus, even if the ostensible topic—chastity, for example—is the same. Some organizations produce religious and nonreligious versions of exactly the same brochure. Pro-life groups are also involved in developing pro-life curricula for schools and churches that deal with chastity, birth control, abortion, sexuality, euthanasia, and so forth. They actively seek out speaking engagements. Pro-life presentations are given in schools, hospitals, and prisons as well as for civic groups, women's groups, Girl Scout troops, and churches.

As in the other streams, those involved in public outreach generally view their work as the core of the pro-life movement. Consider these statements from activists in this stream:

Ultimately, it's changing hearts and minds is what it is. And, you know, whether a constitutional amendment ever comes into existence or not, if the hearts and minds of the majority of the people are against abortion, and the doctors don't do them, there won't be any. The ultimate thing really is that direction.

(MARK, 43, TWIN CITIES)

I just feel like education is everything.

(ANGELA, 30, BOSTON)

The law doesn't seem to be the biggest factor in it. That's why even praying at the abortion clinics or picketing is almost a waste of time. . . . Educating children and making sure they know what it [abortion] is and being there for them is the only way. . . . I don't know if making it legal or illegal is even relevant.

(SHARON, 50, CHARLESTON)

Mark claims changing people's hearts and minds through education is the "ultimate" direction of the movement. Angela sees education as "everything." Cynthia sees educating children as the "only" way. In each case, these activists privilege broad educational efforts over the strategies pursued by other streams. They understand the abortion problem as one of ignorance and misinformation. The only solution, therefore, is to educate people.

Together but Not One: Defining Movement Streams

The pro-life movement in the United States is structured as a set of organizations and activists with a universally held goal of ending all abortion but segmented into four different movement streams: a politics stream, which focuses on legislation and litigation; a direct-action stream, which focuses on street protest and sidewalk counseling in front of clinics; an individual outreach stream, which focuses on individual women and their pregnancies; and a public outreach stream, which emphasizes education and broad societal awareness of the abortion issue. Streams incorporate what Elisabeth Clemens (1997) calls "logics of appropriateness." They are built on different understandings of the "group etiquette" observed by Nina Eliasoph (1998) in suburban voluntary associations but incorporate not just discursive expectations but relational and organizational ones as well.

Organizations and Streams

These four streams of the pro-life movement are remarkably distinct. As the descriptions of each stream show, organizations in one stream are seldom involved in activities outside the stream in which they are embedded. The boundaries become especially apparent when organizations bump up against them. The bylaws of groups in the politics stream often expressly prohibit the organizations' officers, board members, and staff from protest activity in front of clinics (a direct-action activity). Larry, a single forty-nine-year-old in Boston, once dropped his letter of resignation from the board of directors of MCFL, a politics stream organization, in the mail on his way to a protest sponsored by Operation Rescue Boston, a group in the direct-action stream of the movement.

The direct-action stream is similarly insulated from the rest of the movement. None of the direct-action organizations I studied has a lobbyist, for example, while every pro-life organization in the politics stream has at least one lobbyist and sometimes more. The mission statement of Pro-life Action Ministries, the main direct-action group in the Twin Cities, clearly illustrates the difference between direct action and the politics stream: "Pro-Life Action Ministries is a Christian, pro-life ministry established in order to rescue the lives of innocent human beings in danger of being killed by means of abortion, infanticide or euthanasia. We believe that the 'right to life,' from the moment of conception until natural death, is the most basic, fundamental, God-given human right. . . . Through peaceful direct-action and educational projects, Pro-Life Action Ministries, Inc. seeks to protect and save all unwanted, innocent human life from destruction and to offer women non-violent alternatives to abortion." There is no mention here of trying to promote legislation, change public policy, or overturn court decisions.

The individual outreach stream, too, is organizationally distinct from the others. Groups in other streams do not themselves run CPC programs, nor do CPCs include legislative work or sidewalk counseling in their activities. Sharon, a fifty-year-old in Charleston, explains that in many instances, the activities of different streams are incompatible: "If a woman is coming into the crisis pregnancy center, you need to minister to her. If you're standing in front of the clinic holding up a sign, it's too much for her. She needs to trust you, and it's almost like you're giving her some kind of a message that she's not a good person." Sharon's concern is that a pregnant woman might see a person protesting or sidewalk counseling outside of a clinic (direct-action activities) and therefore not trust her if she later sees the same person as a CPC counselor (an individual outreach activity). For this reason, the streams must remain separate.

This view is widespread within the individual outreach stream. CPCs frequently prohibit their activists from participating in clinic protests or sidewalk counseling—and will even ask volunteers to quit if they attend such events. Activists affiliated with the Birthright network are explicitly prohibited from participating in any protest or even pro-life political activity. "We take care of moms and babies," Henry, a fifty-nine-year-old, says in explaining such policies, "and some of the organizations which go out there and picket heavily do nothing for the babies."

Those in one stream not only see their activism as different and separate from that in the other streams but also view it as more fundamental to the pro-life movement as a whole. Sandra, a thirty-four-year-old in Oklahoma City, explains it this way in describing the individual outreach stream: "[Crisis pregnancy centers] are like the little treasures, you know. They don't, they never hoopla anything, they don't really want tons of people to know them or recognize them. They don't want to be in the media for the simple fact that then they cannot function and do what they need to do. But it's these small groups—they're the ones in the trenches. They're the ones that are truly helping people." Sandra begins with an implicit criticism of other streams of the movement, suggesting they are too media-focused. She then likens CPCs to the hard work "in the trenches," suggesting that the individual outreach stream is the only authentic, or "truly," pro-life work. In Oklahoma City, fifty-six-year-old Tony uses exactly the same imagery: "You go talk to the ladies who are volunteers at the crisis pregnancy center and what you will discover is these are ladies whose names are not up in lights anywhere. They are the ground troops, and they are occupying the territory, so to speak." Activists in the individual outreach stream see work through CPCs as the most central and most legitimate pro-life activity. Like those in other streams, they view what they do as the core of the movement. Abortion is a problem because of the individual decisions made by young pregnant women, and therefore, the solution must come through reaching those women and meeting their needs.

directly to source

Attempts to challenge stream boundaries can also be a source of new pro-life organizations. In Minneapolis, Prolife Minnesota, which focuses exclusively on public outreach, was originally founded in 1989 after battles within MCCL—in the politics stream—over a campaign to place pro-life advertisements in public buses. Conflict erupted between those who wanted to adopt more of a public outreach orientation and those who wanted to continue MCCL's exclusively political focus. The boundaries of the political stream were thus being challenged, and ultimately, a group of disaffected members left the organization and founded the separate group Prolife Minnesota, outside the politics stream of the movement.[16] In Boston, MCFL had a fierce debate among its staff and board of directors about providing even financial support for a CPC that was opening in a nearby city. Disaffected activists left MCFL after this discussion to found an organization of their own.

Individuals and Streams

Just as organizations seldom cross the boundaries of the different streams of the movement, neither do individual activists. The activism of most people in the movement is confined to a single stream. Table 5.1 shows the number of streams in which each activist in the study has ever participated. Activists who, at any time in their life, regularly volunteered their time to a project or an organization in a particular stream are classified in the table as being a part of that stream, no matter how limited their involvement. Thus, Jeff, who now works full-time for a CPC in the Twin Cities and is part of the individual outreach stream, is also classified as having been a part of the politics stream because he helped his mother distribute pro-life voter guides in a political campaign while in high school. Even with this strict standard, a remarkable sixty-three of the eighty-two activists—77 percent—have never been a part of more than one stream of the movement at any point in their activism. Only five of the activists (6 percent) have been involved in more than two movement streams, and in each case, these are individuals who have been movement leaders in their respective communities. The relative parochialism of most activists vis-à-vis the range of streams in the movement is a testament to the power of stream boundaries.

Table 5.1 Distribution of activists in movement streams

	Activists	
	Number	%
Stream		
Politics	19	23
Direct-action	21	26
Individual outreach	27	33
Public outreach	15	18
Active in		
Only 1 stream	63	77
2 streams	14	17
3 streams	5	6

Activists sometimes express respect for different streams of the movement, saying that they are all "interwoven" or that each is a "piece" of the larger picture. The public outreach stream is held in especially high regard by the majority of those in other streams. Ultimately, however, the different streams understand abortion in very different ways. These differences lead them not only to pursue different strategies but also to view the other streams with suspicion and in some cases contempt. There is a great deal of underlying conflict among different movement streams, as echoed by the views of Glen and Josh that introduced the chapter. Not only do activists in one stream sometimes denigrate the work of those in other streams, but they also question their very values and motives.

Claire, quoted earlier, believes that abortion will only be ended through the legislatures and the courts and has been active in the politics stream of the pro-life movement in Boston. She initially draws a temperate contrast between the politics and individual outreach streams of the movement. Referring to CPCs, she says, "I think it's much tougher than the other pro-life stuff because you have this particular girl you have to deal with and you have to meet her needs and everything. It's much easier to go speak to two hundred people! But it's a different way. One is changing the world one by one. And one is helping all of them by changing the world." Claire begins by describing the politics stream as simply "easier" than and "different" from individual outreach. But in describing the difference, she makes clear that the latter only changes abortion on the individual level while the former can change society as a whole. She is more explicit later in the interview: "I mean, I think if you only did the Birthright [individual outreach] kinds of things, that you might never change society. And you have an obligation." Claire doesn't reject individual outreach; she sees it as a legitimate, if less important, stream of the movement. But the difference is also more than simply personal preference. Like many activists, she sees the work of her stream as a moral obligation—an obligation those outside the stream do not meet. Andy, an activist in the direct-action stream in Charleston, goes even further and questions the basic beliefs of those involved in individual outreach: "They're only affecting those that want to go [to the CPCs]. I don't see them in front of the clinic. You see, the people who are in front of the clinic have gone to the clinic and have been convinced that killing this child is not the right thing to do. And the crisis pregnancy centers are not in front of the clinics." For Andy, as for many others, it isn't enough just to save individual babies. The country must be saved from itself. Thus, while those in the stream are dedicated activists for the individual outreach approach, those in other streams question their strategy and, by extension, their underlying values and commitment.

The politics stream gets similar kinds of critiques from those outside it. "You could go visit your legislator, you could send petitions, hundreds, thousands of names to your legislators, nothing would get done," says Carol, quoted earlier. "You would do it, you do it the way it's supposed to be done. You do everything by the book, and nothing happens. Nothing." Tim, introduced in chapter 1, was not optimistic when I asked him how electing George W. Bush might affect the abortion issue: "Well, you'd think it would be positive. But I just have, I guess I've become so jaded in believing that the system can help all that I, I think it would be better than what we have now, but it certainly is not a cure-all. The guy more than likely is spouting things he doesn't truly believe to get elected."[17] For Carol, Tim, and many others outside the politics stream, politics is the wrong venue for change. An undercurrent of frustration with the ineffectiveness of legislative and legal strategies runs throughout the conversations I had with activists in other streams of the movement.

Politics might not be merely ineffective; it might be actively harmful to the overall pro-life cause. Erin believes the gains of the politics stream are illusory and thus distract pro-lifers from the cause: "The pro-aborts are sticking to what they want—abortion legal anytime, any reason, no reason. Why can't we stick to ours—no abortion? I really don't think that parental consent [laws save] babies. Or twenty-four-hour [waiting periods], when you get down to it." Amy, a twenty-two-year-old activist in the direct-action stream in the Twin Cities, goes into more detail about why she finds the political arm of the movement distasteful. When asked what she thought of work to end abortion in the political realm, she replied: "I think that whole stuff is really icky. . . . And I think that there's really a risk of running people over in the process of, well, if you say abortion is murder, that abortion is illegal, well, then every woman who has ever had an abortion suddenly has to deal with this image of herself as a murderer. And so then how do you deal with that? I think it depends, when things are in the political arena, if the political agenda is pushed at all costs over the valuing of women." Amy doesn't see the politics stream as always maintaining the principles of the pro-life movement that she believes are important. By hurting women, Amy believes political pro-life efforts can betray what activists such as herself are working for. She holds the politics stream at arm's length, helping to keep the different parts of the movement separate on the individual level.

Direct action, like all the other streams, has its own strong advocates within the stream and critics from the other streams. Andy's comments earlier demonstrate one view from the direct-action side of the movement: activism in front of clinics is the most legitimate form of activism because it focuses on the location where babies are actually being killed. Mildred, a former rescuer who is now eighty years old, argues that picketing the homes of physicians who perform abortions is the most effective approach. "Yeah, honestly I've always thought that was a pretty good idea. It's effective if you're in a war, and that's what this is." Josh, introduced at the beginning of the chapter, feels that direct action represents the "true" pro-life movement.

As has already been noted, however, activists in other streams resent direct-action tactics as ineffective. According to Sharon, a fifty-year-old leader in the movement in Charleston, "Praying at the abortion clinics or picketing is almost a waste of time." Many worry that direct-action activism has led to a negative portrayal of the movement in the press and thus has hurt the pro-life movement overall. Steve, a twenty-eight-year-old in Boston, puts it this way: "Now, I'm sure that there are stories of some people who actually do change their mind. And the question is OK, good, so it's somewhat efficacious. So then I guess I'd say like let's do a study to see. You spent eighty hours doing this and saved one life. Let's say you spend eighty hours doing some other thing, maybe earlier in the chain of events. Would the yield be higher? I bet it would be higher. So you're not making really good use of your time—even though you can show me a few lives that were saved. And then that's also minus all the other people that you've completely like made hate you forever." Opposition to the direct-action stream can be even more basic. Heather, a twenty-six-year-old in Oklahoma City, sees direct action as too strident: "A lot of these women go in scared out of their mind, and they're sitting in the waiting room and a lot of times they can see out at the people outside. And if all they're hearing is screaming and yelling and seeing signs with aborted babies on [them], then why would they ever talk to you? Why would they ever even consider it?" Even within the pro-life movement itself, the direct-action stream is frequently regarded as self-righteous, aggressive, and loud. People such as Heather reject the approach because of this image. "I mean I think there's a lot of groups that assault people almost with their signs," says Judy, a sixty-year-old in Charleston. "Like in front of the abortion clinics. And I've never participated in that. I think that's another way of tearing down, not building up." As with those in other streams, there is a moral valence to Heather's view of other streams. She sees direct action not only as less useful and effective but also as morally suspect. Such beliefs about one's own work and the work of others maintain strong boundaries among the different streams of the movement. These boundaries are well institutionalized and, as table 5.1 shows, seldom crossed.

Why Streams Matter

Too frequently we think of social movements as unified actors. Though most scholars would readily acknowledge that movements are often highly differentiated and heterogeneous, this acknowledgment seldom leads in practice to data collection and analysis of the internal structure of social movements and its effects. The problem extends to existing studies of the abortion debate. An example is Marcy Wilder's (1998) description of pro-life movement history in the 1980s: "The tactics of the anti-choice movement grew increasingly confrontational: what began as picketing in front of clinics turned into 'sidewalk counseling' and then escalated into full-fledged blockades. Death threats against physicians became commonplace, and arson and bombings more frequent. By the mid-1980s there had been a perceptible shift in anti-choice tactics from the rule of law to the reign of lawlessness" (p. 81). Ellie

Lee (2003) takes the same approach when she describes a single master narrative of the movement's changing from a moralizing, woman-blaming focus to a pseudomedical concern for women. In both cases, the movement is incorrectly conceptualized as a single whole, with an essentialized master narrative.[18] Ultimately, these attempts to provide an overarching gloss to the movement's beliefs hide more than they reveal about the moral perspectives of pro-life activists.

The social movement stream concept helps us recognize the internal differentiation within the movement. Streams, however, are more than just a convenient way of categorizing and describing different beliefs among organizations and activists. Streams define the very structure of the movement and as such define both the possibilities and the limits for movement recruitment, coordination, and impact. In this sense, streams are similar to Russell Curtis Jr. and Louis Zurcher Jr.'s (1973) original definition of multiorganizational fields in social movements. Movement streams extend the notion of such fields by focusing attention on the relationship among streams as well as the effects of stream boundaries on both individuals and organizations in the movement.

Tactical innovation, for example, is related to the streams that structure the movement. The end of rescues and civil disobedience in front of abortion clinics in the early 1990s can be easily explained through existing models of resource mobilization (McCarthy and Zald 1977; Jenkins 1983; McAdam 1988; Zald 1992), political opportunity structure (Jenkins and Perrow 1977; McAdam 1982), and movement-countermovement interaction (Lo 1982; Meyer and Staggenborg 1996; Andrews 2002). Pro-life organizations lacked the resources to continue large-scale rescues in the face of state repression won by pro-choice forces. But the organizations and activists involved in civil disobedience did not simply turn to other tactics being used within the pro-life movement. Rather than simply adopt an alternative within the existing tactical repertoire (Tilly 1977; Tilly 1978; Tarrow 1994) of the movement as a whole—which would have required crossing boundaries of a movement stream—the direct-action stream of the movement created a new, innovative tactic: sidewalk counseling.

Similarly, streams inhibit what Russell Dalton (2006/1988) calls hierarchies of participation, in which activists begin with conventional forms of protest and then ramp up to increasingly disruptive activity. The data here suggest that such a process is severely constrained by an activist's embeddedness in a specific movement stream. My data show little or no movement of activists from streams that engage in less disruptive tactics to those, such as the direct-action stream, that engage in more disruptive tactics.[19] Stream boundaries are thus real barriers within the movement, restricting the flow of both individuals and ideas and thereby affecting the tactics within each.

Streams also matter to the recruitment patterns and biographical trajectories of activists within the movement. The first contact and initial activism steps of the mobilization process spelled out in chapter 3 happen with specific organizations, located in single streams of the movement. Activists' understanding of abortion and the development of their beliefs is then circumscribed by the stream they initially entered, for as table 5.1 shows, activists seldom cross stream boundaries. Put another way, individuals tend to stick to those organizations and activities through which they first began their activism in the movement. Stream boundaries are so strong, in fact, that when serious disagreements arise within a movement, activists sometimes drop out of the movement rather than cross them.

This is how Josh handled a period in which he was simply "burned out" from direct action. "I got tired of police sitting there," he says as he explains a time when he disappeared from the movement. "I got tired of going out and wondering if today one of our counselors was going to be arrested or if I was going to be arrested. Or if I was going to be hunted down by the FBI or something like that." Rather than change to pro-life activism in which police and the threat of arrest would not be factors—in other words, activism in a different stream of the movement—Josh chose to simply stop all movement activity. David, a Twin Cities activist quoted earlier, explains his exit from the movement this way: "I've walked away from the issue partly or to a significant degree because I have no respect for the leadership of the pro-life movement in terms of their strategy. Their strategy is so bankrupt in my mind, which I've told them and which other key people agree with me on, but we're powerless to impact it." David's explanation is reasonable, but it also shows that his vision of the movement is limited to the particular stream in which he participated. "Leadership of the pro-life movement" here in fact refers only to the leaders of the main politics stream organizations within the movement. David did not switch streams; instead, he dropped out of the movement entirely. The boundaries of movement streams are sufficiently real and formidable as to pose a significant barrier to individuals' crossing them, even when they are frustrated, upset, or unhappy with the stream they are in.

The study of the social movement streams helps explain the lock-in process by which activists become tied to particular understandings of the issue. It also reveals the importance of ideas in social movement analysis beyond their use as the raw material of "frames" deployed by movement leaders (Snow et al. 1986; Tarrow 1994; Benford and Snow 2000). Streams provide a basis for combining the cognitive and affective components of social movements that critics of frame analysis have argued is needed (Jasper 1997; Goodwin, Jasper, and Polletta 2001). Analysis of the streams of the pro-life movement demonstrates how emotional commitments to particular ways of understanding the abortion issue serve to structure the movement as a whole. A focus on movement streams thus complements existing approaches to social movements by allowing us to more carefully specify how a variety of movement processes—such as tactical innovation, activist commitment, and individual recruitment—work in established social movements. In doing so, the stream concept offers a way to avoid trivializing ideas and beliefs by seeing them as unconnected to movement structure and little more than ideological possibilities that leaders might instrumentally deploy.

Finally, the analysis here builds on a growing literature that has broken down the analytic distinctions that have long been made among social movement organization, strategy, and identity. Elisabeth Clemens (1997), for example, demonstrates some of the complex ways in which organizational forms and the structure of social movement fields are related to movement strategy and ideology. Elizabeth Armstrong (2002) explores these relationships further through her concept of different movement "logics" and the ways in which they have served either divisive or unifying roles in the mobilization of gays and lesbians in San Francisco. In each of these studies, as here in the case of the pro-life movement, the identities of individual activists, understandings of the proper strategies and actions to be taken to address an issue, and the formal organization of the movements all come together to define the ways in which the movements are structured.

Summing Up: Beliefs as Defining Movement Structure

Different streams in the pro-life movement, despite nearly universal consensus on an ultimate goal, have profoundly different ideas about the means to achieve that goal. These ideas are more than just social movement currency designed to persuade. Movement leaders don't simply pick and choose among different ideas in order to frame their activities. The ideas themselves define where in the movement those leaders and activists are located. Differing beliefs about the morally appropriate or most efficacious strategies continue to define and separate pro-life organizations' orientations and pro-life activists' understandings of the abortion issue. These differences split the movement into four distinct streams: politics, direct action, individual outreach, and public outreach. These streams operate largely independently of one another, with organizations and activists in one stream being suspicious and sometimes contemptuous of their colleagues in other streams.

Understanding the patterned variation within the pro-life movement reveals the importance of ideas in shaping the development of the movement as a whole. The movement's structure is defined by differences in belief: belief about the relationship between conscience and action, about the morality of different forms of behavior, and about the most fruitful avenues for pro-life activity. Streams are ultimately defined by profound differences in the ideas activists and organizations hold about abortion and activism. These different streams play an important role in how individuals become activists and how their ideas about abortion and position in the movement become locked in on the basis of how and where they entered the movement in the first place.

SIX

"United We Stand"? Tension in the Pro-life Moral Universe

Glen, the politics stream activist introduced in chapter 2, understands abortion as the root of many problems in society. He explains: "But if we unify again the act of procreation with the fact of procreation, then we are going to see ramifications when it comes to divorce rate, when it comes to human motherhood, when it comes to abandoning their children. . . . I think that's all wrapped up in this. It's wrapped up in things like Columbine. Things like violence and drug addiction." For Glen, abortion is a fundamental cause of social ills ranging from divorce to school shootings to drug addiction. His viewpoint is similar to that of many other activists, but it by no means dominates pro-life thinking about abortion as a whole. Consider the views expressed by Doug, a thirty-two-year-old in Oklahoma City: "We have a society that focuses on symptoms. Abortion is a symptom of a greater thing. It's a symptom of a callousness for life that has developed, that is shown through abortion, that is shown through the amount of murders and crime rate we have, and the amount of child abuse and spousal abuse that exists in society." Doug's perspective is almost the opposite of Glen's: abortion is not in itself the problem but rather a symptom of a larger callousness toward life. Abortion is just one of many pieces of evidence for this callousness. Tom, a thirty-eight-year-old in the Twin Cities, offers still a third view: "The disrespect for life which was started by the Supreme Court's decision is, unless we turn it around, only going to get worse. You know, it's Kevorkian and all these pro-death groups, and it's assisted suicides, and then he'll really want suicides, and then it's the handicapped, and then it's people with who knows. Who is going to be on the list? People with brown skin? Big noses, you know? The master race. It's straight down there. It's all the way out, all you have to do is look at it. It's so easy." Here Tom places abortion at the top of a slippery slope of moral concerns. If we allow abortion, then it is only a few short steps to other forms of killing and ultimately official sanction for genocide.

The views of abortion expressed by Glen, Doug, and Tom illustrate the range of beliefs present in the pro-life movement. This chapter looks at this range in more depth. How do pro-life activists understand abortion in the context of today's world? How do they relate their beliefs about abortion to their beliefs about other important political and moral issues? Once they become a part of the movement, activists face a wide range of different ideas about abortion. Differences about the appropriate means to stop abortion structure the movement into separate and largely mutually exclusive streams, as the last chapter demonstrated. The ideational tensions built into the movement don't end there, however. Crosscutting social movement streams are different understandings of the abortion issue rooted in different basic worldviews. Activists are thus exposed to a surprisingly wide range of differing ways to think about abortion and root commitment to the cause of ending it. Even within social movement streams, then, activists experience conflict and controversy within the moral universe of opposition to abortion.

After examining and assessing the range of beliefs present in the movement, I found that three important themes emerge. First, beliefs about abortion are sufficiently complex that they cannot be reduced to a single worldview (Luker 1984) or gender debate (Ginsburg 1989/1998). This finding challenges prior research beyond just the pro-life movement, where scholars often identify a "core" set of beliefs that everyone shares. Mitchell Stevens (2002), for example, has found such a core for as diffuse and heterogeneous a movement as conservative Protestantism. Second, deep tensions within the movement result from fundamentally different moral understandings of the issue. The differences between Glen and Doug are about more than just how to frame the debate; they reveal disparate moral bases for opposing abortion. Third, beliefs about abortion are not limited to traditionally conservative moral and political ideas; they span a wide range of concerns, from personal responsibility to issues of civil rights and racism. As we continue to examine the movement through the eyes of the activists themselves, such diversity establishes the terrain in which ongoing personal commitment to the cause is made and remade as activists deepen their ties to the movement.

A Universal Core: Abortion as the Killing of Life

"You're killing. You're killing the life. This is life. It doesn't matter whether you get a gun and shoot somebody or do this. They're the same. It's the same thing." Forty-nine-year-old Oklahoma activist Dominique's words reflect the most basic and common understanding of the abortion issue expressed by pro-life activists. The belief that abortion is killing and therefore wrong is central to the movement's moral evaluation of the issue. Mildred, an eighty-year-old in Boston, responded without hesitation when I asked her why she was opposed to abortion. "Well, it's the killing of a life. Life is sacred." This was the end of the story for Mildred; she sees no reason to elaborate on this basic point.

At the core of the pro-life moral universe is the belief that the unborn fetus is a person, and, therefore, abortion is morally wrong because it ends a person's life. This is the central idea around which all other beliefs in the movement revolve. "Killing an unborn infant is wrong," says sixty-eight-year-old Twin Cities activist John. "Killing something is wrong. It's not killing a rabbit or a bird; it's a fellow human being. What do people think it is? A baby is a human being." If the fetus is a person, then it is naturally entitled to all of the human rights afforded any other person in society, including the right not to have its life ended because of the wishes of another person. This common belief is the source of the incredulity pro-life activists show toward arguments about the right to privacy and a woman's right to control her body. If the fetus is as human as a toddler or a child or an adult, then surely its right to life supercedes these secondary rights of others.

Even within this core idea, however, understanding the fetus as a person takes the form of one of two strands: the scientific and the religious. Activists who use the scientific strand root their belief in the personhood of the fetus in their understanding of biology, embryology, and genetics. Donald, a seventy-one-year-old activist in the Twin Cities, says: "The scientific evidence is overwhelming with regard to abortion, that there is a child there. Like any other human, all that's needed after conception is food and time to develop and grow. For a time, there was a question about when there really is life. When is there a baby? But with ultrasound and all the genetic research that's been done and what we know now, I don't think there's any question. Anybody who has studied the issue, I don't see how they can argue that life is not there, that it's not a child." Like many other activists, Donald believes as a matter of science that personhood begins at the moment of conception. In some cases, activists' beliefs are rooted in specific scientific information. "All I ever need to understand," says twenty-eight-year-old Charleston activist Dana, "is that when a sperm and an ovum meet, there are twenty-three chromosomes from the mother, twenty-three from the father, never to be repeated again." In other cases, the activists make no such claims to special expertise. Frank, for example, a fifty-eight-year-old activist in Boston, told me, "We have pictures. We know that it's not just tissue. . . . It's something totally different. I don't have to have a college degree to figure that out."

Activists who use scientific truth as the basis for justifying their beliefs frequently express frustration that abortion is even discussed at the level of personal moral opinion. For them, the issue is no more a matter of opinion than is the process of mitosis or photosynthesis. Linda, the activist introduced in chapter 2, puts it this way: "I mean, I know that the unborn baby is a human being. A first-year medical student will flunk out if he can't tell the difference between a fertilized human ovum and that of an ape. I mean, that's scientific fact. . . . So let's not argue science. Let's agree. Let's say that the issue isn't whether it's human; the issue is whether or not this human has any value."

Unborn baby, child, human being, infant, and *innocent life* are all terms universally used in the movement to underscore a belief in the humanity of the life being ended by abortion. And for activists such as Donald, Dana, Frank, and Linda, this humanity is plainly rooted in firm scientific knowledge.

Other activists use a more religious understanding. Rather than focusing on scientific facts surrounding conception and fetal development, these activists root their beliefs in God's authority over life. For sixty-year-old Judy of Charleston, the fact that her church teaches that life begins at conception is enough: "That's what the Catholic Church teaches, and I support that. We protect life from the moment of conception until death. That's God's domain. He decides when we're born." "It all boils down to the belief that there is a God and He's the author of life," echoes forty-six-year-old Christina of Boston, "and that for some reason, He allowed a life to be created." Because God is responsible for the creation of human life, many activists see it as hubris, if not heretical, to interfere with God's plans by ending such life through abortion. According to seventy-nine-year-old Charleston activist Ben, "God is the author of life, and He has His reasons for things that happen. And we may never know what they are. Even if we don't know, He's a good God, we know that. So we know that He will give you what you need, and this [an unplanned pregnancy] is probably what you need. So we can't play God in that." Ben sees abortion as playing God. God imbues humans with souls at the moment of conception, and abortion disrupts God's plans for those souls.

Josh, the direct-action activist introduced in chapter 5, sums up the implications of a religious basis for the belief that a fetus is a moral agent from the moment of conception: "My thinking has gone away from women having a right to choose. She does not have the right. Once that child is conceived, that is the child of God and only God has the right to determine the life of that child. She doesn't. She's a caretaker. The father and the mother are caretakers of that child, of God's child. Just like them, they are children of God, too." The central tenet of the pro-life moral universe is the belief that the fetus is imbued with personhood and therefore abortion represents the killing of a human being. This belief is so fundamental to the movement that it is not subject to challenge, reflection, or debate. It is also one of the few beliefs about which all activists agree, even if their bases for the belief differ.

Facets of Pro-life Beliefs

Although abortion as the killing of life is a universally held core idea in the movement, it does not follow that everyone puts abortion in the same category as murder or other forms of killing. Will, a sixty-eight-year-old in Boston, differentiates abortion and murder: "Now do I call them [abortion providers] murderers? No. I don't call them murderers because that's not the crime they're committing. The crime is abortion." Others in the movement, of course, frequently refer to abortion providers as murderers. "It's murder. There's no doubt about it." The comments by Glen, Doug, and Tom introducing the chapter show, too, that activists situate abortion differently in their differing moral worldviews. Indeed, whereas everyone in the movement agrees that abortion is the killing of a human life, they differ in how they make sense of this understanding. This fractured moral understanding of abortion needs to be fleshed out to see the extent of ideological diversity accommodated by the movement. Activists describing their beliefs use one of several central narratives for explaining their moral opposition: they understand abortion as (1) representing a lack of responsibility, (2) having dire effects on society, (3) being harmful to women, (4) being a civil rights issue, or (5) being based on the lies of abortion providers.

Lack of Responsibility

Some activists understand abortion as an abdication of personal responsibility. Abortion is wrong because it represents people's not living up to their prior decisions and commitments. Kim, a thirty-one-year-old in the Twin Cities, reflects this view: "If you have the opinion that you don't want a pregnancy, then I think you are responsible to make sure you don't have one. Because you are responsible for your choice. If you chose to make a baby, you made a baby. Deal with it. You know, I don't mean to say that without any compassion for people's situation and the pain or the fear that's involved with that, but, still, now there's another person involved. They're little, they're defenseless, but there's a person involved." Others echo Kim's belief that the issue is tied to choices made before the choice for abortion: "Freedom of choice should start at the time of sex. It shouldn't start after sex," says one. "You're trying to put responsibility down the line instead of back a little bit further and being responsible for your actions from the beginning," says another. These activists see the availability of abortion as contributing to sexual promiscuity and thus reinforcing the problem that leads to abortion in the first place.

Other activists understand what is at stake in more punitive terms. Take, for example, the words of Paul, a thirty-four-year-old in Oklahoma City: "But for me, that's why I never did stuff in the first place. And not to sound judgmental, but I feel like I can kind of say, 'Hey, I was there just like you, I was in the back seats, and I was doing all this stuff, and I chose not to.' So don't give me this woe-is-me crap, because you chose it, you know?" Paul feels as if abortion is unfair because it allows sexual indulgence that he did not permit himself. The underlying idea is that people ought to pay for their indiscretions, not "fix" them with abortion: "The choice is not to have relations without paying the consequences," and "The idea that sex should be free and there aren't any consequences is wrong. That you can have all the sex you want, and if you get pregnant, you just have abortions."

The idea that abortion is wrong because it stems from irresponsibility is the basis for the common conclusion that the pro-life movement is really about the defense of the traditional family and an attempt to exert control over (especially female) sexuality. These beliefs are certainly present in the pro-life moral universe, but only some activists hold them. Fewer than 25 percent express any beliefs that can be related to the issue of personal responsibility, and only a handful of those see the problem in the punitive terms expressed by the previous quotations.

A twist on the belief that abortion reduces individual responsibility for action focuses attention on how abortion might be used to cover up rape and incest, cases in which pregnancy did not result from voluntary action:

I don't believe it [abortion] is ever acceptable. First of all, incest: I think that it is a great way for the incest abuser to hide his abuse and to continue in that abuse, to manipulate more. People who are subject to incest are manipulated. They have been manipulated and continue to be manipulated, and they will continue [to be abused] if they hide this pregnancy.

(NICKY, 37, CHARLESTON)

A father molested his daughter for quite a while when she was younger, and then she got pregnant. He forced her to go and to have an abortion. She was fifteen, fourteen, somewhere in there. But a child that young, the parent has tremendous influence and authority over them. So he forced her to have an abortion. And then not long after the abortion, he started to try and molest her again. But she at some point had grown up enough or was strong enough that she resisted and said, "I will tell." But you see what happened there was he had destroyed the evidence. There was no case against him for incest or rape or anything. He destroyed evidence and had gone right back to his old habits again.

(THERESA, 67, CHARLESTON)

Thus, some activists believe that abortion resulting from nonconsensual sex simply allows abusive men to avoid responsibility for their actions. Abortion is therefore wrong even in cases of rape and incest. Allowing abortion reinforces a lack of responsibility, allowing abuse to continue.

Related to the issue of responsibility is concern over traditional sources of authority: God and men. Abortion is wrong because it takes away the right of conventional power holders to make decisions. I touched on this belief earlier in reference to God: abortion is wrong because it disrupts God's plan for human life. "God's law says that we shouldn't do this," says fifty-four-year-old Boston activist Ron, "and when a Christian country, supposedly, sets itself up in direct conflict with that law, it sets off some alarm bells." As the traditional source of ultimate authority, God's will should not be challenged through abortion, which interferes with the human lives he has ordained. Interference is not only immoral, it is also dangerous. Tim, a thirty-eight-year-old activist in Oklahoma City, explains: "God is not going to be mocked very long. He's allowed it [abortion] to go on now since '72 or '73 or whenever *Roe v. Wade* was decided. . . . The Holy God ain't gonna allow that very long. We're suffering now for that, and you know God isn't gonna be mocked. . . . He is wrathful, He is vengeful, and He doesn't appreciate people killing His creation." Abortion thus represents a challenge to a vengeful God's authority that will ultimately bring ruin upon us all. Josh, the direct-action activist introduced in chapter 5, agrees: "God in the Bible destroyed kingdoms because they were sacrificing their kids." This narrative is evident among leaders of the Christian Right as well. Pat Robertson has advanced the same understanding of abortion and judgment by God in his interpretation of the 9/11 terrorist attacks in 2001 and Hurricane Katrina in 2005, suggesting that both represent God's response to a country that "has killed over 40 million unborn babies" (Media Matters 2005).

Some activists also believe traditional male authority is threatened by abortion. Abortion laws in the United States are seen as taking away the rights of men to be involved in the decision-making process. If some abortions shield abusive men from the discovery of their rape or incest, other abortion decisions are made without giving the men who are the potential fathers a fair hearing. John, a sixty-eight-year-old in the Twin Cities, became increasingly agitated as he explained to me, "There are absolutely no rights at all for the father. You know, he helped create the child. He should have some right; he should have the right to a hearing. At least be heard and be a factor, to consider. No due process whatsoever; it's absurd." Sandra, a thirty-four-year-old in Oklahoma City, expresses the same belief through a more personal story: "When I was a hostess in a restaurant in high school, the bartender was in college and he and I became friends. . . . When I met him, he was engaged to this girl in Houston, who aborted his child. And it devastated him. I mean, I can remember spending like three days on the phone listening to him tell me, 'I have no recourse, I have no legal options, nobody cares what I think.' He didn't want her to have the abortion. He offered to raise the child; he offered to pay her to have the child; he offered to support her for the rest of her life if she would have the baby." For both John and Sandra, abortion leaves men helpless. They are outraged that men—key stakeholders whom they believe ought to have a voice in the process—are legally excluded from the ultimate choice over whether or not to have an abortion.

Activists also see that those who stand up for personal and moral responsibility are persecuted. Take, for example, this passage from my interview with Jacob, a forty-seven-year-old in Charleston: "I usually find myself in battles of injustice. Locally I've got a professor that's being fired from the college where I graduated because he made some stands on some moral issues down there. There are some professors on a Christian campus who happen to be lesbians and who let it be known. He's trying to see that they, you know, get ousted out of the Christian environment. So he's now being fired because of his strong beliefs. So I'm going to meet with the president of the school, and I find myself in a lot of these things. Kind of the weaker . . . [pause] I like to be on the underdog's side." Jacob formulates the situation in such a way that the established professor trying to have two lesbians fired because of their sexual orientation is the weaker party in the confrontation. He tells this story as an analogy explaining why he opposes abortion: he likes to fight battles over injustice, as in this case. Others bring this same formulation to their involvement. Michael, a forty-two-year-old in Boston, describes how people are punished just for expressing pro-life views: "I listened to my teachers and so forth. But sometimes I said some things in class that caused my grade to suffer. Because the grading is subjective. And I just saw that you get punished if you're different, you get punished gradewise." Traditional authority has been turned on its head for Michael and other activists in the pro-life movement; they see political correctness stifling their views and leading to persecution of the regular and ordinary people who once rightfully controlled the public debate over personal and moral responsibility.

Effects on Society

A second way in which abortion beliefs are understood is in terms of how abortion harms society at large. For some, the issue is economic: they focus on the idea that tens of millions of abortions over the last several decades have reduced the number of people working in the economy. This idea is then understood as having a variety of negative effects. "They're doing it to the tune of four thousand or forty-five hundred a day to Americans," exclaims Tim in Oklahoma City. "I mean, no wonder we don't have enough money to support Social Security—we've killed a whole generation!" Shawn, a thirty-three-year-old in Boston, agrees: "And who is going to support the upper age bracket? Are you going to have enough workers to support that population? What do you do about that?" Others understand the issue in the same way but from the demand side. For example, seventy-one-year-old Joe, from the Twin Cities, sees declining food prices and a resulting agricultural crisis as the result of abortion policy: "And this country now, the farm problem. Farms are going out of business every day. If we had those 40 million children that were aborted here, there wouldn't be any farm problem. They'd be eating up all that food that is produced. It's all surplus, you see." Opposition to abortion for Joe and others is tied to the macro-level economic effects that they believe it has on society as a whole.

Others focus more generally on the potential loss of those who could make valuable social contributions. "And with each life that we destroy, I think of the generations," says seventy-one-year-old Ruth in the Twin Cities. "Generation after generation of children. It's not just one child that is lost." Activists dwell on the "what-if" question: What if an important future leader was aborted? What if a potential future husband was aborted? These what-if ideas are summed up by Allen, a fifty-eight-year-old in Charleston: "See, there's so many abortions, and who is to say that one of these, you know babies being aborted, isn't the very person that if they'd been allowed to reach adulthood, they might be the very person that could discover the cure for AIDS or cancer, be the twenty-first-century Beethoven or Mozart. I mean, it just stands to reason that, somewhere in all those millions of innocent lives that are being snuffed out, that there are a lot of geniuses there." Abortion is thus devastating to society not only because it is the killing of human life but also because it deprives us of those who might make the world a better place.

This understanding of abortion puts a particular emphasis on its threat to medical progress, especially innovations designed to correct genetic and in utero problems. Abortion is used as a "shortcut" to simply ignore these problems rather than focus on finding cures or new technologies that might be able to correct them. This is the view of fifty-four-year-old Robert in the Twin Cities: "It [abortion] stops medical research. We aren't able to do in utero repairs of children. If it's easier to eliminate them, why put money into fixing them up?" Fifty-year-old Suzanne of Charleston echoes Robert's beliefs: "If you have fetal defects, then the treatment is to kill the patient. And I mean people just don't understand. That's what a lot of people say these days: if you have a defective fetus, then the way you treat that is you abort." Such ideas are the basis for the belief that we would be better off without abortion, forcing scientists and physicians to develop alternatives for treating genetic or developmental defects in the fetus.

The concern over fetal defects is in fact an important focal point for many ideas about the negative effects of abortion. Not only does abortion hinder medical progress, but it also creates disrespect for those who are living with genetic or other kinds of disabilities used as a rationale for abortion. Robert says that abortion "has become a way of eliminating the handicapped" and then wonders, "What does that say about the living handicapped, do you know what I mean?" Activists thus see the most harm from abortion in the circumstances under which the public is least likely to oppose it: abortion in cases of fetal anomalies.[1] These kinds of beliefs are often explained through anecdotes of people who were told of such problems during their pregnancy but who ultimately gave birth to children who are now growing up normally or with a seemingly high quality of life. Erin, the individual outreach activist introduced in chapter 3, relates a typical story:

Her first baby had been diagnosed with, I can't even remember the name of it, but it was some huge brain problem I guess. Before she was born. And, of course, the doctors encouraged her to abort, that this baby would not function properly. She would have all these problems. . . . The doctor even went to the point of saying, "I will not do a cesarean section on you." Which, a cesarean would help the chances of the baby. He said, "I don't believe the baby has a chance, so I believe she should go through the typical birth canal and the trauma will probably kill her during birth. And that's the best thing. I will not do a cesarean." So they chose to find a different doctor, and now they have a girl who will be two or three in August. . . . She was delivered, and she's doing real well. She's had very slow development; she's had some surgeries and so forth. But she's doing very well, almost walking now.

For those such as Erin, the abortion issue extends beyond simply the life of a fetus or the choice of abortion; they understand abortion as based on false medical certainty about potential problems, which can ultimately lead to a range of negative social effects. They believe abortion is wrong because it is wrong for society and the individuals who live in it.

Harm to Women

Some activists focus on the ways in which abortion is detrimental to women in explaining their abortion beliefs. This focus represents still a third way of understanding the issue. "I think they're selling a bad bill of goods to women," says one Boston activist. Says another, "When you look at the needs of women, they are suffering much more by being able to go and have an abortion." There are two themes to the basic idea that women are the victims rather than the beneficiaries of abortion. First, there are activists who understand a woman's choice as resulting from pressure by others and thus not representing a real choice at all. Second, there are those who believe abortion is degrading to women, leaving them with emotional and psychological scars that are worse than what they would suffer if they carried problem pregnancies to term.

Many in the pro-life movement believe that women seldom freely choose abortion; rather, they are forced into it. Boyfriends and husbands drag their girlfriends and wives to abortion clinics. Families pressure young pregnant women to "deal with" or get rid of their pregnancy "responsibly." Planned Parenthood and other abortion providers don't give women information about all their options, instead pushing abortion as the only alternative to a crisis pregnancy. Fifty-year-old Charleston activist Suzanne sees the legal choice to have an abortion transformed into a duty: "I've learned that so many times, it's not the woman's choice. It's not her choice. It's just that's the only option she was given. I mean, she had people that threatened to abandon her. I mean, it's like the right to abort has become the duty to abort." The belief that women do not really want abortions can be couched in very gendered terms. For example, Glen sees abortion as part of a larger pattern of male domination in society: "One of the things that drives me about the abortion issue is I look at it as the abandonment of women by men. All-male Supreme Court [that decided *Roe v. Wade*]. Male-dominated legislatures. Male-dominated corporations that have kept abortion legal. You know, this whole line that if women ran this world, abortion would be safe and legal. It's not true! Women are less pro-aborts than men."[2] According to these beliefs, abortion is thus not a vehicle for opportunity and equality for women; it is a tool for men who are inconvenienced by female pregnancies and for a male-dominated society that insists on deciding when women can and cannot be pregnant.

Activists also believe that abortion can be directly harmful to women by causing long-term emotional and psychological scars. They point to abortion as a source of posttraumatic stress for women and sometimes cite statistics supporting the view that abortion hurts women's lives rather than helping them. "The majority of the women who have been raped and have abortions commit suicide," one activist in Charleston tells me. "Ninety percent of the people who have abortions usually end up in divorce or separation"; "Ninety-four percent of women who have abortions regret it and wish they hadn't,"[3] say others. The harm caused by abortion is seen as staying with women the rest of their lives, a trauma that can only be overcome with psychiatric help: "I guess the biggest thing I have seen in postaborted women is the wounding of their spirit. And I've worked cross-denominational: I've had Buddhists, American Indians, you know, Lutherans, Catholics, whatever. But there's a spiritual violence that these women have experienced, that they then have to reestablish in therapy." This the perspective of Joan, a sixty-nine-year-old activist in the Twin Cities. Her views reflect those of many who understand abortion as a procedure that leaves long-term scars on the women who have them. Such activists believe that instead of performing abortions, underlying issues need to be addressed—issues such as the breakdown of traditional families, premarital sex, and a lack of options and support for women who become pregnant. "A lot of times, they [pregnant women] are facing very real problems," explains twenty-four-year-old Mariah, an activist in Boston. "And the answer isn't just to kind of Band-Aid it with an abortion and move on and forget it and not address the underlying issues."

Ultimately, then, abortion is not liberating but degrading to women in the eyes of some activists. Patricia, a fifty-five-year-old activist, began crying as she related her beliefs about what abortion does to women: "We're talking about a woman who's made to crawl up on a table and put her feet into stirrups and hear a machine sucking out bits and pieces of a little baby. And made to feel that she's so poor or she's so ignorant or she's so stupid or she's so abandoned by the father of the baby that this is her 'choice.' You know, we can't do this to women." The link between the poverty, race, or marital status of women and abortion is a recurring theme in the ideas of some activists. Abortion is seen as perpetuating women's second-class status by confirming that they are weak and unable to handle the challenge of pregnancy. Sandra, a thirty-four-year-old in Oklahoma City, puts it this way: "How can you believe that a woman is as strong as a man if you're telling her she can't do this on her own? She's too poor to do it, she's not educated enough to do it, she's too young to do it, she can't do it without having money, she can't do it without having a man? That's degrading women. That's not saying that they're equal in any way. That's like saying they're cattle, and unless somebody owns them and feeds them and takes care of them, their life is over." Sandra and others contest what they view as the feminist appropriation of abortion as a tool of women's equality.

They see it as the opposite—a tool for male domination—and thus ultimately harmful to women and their place in society.

A Civil Rights Issue

Beyond the matter of gender, activists frequently understand abortion as being at its core a civil rights issue. This fourth way of understanding abortion sees unborn children as being discriminated against by the law and powerless to change their own condition. Because of their powerlessness, some activists feel a moral obligation to work on behalf of unborn children. Frank, a fifty-eight-year-old in Boston, puts it this way: "There's a responsibility to the unborn woman, little girl, little boy, gay little boy, lesbian little girl, Down's syndrome kid. Hey, they have rights. I'm an American, and that's what America is all about, our weakest voices, our little people. So I feel committed to speaking for these people; they can't speak for themselves." These kinds of beliefs are frequently articulated in terms of analogies to abolition or the civil rights movement of the 1960s. Maria, a forty-nine-year-old in the Twin Cities, reflects the views of many in the movement when she describes the acceptance of legalized abortion as the moral equivalent of the acceptance of legalized slavery: "How much different is it to say that you have friends who, although they themselves would say they won't have an abortion, they're willing as a taxpayer to fund someone else's or drive someone else there who is in need? How is that different than someone who might say, Well, I probably would never have a slave myself, but I'm going to support someone else, or I'm going to keep laws that keep slaves from escaping. How is that different? They're both oppressive of human rights." The fight over abortion is thus formulated as the most recent in a long string of battles in U.S. history over the rights of the weak and those who face unjust discrimination. Abortion is a means for one group to oppress another that it sees as unwanted or inconvenient.

The idea that abortion is fundamentally the tool of a racist society represents another side to this understanding. "So in the early pro-abortion movement," explains fifty-three-year-old Lisa of the Twin Cities, "they talked about rape by a black man or the possibility of a handicapped baby. It's the same thing they're talking about today. It hasn't changed; it's just that they've become more sophisticated in the way they present their issue." Activists see the arguments for abortion as racist and the fact that abortions are performed disproportionately on black women in the United States as proof that abortion is really about the continuing battle over race.[4] Tom, quoted at the beginning of the chapter, reflects the beliefs of a number of activists in his explanation of the issue:

I was listening to this woman from Australia talk. . . . And she went on and on about all the world's problems, and they all boiled down to there being too many people in Central America. And I thought, well, there's not too many people in Sweden, there's not too many people in Germany, there's not too many people in Norway, you know, or Latvia. It's Central America. . . . People who are really for abortion, it's no accident that they're always trying to, under the guise of trying to help people, there's some deep-seated racism, or at least some elitism. Because it's always the poor people that gotta have them. It's always these immigrants; it's always the people from India or China or Africa. It's never the Irish, it's never the Germans, it's never the Swedes. It always just happens to be that the people they want to have less of are the people with brown skin.

Abortion is thus a population control measure, applied unequally across different populations. Allen, a fifty-eight-year-old in Charleston, agrees with Tom. "You know, it's a eugenics type of thing," he says. "And I still think there's an element of eugenics in the way people are pushing abortion in the United States. . . . The population groups that are poor and that are minorities, that is a eugenics thing." These activists worry about how abortion impacts the civil rights of different groups in society.

An understanding of abortion rooted in concern over civil rights is often coupled with the belief that legalized abortion is the first step down a slippery slope of disregard for human life. "When you get people to accept abortion, accept the killing of a person, then you can accept what's next," says seventy-nine-year-old Ben of Charleston. "Infanticide is next. Then euthanasia is next. . . . Those are the progressions, and that's what is happening to the human race." Like Tom, whose concern about a slippery slope introduced this chapter, Ben and others express a fear of not only abortion but also a much larger set of evils to which they see abortion leading. Activists will use the idea of a slippery slope quite explicitly. "I think the scary thing is that we're edging now towards that slippery slope of a 100 percent relativistic belief system," explains thirty-seven-year-old Nicky in Charleston. Abortion for Tom, Ben, Nicky, and others cheapens life and is thereby partially responsible for the increase in murders, domestic abuse, newborns abandoned in trash cans, and myriad other problems our society faces.

Activists are also concerned about the slippery slope of what they see as excuses used to justify abortion. They believe that acceptance of abortion in some cases or under some circumstances will inevitably open the floodgates to abortion for any reason, no matter how reprehensible. If abortions are performed because of medical problems with the fetus, for example, where will the line between "healthy" and "to be aborted" be drawn? An activist in Oklahoma City, a diabetic, wondered: "Would the doctors [have] come to my mom and said, you know, we know your son is going to be a diabetic. His quality of life is going to be less than the normal person. You know, he's going to be embarrassed because at times his blood sugar is going to get low in the middle of an interview . . . and he's going to have to excuse himself, and we think you ought to abort. Well, I wouldn't be in favor of that! So the line drawing that takes place on abnormalities, you can make some pretty horrific predictions." Should unborn children be aborted because they will be poor? Should they be aborted because they will be blind? Should they be aborted because they might be gay? These are the kinds of questions activists ask themselves in working through an understanding of abortion as the first step in a long string of potentially appalling decisions.

Beliefs about the slippery slope of abortion find their ultimate expression in analogies made between legalized abortion in the United States and the rise of the Nazis. Donald, quoted earlier, had difficulty containing his emotions as he explained the idea this way: "We talk about that slippery slope and how Hitler got started by eliminating the handicapped and the elderly, those who didn't have the quality of life or any utility. What could they provide? It's just hard for me to understand how intelligent, apparently caring people can favor abortion. When you think of it, you almost have to cry." Some see the Holocaust during World War II as the end point to which abortion is leading us. For others, the Holocaust serves as a comparison that underscores the evil they see in abortion. "I think you've got to compare, the only comparison I think is the Holocaust of the Jews," says Ron, a fifty-four-year-old in Boston. "There are people that are here that are not going to be here. There's not going to be a second choice. It's definitive." Josh, introduced in chapter 5, puts it this way: "I look at abortion clinics like I do the gas chambers that the Jews went to. Same type of thing." In fact, many understand abortion as the moral equivalent of the Holocaust, highlighting a view that the country has completely lost its moral bearings. Abortion puts everyone's civil rights at risk.

Deceit of Abortion Providers

For some activists, the abortion issue is as much about the lies and ulte-
rior motives of pro-choice advocates as it is about the substantive harms
of abortion itself. "It's very common for abortionists to be alcoholics,
drug addicts, pornography addicts," an activist in Boston tells me. Another says, "Most physicians consider abortionists bottom-feeders."
Vilifying the opposition is not surprising in any social movement.
What is interesting here is that impugning the character of pro-choice
advocates is not just a rhetorical strategy but also a part of some pro-life
activists' understanding of their own position. For these activists, the
abortion debate is not between two different points of view or different
understandings of the world or different cultural perspectives. Their
battle is one in which the enemy is a small cadre of utterly corrupt
opportunists. That corruption, more than anything else, invests their
activism with meaning.

Many pro-lifers believe money is the ultimate motivation behind the
work of abortion providers. This is the perspective of Tammy, a thirty-
two-year-old in Boston: "I think economics is a big reason [motivating
pro-choicers]. Global control of population and economics. And that's
a big reason. . . . Because some people feel the population is growing
too fast, and that has a big impact on economics. Some feel like if teenagers become pregnant, that would be a burden to the government."
More common than this interpretation of macroeconomics, however,
is a focus on the greed of individual abortion providers. "What are
abortionists in it for?" asks forty-five-year-old Susan in the Twin Cities.
"They're in it for the money. The bottom line is money. Money, money,
money." Henry, a fifty-nine-year-old in Oklahoma City, captures the
ideas expressed by a number of activists:

If you need to have your gallbladder taken out, they worry about getting paid later.
Because the first, primary effort of the physician in the hospital is the wellness of
the individual that comes to them. However, in an abortion clinic, what is the first
thing you do? You pay. No money, no abortion. Why do they want the government
to fund it? Because that's more money. It's all about money! They don't give a fat
rat's ass about any of the women that go through their doors. Just the money. You
figure that an abortionist, it's going to take him roughly fifteen minutes to do it.
And in most cases, they're running an average of actually even less. Because some
of the abortionists are aborting women that are not pregnant. Roughly 10 percent
of the women who have abortions are not pregnant, and the doctor knows it. But
it's going to take him, say, fifteen minutes. That's four an hour. Going rate is $450 a

pop. That's $1,800 an hour. He operates his shop for seven hours a day, five days a week. Do the math. There is a huge sum of money there. No matter how many staff members he's got, it works out. It works out that the guy is making on the average at least one-third, $600 an hour. Pocket change, right?

Henry's understanding of the issue contains a number of elements, including a view of abortion as financially lucrative, abortion providers as greedy and uncaring, and abortion clinics as the sites of a conspiracy to get government money and to perform procedures on women who aren't even pregnant.

Others tell similar stories of the abortion industry as a multibillion-dollar enterprise built on the lies needed to perpetuate legalized abortion. "Frankly, the pro-choice position, it's just simply a falsehood," says Max, a forty-nine-year-old in Boston. "They're selling a bad bill of goods to women." Judy, a sixty-year-old in Charleston, was much more specific in discussing how Planned Parenthood in particular operates: "Their practice, their method of operation, is to talk to young girls about getting pregnant and to put them on low-dose pills, which, if you don't take those at the same time every day—and what teenager do you know that will?—then you can get pregnant. In fact, it makes you more fertile if you don't take them at the same time. So it almost guarantees that these women will, well, their goal is to have every woman in her lifetime have three abortions so they can get the money." Other stories depicted clinics that lie about the stage of pregnancy to increase the price of abortion, companies that deliberately weaken the strength of birth control pills to increase pregnancy rates, and rumors of a black market for body parts taken from aborted fetuses. These kinds of beliefs all add up to opposition to abortion rooted in an understanding of abortion's defenders as deceitful and unprincipled. William, a sixty-eight-year-old in Boston, says it simply: "The other side relies on lies."

Tensions in the Pro-life Moral Universe

There is no consensus, even within the pro-life movement, on how to understand the abortion issue. Even among those most committed to ending all abortion in the United States, there are marked disagreements about how to understand abortion, why abortion is wrong, and how it is tied to other moral issues. These are more than cosmetic differences in how people explain the issue; they are fundamental tensions within the movement.

The issue of personal responsibility is one good example of how this tension cuts to activists' core worldviews. Although some people understand abortion as opening the floodgates to immorality and lack of responsibility, others suggest that this belief is actually a betrayal of the movement's central principle—that the fetus is a person. Ideas about abortion rooted in concern for personal responsibility lead people to sometimes accept the possibility that abortion in cases in which a woman has been raped (and is thus not morally responsible for her position) might be justified. Others, however, strenuously disagree, seeing the personhood of the fetus as trumping any circumstances surrounding the conception, however horrific. "If your reasoning is really around the life issue," explains twenty-eight-year-old Steve of Boston, "then I don't see any exceptions. But if your reasoning is around moral policing, not life issues, then you can make assumptions like that [justifying abortion in some circumstances] because rape or incest wasn't your choice."

The difference between these views is crucial, because people such as Steve are questioning who is "truly" pro-life based on their beliefs. Twenty-four-year-old Mariah, also of Boston, explains that "the majority of the pro-life movement—which really hasn't been expressed well in the media—is not judging anyone. This isn't, you know, we're not self-righteous and trying to force our views down everyone else's throat." Mariah is not entirely correct. My data show that both kinds of moral understanding exist in the movement. The point is that there is no majority or common position among activists on how to understand why abortion is wrong.

The idea that abortion providers are all greedy liars is also a source of tension among activists. Some express frustration that their compatriots vilify clinic workers and those in the pro-choice movement. "I get pretty impatient with pro-life people who paint pro-choice people as, you know, villains or murders or whatever," says forty-six-year-old activist Debbie in the Twin Cities. Sidney, a seventy-two-year-old in Oklahoma City, echoes this view: "I know numbers of people who are pro-abortion, and they are very, very good people," he says. "They lead good lives, and they're good people. In my view, it's a flaw that they have this opinion, but it's still a free country." Activists are thus divided over whether abortion is a fundamental force of evil or a simple (albeit important) difference of opinion.

Differences in the way pro-lifers understand their opposition have implications for the movement. If abortion providers are greedy, lying, scheming criminals, there is little room for negotiation or respect between the two sides in the debate. By contrast, if providers are seen as similarly committed to a moral conviction, even if ultimately flawed, there is a great deal of common ground for working out at least some of the many tensions between the two camps. Forty-nine-year-old Alicia in Oklahoma City actually identifies with abortion providers, seeing them as genuinely concerned with helping women: "I think they evidently have an opinion that a woman is entitled to choice. And they believe that they're going to help a woman. If that's what she wants, then they'll help her. I want to help them make the right choice, too. I mean that's why I do what I do. I'm sure they really believe that they're helping them. But they're really deceived." Alicia's beliefs thus dramatically narrow the divide that separates pro-life activists from those on the other side of the debate. They also situate the abortion issue with respect to other social and moral issues in a much different way from those that focus on the deceit or immorality of pro-choice advocates.

The connection between abortion and race is another way in which the deep divisions within the movement can clearly be seen. As noted earlier, some activists regard abortion as fundamentally racist, rooted in a desire to limit minority populations and disproportionately affecting blacks and Hispanics. Others, however, exhibit clear racial animosity in their opposition to abortion. This is most evident in discussions of how abortion amounts to national suicide, as it results in negative population growth among (white) Americans and therefore requires reliance on (nonwhite) immigrants in our marriage and labor markets. In other cases, activist beliefs reflect crude racial stereotypes. A woman in the Twin Cities, for example, described the rape of a black woman by a white man as "one of those sort of strange things, you know, a little reverse on what is common." In Charleston, thirty-five-year-old Andy explained his belief that abortion exists as one leg in a triad of evils consisting of the abortion clinic, the porn shop, and the crack house: "And what happens is they get hooked, they get all fired up on crack. So then they go to the pornography shop, they get all fired up on the pornography shop. Then they go to their girlfriend and they have sex with their girlfriend or wife. She gets pregnant, and they go to the abortion clinic and kill their children. The majority of abortions taking place are done on black women." Andy is firmly opposed to abortion, but he understands the issue in racial terms as a problem rooted in his vision of the black community and the lifestyles "they" lead. His view is incompatible in many ways with the concerns of other activists who root their opposition to abortion in ideas about civil rights.

The various beliefs about abortion in the movement are thus not simply different rhetorical strategies for pushing the same underlying issue; they represent fundamentally different understandings of abortion and how it is connected to individuals, institutions, and other social problems. Factors beyond abortion also bleed into the tensions created by these differences in belief. One is religion. Differences between Catholics and Protestants within the movement are frequently a source of conflict, particularly on the hot-button issues of capital punishment and contraception. "That's another one of the things I find very irritating is people want to be pro-life, but they're pro–capital punishment. . . . You know, if you're going to be pro-life, you need to be for it on all sides," says twenty-nine-year-old Twin Cities activist Chris, a Catholic. Doug, a thirty-one-year-old activist in Oklahoma City and member of a nondenominational Protestant congregation, disagrees: "God Himself said 'An eye for an eye and a life for a life' to teach us the value of life. That if you don't value it, if you take it from that person, then you give your life in return. Why should someone be allowed to live who has no value for someone else's life?"[5] These religiously rooted differences don't fall neatly into any of the categories of belief about abortion. Catholics who understand abortion principally in terms of personal responsibility still frequently oppose the death penalty, while Baptists with a more civil rights understanding of abortion nonetheless support capital punishment.

Birth control is another issue that divides the movement. Compare, for example, these two views of birth control:

There's a difference between being pro-life and anti-abortion. There's a lot of people who are anti-abortion and yet not truly pro-life. . . . The idea being contraception. They [some activists] don't know what to do with contraception. And research has shown over and over again that the pill is an abortive agent.
(MELISSA, 37, CHARLESTON)

Even if I am personally against birth control, a good pro-lifer does not intermingle those two issues. And that's what has been divisive to the movement.
(SHARON, 50, CHARLESTON)

Both of these women are Catholic, and both are opposed to the use of birth control. Melissa links birth control directly to the abortion issue, however, while Sharon does not. Moreover, each woman thinks that her belief is a defining criterion for a "true" or "good" pro-life activist.

Why Care about Moral Tensions in the Movement?

There is a tendency to try to boil social movements down to a single underlying idea or belief. This is especially true of movements with which one disagrees: it is easier to dismiss an opposing viewpoint by reducing it to a sound bite or a simple (and ugly) message. Until now, the pro-life movement has been examined in this manner—as a countermovement that is "really" about gender relationships, changes in sexuality, and the role of women in society. These ideas are evident in the moral universe of pro-life activism, but they neither define nor organize the different constellations of ideas about abortion that make up that universe. Although everyone in the movement agrees that the fetus is a person, and, therefore, abortion is the killing of a person, there are many different ways in which this core idea is understood. Activists' beliefs about abortion do not fit neatly into a single ideological camp.

In practical terms, this means that people mobilized into the pro-life movement are exposed to a wider array of different moral understandings of the issue than previously believed. In particular, not all the moral understandings of abortion come from commitment to a politically conservative set of ideas. Concerns over civil rights, racism, and the protection of the weak coexist in uneasy company with concerns over personal responsibility and female sexuality, the deceit of abortion providers, and the will of God. Becoming an activist involves a need to negotiate this complex moral landscape, providing a cultural connection to some in the movement while straining relationships with others. Such ideational complexity means that social movement activity, at least in this case, somewhat ironically represents an opportunity for exposure to a range of different perspectives on the issue.

Theoretically, recognition of profound differences in the way activists understand the abortion issue requires that we talk less about a single monolithic movement and more about the different pieces that compose it. This makes the movement distinct from the gay and lesbian movement in San Francisco (Armstrong 2002) or the working-class advocacy organizations in the American Southwest (Warren 2001) or even the more general national movement of conservative Protestantism (Stevens 2002). In all of these cases, scholars have found a basic ideational core around which all the beliefs in the movement can be organized and understood.

By contrast, activists with very different moral bases for their opposition to abortion can and do intermingle and work together in the same movement streams. This fact says something important about the role of ideas in the pro-life movement specifically and perhaps in other movements more generally. Differences in belief within the movement over the proper *means* to end legalized abortion keep the movement fractured and define the movement's structure, as the last chapter demonstrates. The analysis in this chapter shows that the differences over how abortion *itself* is understood create tensions within the movement, too, but do not ultimately define or maintain the same kinds of structural divisions. Activists with very different moral bases for their opposition are evident in each movement stream, working side by side. Different kinds of beliefs thus play different roles in the movement, even when they are ostensibly held with the same "strength" or fervency. Ideas about action—what people actually *do*—turn out to be more consequential in the pro-life movement than the underlying basis for that action.

These findings suggest the need to ask new questions about ideas in social movements. What, for example, are the factors that allow groups and individuals to cohere in a single movement in the face of profound ideological differences? Can social movements be arrayed on a continuum of diversity of beliefs, or do all movements exhibit similar differences and tensions in how activists understand the issues being contested? How do differences in belief influence tactical innovation in movements, their relationship to elites, the ability of movement leaders to frame their messages to the public, and so forth?

These findings also matter to partisans on both sides of the abortion debate, as the composition of the pro-life moral universe has implications for the future development of the movement as well as the dynamics of its relationship with others. In particular, it affects the likelihood of coalitions among different organizations and the degree to which the movement can forge close relationships with various outside actors, including political parties, social service organizations, and religious congregations. Internal tensions over beliefs affect the ability of actors in the movement to work together and accomplish goals. They limit the possibility of collaboration within the movement as well as create opportunities for alliance between the movement and other organizations and institutions in the larger society.

SEVEN

"My Life Is My Argument": Religion and the Movement

I think that the message of repentance is going to be broadcast in a big way and that the time of the waters is near. For some folks, it will be the second time, and for others, it will be the first. In either case, there is time for people to have great anticipation. Their cries and their pleas have not fallen on deaf ears. So it's a time of great expectancy, and it's almost as we talk, the world is travailing and groans and so on and so forth. The world is about to go into convulsions and transitions and give the new birth to the new heaven and the new earth. But the good thing about it is that before the labor can begin, those who subscribe to the belief and the trust in Him have to be taken out and honored. That's the sign of the water breaking right there.

These words from fifty-year-old Boston resident Albert richly tie together a theological worldview with imagery of pregnancy and birth so important in the pro-life movement. His comments highlight the widely cited—but poorly understood—connection between the movement and religion in the United States. Those who become pro-life activists are immersed in a complicated religious terrain, one that is more limited and more profoundly influential on individual activists than previous research has indicated.

This chapter examines two main findings from my data on the pro-life movement. First, it demonstrates the relatively modest ways in which religious organizations and religious beliefs exert a direct influence on the movement. Contrary to common belief, the pro-life movement today is not fully immersed in the American subculture of conservative Christianity. The movement is influenced by, but by no means relies on, religious institutions for resources and support. Activists' moral worldview includes, but is not reducible to, religious ideas. I suggest instead that the everyday activity of pro-life activism frequently constitutes religious practice. I argue, then, that religion and the pro-life movement represent overlapping spheres of action whose boundaries are blurred and thus hard (if not impossible) to disentangle. Much of the impact of religion on the pro-life movement therefore occurs as religion "happens" outside of traditional religious spaces—churches, ministry events, and so forth.

Second, my data show that some activists within the movement have found their religious faith *after* first becoming involved in pro-life activity. Activists who participate in the discussions, meetings, rallies, events, and campaigns of the pro-life movement reinforce, or sometimes create for the first time, an interest in religious faith in their own lives. Activism can lead people back to a religious commitment they had lost years ago. In some cases, it can lead to outright religious conversion. Overall, more than one out of every five activists in my sample found their religious faith either contemporaneously with or after their mobilization into the pro-life movement. This finding offers an important lesson about the role of religion: religion may be a dependent variable in the mobilization process, not just a "cause" of or resource for social movement activity. Becoming an activist, then, can involve substantial reworking of other aspects of a person's identity and system of practices and beliefs.

Religion and the Movement: A Traditional View

There is no shortage of books and essays that focus on the relationship between religion and the pro-life movement. Whether based on scholarly research or partisan opinion, almost all of this work examines the relationship by conceptualizing religion in one of two ways: religion as churches (or other houses of worship) or religion as sets of ideas and belief.

Religion as Churches

Movement scholars have typically treated religion in organizational terms (for example, Morris 1981, 1984; McAdam 1982; Warren 2001). Churches are seen as social institutions that provide various resources needed by movements.[1] In his seminal work on the civil rights movement, Aldon Morris focuses on the importance of religious institutions to the mobilization of southern blacks in the 1950s and 1960s. His work documents the specific ways in which the black church was crucial in the origins of the movement. In particular, he found that churches furnished many of the material resources, organized audiences to serve as a mass base, and provided the seasoned and independent leaders necessary to the civil rights movement.

Like the civil rights movement, the pro-life movement has been rooted in church institutions in a number of ways. Churches often directly support pro-life organizations, either by making financial contributions to such groups or by hosting fund-raisers for the organizations in the churches. An example of the former is Minnesota Citizens Concerned for Life (MCCL), which receives several thousand dollars annually from the Archdiocese of Minneapolis/St. Paul. Many crisis pregnancy centers (CPCs) rely on the support of churches for part of their annual revenue. Fund-raising takes many forms: special collections, Pennies for Life campaigns, talent shows, bake sales, church "lock-ins" in which children receive pledges for fasting for twenty-four hours, Mother's Day corsage sales, and so forth. Churches can also provide in-kind financial resources, such as when they rent buses to transport people to rallies and protests. Physical space is also an important resource. In South Carolina, board meetings of South Carolina Citizens for Life (SCCL) are held in a small independent church that itself has so little space that the altar in the church must be moved during the meeting to accommodate a portable table for the dozen or so attendees. Organizational and inspirational rallies by Operation Rescue Boston were often held in churches on the eve of major civil disobedience campaigns.

Beyond providing material resources such as money and meeting space, churches command enormous potential audiences for the movement. Pro-life groups are permitted, and in some cases encouraged, to display pro-life posters around some churches, make announcements of upcoming pro-life events during services, screen pro-life films such as *The Silent Scream*,[2] and set up tables or bulletin boards to distribute pro-life pamphlets, newsletters, and fund-raising appeals. Weekly church bulletins are one of the most common ways in which pro-life groups use church congregations as an audience. Many churches allow small advertisements in their bulletins by pro-life groups offering help, soliciting new donations, or recruiting volunteers.

In both the Twin Cities and Boston, the Catholic archdioceses maintain a Respect Life office that distributes pro-life information and helps coordinate pro-life programs in individual churches. Respect Life or social ministry directors hold regular meetings with volunteer committees, make pro-life information available to parishioners, and in some cases grant limited funds for individual parish programs.[3] Churches can also provide an audience for the movement in purely symbolic ways. There is a reading of petitions every week in an independent Twin Cities church in which congregants are asked to pray for pregnant women "in the midst of a difficult choice." In Charleston, a Catholic church hosts a special service twice each year in which pregnant women are asked to come to the front of the congregation for a special blessing.

Leadership is the third important way in which Morris (1984) identifies churches as being consequential to the civil rights movement. He argues that religious leaders offer a number of advantages to social movement groups: their churches pay their salaries and thus make them available for social movement work, they already have experience with leadership tasks and responsibilities, they are often well respected in the community, and they are generally well educated. A number of leaders in the pro-life movement have come from churches with such advantages. Richard is a fifty-seven-year-old Catholic priest in the Twin Cities who was once very active in the movement. He became involved in social justice activism while attending seminary in the 1960s, especially around the issue of racism. His first parish posting, however, was to a white, middle-class suburban church in which racism and poverty were not particularly salient issues. Richard decided then to get more involved in the emerging pro-life movement. As he explains: "I wasn't in a position to be involved in interracial affairs in a first-ring suburb like Maplewood. And issues of homelessness and poverty weren't present there. I mean it was kind of an awkward situation. So this [abortion] seemed to be a logical place where justice could be pursued—in a pro-life dimension, which actually affects everybody."[4] Soon after mobilizing his own parishioners to oppose the reelection of a local pro-choice politician, Richard was approached by MCCL: "The leadership of MCCL heard about me, and they came to me—in particular Darla and David—and they asked me to join the board while I was at Sacred Heart in those first three years. Which was very unusual, because I was just starting out. Of course, they were just starting out, too. But they wanted a priest representative on their board, and they felt that I would [pause] They talked to me awhile to screen how I was and where I was, and they felt that I suited their purposes." Richard was a leader in his parish and sought out abortion as an issue in which he could make a difference as a social movement leader. At the same time, the movement itself sought Richard out precisely because of his religious credentials. He spent many years as a pro-life leader, involved in the church, on the board of directors of MCCL, and in local and state politics.

Religion as Beliefs

Thus far, I have conceptualized religion primarily as formal organizations, especially churches. But focusing on the role of church organizations is not the only way to evaluate the impact of religion on the pro-life movement. Religion can also be conceptualized as a body of values, beliefs, ideas, and teachings. Morris (1984, 282) recognized that "cultural factors such as religious beliefs" played a role in the civil rights movement, but his analysis does not explore the way in which such beliefs mattered to the movement or how such beliefs are related to the moral understandings of movement participants. The sociology of religion, however, has focused more closely on religion as a set of beliefs (for example, Williams 1996, 1999; Darnell and Sherkat 1997; Wood 2002; Hart 1996). In this conceptualization, religious ideas are seen as important for the values and beliefs they represent and the religious language and imagery they offer to both their members and the larger society.

Religion might be thought of as a source of values and ideals on which pro-life activism is based. Rhys Williams (1999), for example, demonstrates how beliefs about the public good come out of different religious visions: the covenant model, the contractual model, and the stewardship model. In his analysis, religious beliefs provide the values that are used in other debates and struggles. Religion can also provide a vocabulary or language for understanding the abortion issue. Religion is thus a "generator of religious culture" (Wood 1999) that a social movement can use to articulate its ideology and goals. Ann Swidler (2001) has noted that discourses can have power not just because of the beliefs embedded in them but also because they are easily called to mind and understood in multiple contexts.

The beliefs expressed by pro-life activists are at times rooted quite explicitly in religious values. Some see the whole issue as being rooted in religious ideals: "The pro-life versus pro-abort debate is really a struggle between the spiritual view of the world and the materialistic view of the world," says Glen, an Episcopalian. Values can also influence individuals by establishing norms of belief and conduct that are tied to their identities. Take, for example, the comments of Jeff, a thirty-five-year-old Catholic: "You know, if we're not open to life occurring, not necessarily spontaneously, but if we're going to be the ones in charge of deciding when life comes about, you know, in a sense playing little gods, are we still open to the Creator of all life?" Jeff sees the abortion issue as one in which ideas about what God is and the role of God in our lives is jeopardized if we allow abortion, which is tantamount to "playing little gods." Monica, a forty-one-year-old Baptist, understands the issue in much the same way, seeing her opposition to abortion as a reflection of her being a person who believes in the Bible: "I don't believe that anyone believing the Bible can think that it's OK to end a life through abortion. I mean, I think we can all have our different interpretations of the Bible, but I'd be hard-pressed to ever side with somebody trying to find in the Bible that it's OK to do that." In Monica's mind, opposition to abortion is a litmus test for being a believer. Being a pro-lifer is a reflection of her values, a core piece of what it means to be a Christian.

Activism itself can also be understood as being prescribed by religious teachings. Activists with this view are fulfilling their values and making claims to a particular identity by living out religious beliefs. In Charleston, fourteen-year-old Justin, a Baptist, explains that his activism is his way of proving God's existence:

As far as pro-life goes, I mean, how can I persuade somebody to be pro-life, what would I do? Let's say I argue the Bible, and they doubt its authenticity. I argue justice, and they argue choice. I argue life, they argue choice. I argue freedom, they argue liberty. I argue justice, and they argue liberty. I mean, there's two sides to everything. So how can I persuade them? I can't argue morals if everything is postmodernistic. There's very few things I can argue, but Saint Francis of Assisi said, "Preach always. If necessary, use words." So my best argument for pro-life is how I live. I mean, I don't think you can really prove there's a God. I don't think there's some system of mathematics or whatever that equals God. But I can prove God because of what He's done in my life and the joy that He's given me; that's my argument for why God exists. And my life is my argument. And how I live my life and my morals and what I do is my argument.

Justin ties the pro-life issue intimately to his faith—to argue about abortion is to argue about the Bible and life and God. He never mentions abortion or the pro-life movement after the first sentence of the passage, an indication that he sees the question of how one disseminates a pro-life message as answered by an explanation of how one demonstrates one's faith. Religious values thus serve as a motivation to action. They inform how people think about the abortion issue as well as how they understand their own involvement. People draw on the teachings of their faith, applying them to the issue and to the movement in important ways.

Language is a second way in which religious beliefs might impact the pro-life movement. Activists need to discuss the issue with fellow activists and explain their involvement in the movement to family, friends, and potential new recruits. Religious ideas provide a powerful vocabulary for thinking about and expressing opposition to abortion. If the development of pro-life beliefs after movement contact is an important step in the mobilization process, as I argue in chapters 2 and 3, then activists old and new need a language in which they can discuss and learn about the issue once they have become involved. Activists quote from Exodus that thou shalt not kill and from Genesis that men are made in God's image. Michael, a forty-two-year-old Catholic in Boston, articulates the source of the abortion problem in religious language, drawing on the notion of sin, which he believes has been left out of the debate: "One of the most important things that isn't taken into consideration is the whole idea of sin. It seems to be something that's just brushed under the rug. You know, even some Catholic priests think that there really isn't such a thing as sin, that there isn't such a thing as evil or something. 'Those rotten conservatives' or 'those racist homophobic antiwoman, anti-Semitic conservatives.' That those are the only evils out there. It seems to me that there is this thing where there is no such thing as right and wrong, because all these things are victimless anyways. As if there's no victim in abortion, you know?" Here Michael rejects the vocabulary of secular liberals in labeling some as "rotten conservatives" and argues that the religious language of sin is more appropriate. Others describe abortion as the result of a fallen society, one that has stepped outside the grace of God.

The dominant language of motivation in American society puts an overwhelming premium on self-interested behavior. Even participation in charitable, volunteer, or self-sacrificing activity is understood by both scholars and the public alike in terms of the satisfactions it brings to the participant ("I enjoy volunteering," or "I feel good when I give money") or possibly the social capital it builds for later use in finding a job, attracting a marriage partner, or gaining political power. This kind of language can also be found in the pro-life movement, but the language of religious faith offers an alternative to understanding one's own involvement solely in self-interested terms. Nicole, a thirty-seven-year-old member of an independent church in Charleston, describes the religious call in even stronger terms, seeing herself as unable to do anything other than be an activist: "The apostle Paul did describe being a prisoner of Christ. And it's funny, when you read the Bible, you tend to romanticize things, and you romanticize statements people are making. And he's like, 'Well, maybe it wasn't this matter of love kind of thing. It's more like I really am a prisoner of this.' So I feel like a prisoner of this cause in a sense. And not in a bad way, but in a way where I feel like I'm driven on a track that is meant for me." Mobilization into the pro-life movement forces activists to confront the question of why they do what they do, both for others and for themselves. Religious ideas offer a language through which activists' large commitments of time and resources to the movement can be understood. Altruism, because God wants it or requires it, helps make sense of social movement activity in a world where many doubt any motive not rooted in self-interest and economic advantage.

Problems with Existing Models

Thus far, I have outlined how two approaches—religion as churches and religious ideas—help to illuminate religion's impact on the pro-life movement. Religion is a source of resources, leadership, audiences, ideas, and language, but its overall impact is surprisingly limited. Although churches and religious ideas have provided important advantages to the pro-life movement, their impact and influence are also clearly circumscribed.

The Limits of Religion as Churches

Churches do offer the pro-life movement a number of advantages. The financial resources they provide, however, represent only a small fraction of those used by the movement. Archdiocesan financial support of MCCL in the Twin Cities, for example, amounts to several thousand dollars a year. MCCL's annual budget, by contrast, is more than $1.4 million (see table 4.1). This is a fairly common pattern within the movement: churches provide support but often in only very limited or token ways.

Churches—even conservative churches—frequently shy away from the issue because they see it as controversial and divisive. Congregations are thus reticent to address the issue or allow the movement to use their churches as a venue for mobilization. Dan, a seventeen-year-old Baptist in Charleston, believes the controversy hurts the bottom line of church finances, and thus church leaders back off: "It's because it's a very controversial issue. I think there are a lot of people in the church who are maybe on birth control or who have had abortions, and [the churches] don't want to do anything to offend them, or they don't want to take a stand because then people start leaving. I think once you get off 'God is love' and you start focusing on real issues that are kind of not so positive, then you get people who get uncomfortable and you lose some of the money." Because churches cannot count on broad consensus on the abortion issue even within their congregations, they are uncomfortable having abortion be the centerpiece of sermons or church activity. "But, see, even in the Catholic Church," explains Josh, introduced in chapter 5, "all the churches are sort of shy. You mention the A-word [abortion] in the churches, and the churches want to hide the A-word. They really do." Josh is at least partially correct. Churches are bureaucratic organizations that require continual resources to survive. They can't afford to alienate too many of those who don't believe in the pro-life cause. Jason, a twenty-three-year-old in Boston, was not allowed to start a pro-life "club" in his Catholic high school because administrators felt it was "inappropriate." Others have been asked to "tone down" their pro-life activism in church or broaden their activism to less controversial issues. Despite the stereotype of the marriage between churches and the movement, I consistently found most churches in all four of the cities I studied to be circumspect about their involvement. This finding is consistent with what both Mark Warren (2001) and Richard Wood (2002) have found about religious organizing more generally: divisive issues such as abortion are avoided.

Many conservative churches and religious leaders shy away from active involvement as a matter of principle. Their concern is rooted in theological traditions that shun any kind of social activism. Mobilizing for the pro-life movement within congregations, they believe, detracts from the church's overall mission. Ben, a seventy-nine-year-old member of a Presbyterian church in Charleston, reflects this view as he explains that the abortion issue is seldom raised in his congregation: "Well, it's not very often now because it's not an issue that's being accepted. If we're going to pass the word to go do something, like the January meeting, we pass the word to participate.[5] But we don't discuss it otherwise. Part of our purpose is to teach the word of God. And we don't get sidetracked on other things very often. . . . We strictly stay with the word of God." Of course, others understand the pro-life position as coming directly from the word of God, but Ben is not alone in understanding that the divisiveness of the abortion issue tends to lead churches away from active engagement. "I don't know that they support this issue [abortion] or not," says Dominique, a forty-eight-year-old Baptist activist in Oklahoma City. "The church I go to, our pastor doesn't want anything to do with politics and those issues, and he makes it clear. Only the word of God and teaching the word of God." Popular conservative leaders Cal Thomas and Ed Dobson (1999) have contributed significantly to this view with a popular book that makes this argument generally for the Christian Right. Commitment to religious beliefs that shun this worldly involvement in politics—and especially controversial politics—places significant limits on the relationship between many churches and the movement.

To the extent that some churches are involved in the movement, it is often in only partial or symbolic ways. I spoke with several people, themselves pro-life activists, who had never heard of any pro-life activity in their church, even when I knew from other sources that church pro-life committees and fund-raisers existed. For others, the level of pro-life commitment in their church, if it does exist, simply isn't strong enough to warrant much time or effort. Jennifer, a twenty-eight-year-old in the Twin Cities, sees this as the reason her charismatic Catholic church doesn't provide any movement leadership: "I haven't been real impressed with them. To me, it seems like they just do meetings, but I've never heard any of them speak; I've never heard any of them say, 'We need to get people out doing things.' So I just haven't been impressed, and I've never been involved in that." Lisa, another young Catholic activist from the Twin Cities, signed up for the pro-life group in her church when she first moved to her new home; it was years later before anyone contacted her. Many activists have no memory of the issue's ever being raised in their church. "Even having gone through twelve years of Catholic education, I can say I had probably never been talked to about abortion. I don't know if I'd even heard the word," reports Brenda, fifty-three years old, of Oklahoma City.

The pro-life movement is far from the image Morris paints of the civil rights movement, as being led by energetic and charismatic pastors who mobilized their congregations behind the cause. Although some religious leaders have become part of the movement, their overall impact has been small. Only one of the fifteen major pro-life organizations in the Twin Cities is headed by a religious figure. Of the forty-seven people on the board of directors of Massachusetts Citizens for Life (MCFL), only two are clergy. None of the officers or executive committee members of MCCL are also church leaders, and only one of the fifty-seven founding members of Human Life Alliance was also a minister. On the national level, only one of the fifty-three members of the board of directors of the National Right to Life Committee (NRLC) is also a religious leader. Neither David O'Steen nor Darla St. Martin, longtime executive leaders of the organization, have a professional religious background.

Activists themselves recognize the limits on the leadership and resources the church provides the movement. As a result, they frequently have harsh words for the work of churches:

The local priests seem very quiet on the issue. They're only interested in attendance. It [abortion] comes up once in a while, nothing that strong. And the worst of the lot are the Jesuits. The rottenest of the lot are the Jesuits. They are completely invisible on the issue of abortion, and they're in positions, running the universities and high schools, where they could have a positive impact. You know, I say only partly tongue in cheek that the Jesuits seem to be the Catholic Church's Unitarians. No spines.
(MICHAEL, 42, CATHOLIC, BOSTON)

The churches are not in front of the abortion clinics because they have hirelings in the pulpit, they don't have pastors. When they took prayer out of our schools, the churches should have rioted. When they took the Ten Commandments off the wall, the churches should have come out and said something. They should have spoken. They didn't.
(ANDY, 35, MEMBER OF AN INDEPENDENT CHURCH, CHARLESTON)

I find that we have more sincere Baptists supporting right to life, pro-life movements, than we do Catholics. All too often, you have [pause] Well, some Catholic churches mention it probably once a year, and that's about it.
(JOHN, 68, CATHOLIC, TWIN CITIES)

Activists see churches as having failed in their mission to both their own congregations and the larger society. I asked one Twin Cities activist if he thought his parish priest was pro-life: "Oh, I'm sure he's pro-life. But they don't bring it out strongly enough; that's my opinion anyway. I mean, if you believe in a moral issue, if you believe it's morally wrong, that killing of a baby is totally absurd and ridiculous and morally wrong, you should speak out on it." This sentiment is widespread among activists; few are fully satisfied with the way churches in general—and their own church in particular—address the issue. Many believe the churches have the power to bring an end to abortion if they would just put their collective will behind the pro-life movement. "I mean, if the church would wake up and do what the church is supposed to do, abortion would end tomorrow," says Erin, the individual outreach activist introduced in chapter 3. In Charleston, many activists were upset because Baptist churches had recently mobilized a great deal of resources and support to eliminate video poker in the state but are not nearly as unified or supportive in their opposition to abortion.[6]

There is also a theoretical limit to conceptualizing religion as churches. Although the treatment of religion as organizations with potential resources is evident in scholarship on the civil rights movement, the relationship between religion and social movements has not been developed further (Smith 1996). A problem with an organizational approach to churches is that it provides no place for what is particularly religious about church institutions. To the extent that social movement scholars have looked at religion, they have analyzed it as just another site of social organization from which to draw resources (Hannigan 1991). Thus, churches have no more to offer a social movement than does, say, NASCAR—both are institutions that can provide resources, audiences, and leadership. Religion is reduced to just another variable that satisfies these social movement needs.[7]

The Limits of Religion as Beliefs

We saw earlier that religious ideas permeate the pro-life movement. They serve as a source of values and teachings about the issue for activists as well as a language in which abortion can be debated and understood. Conceptualizing religion as a set of beliefs also has a number of limitations, however. As chapter 6 demonstrated, the pro-life moral universe consists of substantially more than just religious ideas. Talk of individual rights and freedoms drawn from a more republican language (Bellah et al. 1985), historical analogy linking the abortion issue to American slavery and the Holocaust, and social conservative ideas about personal responsibility are all a part of the moral universe of pro-life activism as well. There are also both empirical and theoretical problems with addressing the relationship between religion and the pro-life movement solely through an examination of ideas.

Although many activists within the movement see the issue in religious terms, many do not. When forty-six-year-old Twin Cities activist Debbie first became involved in the movement, she explained, "I didn't see it as being primarily a religious issue. I mean, I didn't feel like I was against abortion because I was Catholic; I felt I was against abortion because it made sense, you know?" "Life is the most precious thing on this earth. Without life, nothing could exist," says Stephanie, a twenty-six-year-old Catholic. "Why am I pro-life? Because I think life is beautiful and I love people. Nothing religious. Nothing religious." Activists in the movement can be uncomfortable with religious ideas, especially when they first get involved. Some come at the issue from a more secular, scientific point of view, as shown by these remarks from Jeff, a thirty-five-year-old in the Twin Cities: "The pro-life movement for me has not always been so much just religious. For me, well, abortion itself is kind of a moral question. Which, you know, you don't have to get into religion at all to discuss abortion. It just seems to me that medical science has made so obvious, so clear, what the beginnings of human life are, and if you start degrading human life at any point in time, it seems to me fairly obvious that there's not much standing between that person who is getting killed, getting devalued, and somebody else arbitrarily deciding that I'm not needed or that any person is not needed." None of this suggests that religious vocabularies play no role in the movement, but it does suggest that the role religion plays in activists' beliefs can be overstated. Religious ideas are important but limited in the ways they function in the movement.

Activists recognize, too, that religious conflict is a source of divisiveness. The mobilizing potential of religious ideas thus comes with a concomitant danger of schism and arguments that have demobilizing effects within the movement. Twenty-eight-year-old Dana wasn't allowed to work at a CPC in Charleston because of her faith: "I was Catholic, and they didn't want me because I was Catholic. That's the Bible Belt issue that I've struggled with forever, but that really upset me because the division—this is about the babies, and the mommies and the daddies, it's about our culture." In many instances, religious ideas are a hindrance rather than a help to the movement because of conflict over what constitutes "true" religious faith. Take the beliefs of forty-four-year-old Jim, a Presbyterian in Charleston: "A fair amount of the Christian community doesn't know a lot about what God's word says. . . . Because most churches don't preach God's word. And I've been to a number of them." Marsha, a forty-year-old Catholic in Oklahoma City, was even more specific: "There's people who say they're Catholic, but in my personal opinion, I don't think they are Catholic if they're not following all the doctrines of the Church. If they miss mass on Sunday, and if they're not teaching their children the faith, they're not teaching them the prayers and the richness of the saints' lives and things like that. You know, these people say they're Catholic just like some people say they're American. And they're not! You know what I mean? They're just putting on a façade; it's not really true." Although activists sometimes explicitly downplayed such divisions, others brought

Table 7.1 Measures of religiosity

Measure of religiosity	Study participants		
	Activists	Nonactivists	Public (%)
Attends church at least weekly	99% (69/70)	96% (26/27)	27
Participates in church activities	68% (39/57)	77% (17/22)	59
Participates in religious activities outside of church	47% (27/57)	58% (14/24)	n.a.
Has considered a religious vocation	28% (15/76)	28% (8/29)	n.a.
Approves of mandatory school prayer	61% (41/67)	58% (14/24)	62
Approves of mandatory teaching of creationism in schools	56% (40/71)	57% (16/28)	58

Sources: Figures in the "Public" column come from 2004 General Social Survey (church attendance and school prayer); Pew's 2005 Religion in Public Life survey (creationism); and August 24, 2000, Princeton Survey Research Associates poll (church activities).
Note: Figures in parentheses are actual counts. N.a. = not available.

up conflicts between Catholics and Baptists, Anglicans and Lutherans, Catholics and Catholics (as the previous quotation reveals), and more. Religious ideas are not always the most important ideas in the movement, and they can at times be as troublesome as they are helpful to pro-life mobilization.

Religious beliefs also do not seem to be a major factor separating activists from nonactivists—making them a difficult basis for understanding individual mobilization. Table 7.1 compares the two groups on a variety of different measures of religiosity. Both activists and nonactivists in my sample attend church far more frequently than the general population and are also more involved in church activities outside of regular services. There is less evidence of a difference in religious belief, however. Activists and nonactivists are virtually identical on every standard behavioral and attitudinal measure of religiosity.

Conceptualizing the impact of religion on the pro-life movement in terms of religious ideas also has an important theoretical weakness. Understanding religion as a set of beliefs does not suggest the vehicle by which such beliefs are formed and elaborated. Nor does it reveal the processes by which such beliefs become part of the pro-life movement. The question then becomes, why religious ideas and not some other body of belief? Conceptualizing religion solely as ideas, for example, can't explain why it is a language of Christianity rather than a language of rights or the language of Rawls's *A Theory of Justice* that is common in the movement. While recognizing that religious ideas permeate the movement, it is necessary to see their limits as well.

Religion and Activism in Practice

Conceptualizing religion as churches is the primary way the social movement literature has understood the role of religion, and it captures some of the relationship between religion and the pro-life movement. Conceptualizing religion as ideas is the primary way sociologists of religion have understood the relationship, and it captures something, too. In both cases, religion has an impact on the movement, but as the previous discussion reveals, the role of religion in both these respects is limited. Two pieces are missing from the picture painted thus far. First, we lack an understanding of how these two dimensions of religion— the institutional and the ideational—combine to produce distinctively religious effects on the pro-life movement. Second, neither conceptualization takes into account the importance of the regular religious activity of adherents. Rituals, ceremonies, and other forms of religious practice are a critical element in the dynamic link between religion and social movements. To fully understand the relationship, it is necessary to synthesize the previous two views as well as introduce the ways in which both religion and activism are constituted in practice.

The actual lived experience of religion is frequently forgotten with the increasing use of polling data and large survey data sets to measure and study religion in American life.[8] Although some kinds of religious practices are easily quantified through such methods—such as attendance at formal church services—many more are not. I argue that the full impact of religion on the pro-life movement can only be understood by focusing on religious practice enacted outside of specifically religious institutions and without explicitly religious language. By "practice," I refer to involvement in an activity socially understood to be meaningful in a given context.[9] How such practices are constructed turns out to be the crux of the issue in understanding the relationship between religion and pro-life activism. In many cases, the religious meaning and the social movement meaning in particular practices cannot be separated.

The enactment of religious practices is typically seen as something that takes place within the walls of a church or at minimum under the official auspices of church leaders and programs. People come together each week in congregations to pray in churches or other houses of worship. Christenings, marriages, and funerals all take place within churches or are presided over by religious leaders. Missions, recruitment campaigns, and evangelism often take place as part of a church's official ministry or outreach. People's religious commitments have an impact outside of church walls, but the ritualized practices that renew their faith are seen as the province of the religious world.

Such "official" religious practices are important, but they are by no means the only kind of religious practice that matters. Consider simply the issue of time: even the most devout and religiously focused individuals spend only a small fraction of their hours every week in church or participating in church activity. A particularly committed Catholic might attend mass every morning and devotions several times a week and work with a variety of church groups and committees, but this time still represents at most twenty hours in a week. A devoted Baptist might attend services Sunday mornings and Sunday and Wednesday evenings, attend a weekly Bible study class, and participate in several of her church's ministries every week and still spend fewer than ten to fifteen hours in religious activity. Except for those who have undertaken a religious vocation, the sphere of "official" religion in today's society is relatively small. By limiting our view of the religious strictly to activity taking place in a designated religious sphere, we will also necessarily (almost by definition) be limiting our view of the relationship between religion and social movements.

The more dynamic, performative view of religion as everyday practice builds on recent work in the sociology of religion about the way in which religion is actually understood and practiced. Courtney Bender (2003) has shown how religion "works" in the everyday activity of the members of a social service organization in New York City serving AIDS victims, even when religion is seldom if ever explicit in their work or conversation. Looking at public protest in Venezuela, David Smilde (2004) has documented how religious ideas and identities play an important role outside the churches, in the "popular publics" of the underclass. Nancy Ammerman and her colleagues (2006) have shown how everyday religion is the rule, not the exception, in the way in which both Americans and Europeans relate to and practice their faith. All of this work suggests we need to see the ways in which the religious sphere is incorporated into the many other spheres of life, not simply the formal domains of official religious activity.

A look at the range of pro-life activity suggests that religious practice does not take place completely or even principally within religious institutions. Religion is continually enacted in a wide range of contexts in daily life, and the pro-life movement is one such venue. The practice of activism is thus at the same time often religious practice. The issue does not involve simply translating one interpretation of actions and events into another; that is, seeing pro-life action as more fundamentally religious action or vice versa. Instead, the practices can be irreducibly meaningful as both religious and social movement practice. At least four different kinds of religious practices are enacted as social movement activity: prayer, rituals of birth and death, the gathering of the flock, and doing God's work. In each case, these different forms of practice become simultaneously activism in the movement and engagement with one's faith. Activism can thus be a generator as well as a result of religious participation.

Prayer

Perhaps the most obvious and the most widespread practice of religion in the movement is prayer. Prayer is the most common religious ritual within the Christian tradition and is also a common feature of pro-life work. Activists pray during pro-life meetings, on the steps of courthouses and state capitols, in front of abortion clinics, or simply in their own homes, offices, and schools. In one prayer event I witnessed, activists holding hands and praying together told me to hold up my own free hand as well so that "Jesus could hold my hand." A group in the Twin Cities, Rosaries for Life, devotes all of its attention to prayer; it does nothing else in the movement. Jennifer, quoted earlier in the chapter, explains how prayer is part of her organization as she describes the "spiritual adoptions" sponsored by the group: "It's a prayer where you adopt an unborn baby and you just pray that somewhere out in the world a life would be saved, that it won't be aborted. A child that is in danger of abortion. I pray, 'Jesus, Mary, and Joseph, I beg you to protect the life of this unborn baby that's in danger of abortion.' Just say it daily. I usually give a name to the child." Prayer is understood not only as a religious ritual but also as part and parcel of a person's commitment to the pro-life cause.

Many see prayer in this context as also a bona fide tactic to be used in the struggle to end abortion in the United States. In Charleston, one activist described how the pro-lifers in front of an abortion clinic would divide the cars in the parking lot and each pray for the people who had come to the clinic in those allotted cars. The prayers in these cases are not a performance intended to show religiosity but are action intended to bring the people out of the clinic and thus stop an imminent abortion. To these activists, ending abortion is ultimately the work of God, not man, and individuals make their contribution by praying to God for action. This is the perspective of Suzanne, a fifty-year-old Episcopalian in Charleston, who sees her vigil outside an abortion clinic as making way for God's will to be done: "For a long time, I did a vigil even when nobody was there and the place was closed, like some Saturdays. I was just reading straight from the Psalms because God's word is powerful and it has a lot of spiritual power. And I would just, in a normal tone of voice, I would walk the public, as close as I could get to the public route around the building, and just read out the Scriptures. And I felt like in a way I was kind of claiming that land for holy work." If the abortion debate is a battle between good and evil, then prayer is an important weapon activists bring to the fight. "It's a draining, draining emotional experience to go there and pray," explains another Charleston activist, Catholic fifty-year-old Sharon. She continues: "I used to stand there and see the devil shrouded around the place. And I would see those women going in, and I just thought I was valueless, I was worthless. So I stopped going. And then I got strong and I was able to do it. And another woman that was with me, who seemed to be just so great at this, said she sees angels surrounding the place, taking the babies and the souls." Prayer thus transforms the situation. In Sharon's case, the evil of abortion is transformed to a set of angels helping unborn children.

Prayer as pro-life activism is also seen as effective activism in this world. One Boston man expressed hope that one day they would simply be able "to pray the abortion clinics out of business." Another man reasoned that prayer contributed to the fall of the Soviet Union and so it would be the same for abortion. Prayer thus does not simply legitimate pro-life activity; it *is* pro-life activity. Charles, a sixty-four-year-old Catholic in the Twin Cities, summarizes a common view within the movement: "At least from the Christian perspective, but probably from any religious perspective, if you believe in God, you know the solution to these problems is going to come from some kind of divine intervention, however you understand that. And so I would say prayer should be the beginning, middle, and end of any kind of serious approach to the abortion issue." The practice of prayer for Charles and many others in the movement is both a religious and a pro-life practice. It is a "strategy of action" that comes from the same cultural toolkit (Swidler 1986).

Rituals of Birth and Death

Prayer is the most frequent, but not the only, way in which religious practice is conducted in pro-life work. Birth and death rituals also take place in the movement, an extension of a moral universe in which the fetus's humanity equivalent to any other human life and thus entitled to the same life course rites as any other person. In Charleston, pro-life activists attend a special service at a local church every year in which babies whose mothers considered abortion are given a special blessing. More common are memorial services and funerals to honor babies who have been killed by abortion. Tombstones are used to commemorate their lives, set up either as temporary graveyards as part of a pro-life campaign (as has occurred on many college campuses) or as permanent markers (as was done by the local Knights of Columbus lodge in Watertown, Massachusetts). In the Twin Cities, Pro-life Action Ministries established a permanent "Chapel of the Innocents" to remember aborted babies. Its June 1999 newsletter describes the chapel this way:

At the beginning of this year, through the generosity of two families, we were able to purchase the property next to the Robbinsdale abortuary. Our plan is to use this as a memorial chapel to the aborted babies. We intend for it to be a place of prayer, where Christians from all denominations can come and offer prayers for an end to the killing of defenseless babies by abortion. We are also setting aside an area as a memorial to the aborted babies, keeping alive their memory through pictures, plaques, and other memorials. We envision this as not only showing the reality of what abortion is, but also as a means of healing for those who have been involved in abortion.

In some cases, funerals and similar rituals are held as part of a public relations or publicity effort, consciously designed to draw public attention to the humanity of the fetus. But these strategic efforts by movement leaders don't make the experience of engagement with the ritual practice itself any less real for the participants, who are affected in the same ways as if it were the funeral of a person they knew (Munson 2006).

Nicole, quoted earlier, recognizes the role events such as funerals play in the lives of participants and observers. She criticizes abortion rights advocates for failing to recognize their importance: "This is what doctors don't think a lot about, too. Even just from an anthropological point of view, so many cultures spend so much time around the death and dying process and have rituals around that. Well, you have an abortion, and there's no funeral for aborted babies. It just doesn't happen that way. The whole point is to get that baby out, get it incinerated or whatever; it's to get rid of it. Out of sight, out of mind." The pro-life movement has tried to rectify this perceived problem. "As pro-lifers went through garbage cans at abortion clinics," explains twenty-six-year-old Catholic Twin Cities activist Michelle, "they ran across bodies of the unborn, of aborted babies. And there were various services at the university, so whenever they had a memorial service, I would attend the funeral and the memorial service." The lines between religious ritual and pro-life activity are blurred in these situations. The movement does not simply borrow or mimic religious practices; the events taking place within the movement can be as "genuine" as those that occur outside it. Consider how thirty-one-year-old Kimberly, a member of an independent church in the Twin Cities, explains the funeral she had for Jeremiah, the name she gave to her unborn child. Doctors performed an emergency abortion to save her life after discovering her pregnancy was developing in her abdomen, outside of the uterus:

And I knew that He knew Jeremiah since the day that he was born. He knew that he wasn't in the womb, and that his days were ordained. And I think the sovereignty of God helped both Luke [Kim's husband] and I cope with that loss. Because God knew. He knew that his days were going to be as many as they were. He knew that he was going to be outside of the womb. And actually I've seen God use that a lot, too. We had a memorial service, and one hundred people came, and we did a graveside burial and stuff for him. And a few people came up to Luke and me after that, within a few months after that, and said that they had had abortions. And that the service was very significant because they had never grieved that loss.

Kimberly's telling of the story leading up to this passage took well over an hour. At one point, she interrupted the conversation to show me a large photo album filled with pictures of her and members of her family holding Jeremiah's remains in the hospital. Needless to say, the experience was a powerful one for her. The funeral service—the ritualized farewell to a departed loved one—takes on multiple meanings in this case. Her memorial service was both a pro-life act and a religious act. The spheres of movement action and religious action overlap here, an important element in the power such events have as both religious and pro-life experiences.

Gathering the Flock

The ways in which pro-life practice overlaps religious practice can be much more mundane than funerals or even prayers. Much of activists' time together is spent discussing the abortion issue among themselves, exchanging ideas, information, opinions, and experiences. The regular bringing together of activists for banquets, discussions of the abortion issue, public outreach campaigns, and other activities takes on the same tone and meaning as the gathering of the faithful and fellowship in Christian traditions. People talk about how "nice" it is to get together with "other Christians" at pro-life events, whether these events are prayer breakfasts or abortion clinic protests. "We kind of talked, but we were supposed to kind of be praying," says Jean, a forty-six-year-old Baptist in Oklahoma City, "but, to me, it's fellowship. You're standing; you're not afraid." In Jean's mind, activism is communing with other people of faith. A pro-life gathering is thus a Christian gathering as well.

The relationship between religious gathering and pro-life gathering is not simply a parallel drawn from my analysis; the people involved themselves see that both are at work in pro-life practice. When I asked Anne, a forty-year-old Catholic in Charleston, to describe her first abortion clinic protest, her immediate response was: "We got up real early in the morning and went and saw really neat Christians. It was kind of exciting and fun. We stood together and we prayed. It was very loving. In fact, I don't even remember anyone going in." Her experience is one in which the event was defined by a gathering of "neat," "loving" Christians and action against abortion. They met in front of the clinic to express their faith in God and the evils of abortion. The event was a success even though they didn't encounter a single woman considering an abortion—no pregnant women even entered the clinic that day.

Doing God's Work

Gathering together to do pro-life work, or expressions of religious faith and commitment to the movement, are combined in some cases with a sense of doing God's work—a fourth way in which the practice of activism overlaps with religious practice. To engage in pro-life activism is to live out one's religious life by doing God's will on this earth. This twin meaning of activist practice came out to some extent in the earlier discussion of religion's contribution of values to the movement. As Justin, the teenager from Charleston, said earlier, "My life is my argument."

"I am driven, there's no doubt about it, there's a zeal," says fifty-five-year-old Patricia, a Catholic in the Twin Cities. "It's an obsession; it's something that I know God calls me to do." Activist practice in a case such as Patricia's is also a religious calling.

Elements of personal sacrifice and persecution are often part of doing God's work:

If you believe that you're being called or that there is a need to do something and that your religion is speaking on something—and even deeper, that there's a moral reason to do something—you stand up for it. You get out in front when you have to and lead, and you take what comes your way in the way of pain and suffering.
(JEFF, QUOTED EARLIER)

It would be, as Saint Paul says, an honor that I could suffer for Christ. And, of course, I would never fight back or anything, but to say it would be an honor to suffer like that may sound crazy to the third person looking at this, because what is he going to do? I mean that sounds like a jihad. But, no, it's more like if I was to be arrested for doing something peaceful like saying the rosary, that would be something to give thanks for.
(JASON, QUOTED EARLIER)

The introduction of personal sacrifice in the activities of the movement provides the opportunity for events to be simultaneously pro-life activism and religious practice. Individuals can be thankful that they were given the opportunity to do God's work while they also sacrifice for the cause.

———

In each of the contexts I have described—prayer, rituals of birth and death, gathering of the flock, and doing God's work—activist practices in the pro-life movement possess the important quality of also being recognizably religious practices. Practice in these cases is polysemous, being part of religious and activist spheres of action at the same time. The result is a phenomenon similar to that which Karen Fields (1985) describes in her study of the Watchtower movement in Africa. Attempts to separate the political from the religious in these cases are based on faulty theoretical assumptions that require that the instrumental and the expressive, as well as the political and the religious, be separated analytically and empirically. Fields helpfully shows how such distinctions actually get in the way of full understanding of the circumstances in which "flesh-and-blood human beings" (p. 21) actually live out their lives. Those lives, in the case of the pro-life movement, involve engaging in practices that are not reducible to either religion or activism; they are both. More recent qualitative studies have reinforced this basic insight: religious practice cannot be separated from the everyday and political happenings of the contemporary world (Smilde 2003; Bender 2003; Hondagneu-Sotelo et al. 2004).

Understanding the relationship between religion and pro-life activism ultimately requires us to rethink the way in which we view both of these concepts. The clean, analytic concepts we often use in the social sciences sometimes do a poor job of capturing the much messier reality of individual, everyday experience. This is why the concept of religion as either churches or sets of belief is not fully adequate for us to understand the relationship between religion and activism. Rather than thinking of religion as a separate, distinct social phenomenon exerting an independent influence on the pro-life movement and the way in which people become activists, it is necessary to see religion and activism as overlapping domains of action, each continually constituted and reconstituted by the practices of those who are involved in them. The boundaries between the two are blurry, and events can speak in two voices—they are simultaneously part of institutionalized religion and the pro-life movement. This more dynamic conceptualization also opens up a further possibility: in addition to looking at the impact of religion on the movement, we must also consider the impact of the movement on religion.

Activism and Religious Change

Max Weber's *Protestant Ethic and the Spirit of Capitalism* is the prototype for conventional thinking about religion in sociology. Weber identifies the Calvinistic threads of Protestantism as producing a mind-set, or spirit, that was instrumental in the "qualitative formation and the quantitative expansion" of global capitalism (Weber 1958, 91). In Weber's view, religion is the independent variable and capitalism the dependent variable that religion helps to explain. Although Weber's focus on the ideational side of religion is complemented by more materialistic analysis, the basic idea of religion as a causal force used to explain other social facts is virtually universal in sociology and political science. We tend to think of religion largely as an ascribed and relatively immutable characteristic of persons, logically and temporally fixed prior to whatever phenomenon we are studying. Did religious forces influence the outcome of the presidential election? Do religious variables help to explain crime rates? How does religious faith affect social movement frames? These kinds of questions come from the conventional toolkit of social science.

The relationship between religion and the pro-life movement shows that this conventional wisdom can obscure the important ways in which the concepts overlap. Rather than being independent, religion and pro-life activism often overlap in the practice of those involved. Moreover, the causal arrow can point in both directions. Activists who participate in the movement's discussions, meetings, events, and campaigns are not simply influenced by religion, whether conceptualized as churches or as ideas. They are also simultaneously reinforcing the vitality of religious faith in their own lives and in their social worlds. In doing so, they sometimes change their existing religious commitments or create entirely new ones.

The dissatisfaction of many pro-life activists with their churches' stance on the abortion issue is a significant source of pressure for priests, pastors, and church institutions. "How to Encourage Your Priest to Be Actively Pro-life," "Establishing a Pro-life Presence in Community Churches," and "Helping Shepherds Give Leadership on Life Issues" are some of the many brochures pro-life organizations distribute to help activists transform the work of their churches. Despite the Catholic Church's already strongly pro-life stance, Catholic parishes continually spend energy defending themselves against activists' criticism that they are not sufficiently pro-life. Because much of the religious practice of activists takes place within the movement, activists also seek to move more of the movement inside the churches.

Patricia, quoted earlier, reflects the orientation of many activists toward their church: "I suppose I did [hear about abortion in church], but, frankly [pause], I don't know if I want to say this, but I probably had more fights with priests about the issue. Because I wanted it said more, and I didn't hear enough of it. So if I did hear it, I don't remember any barn burners." Fifty-year-old Charleston activist Sharon is more proactive: "I've handed out literature and prayer cards, and we discuss it. And I talk to the priest about just talking about it in church." Activists such as Patricia and Sharon pressure their churches for change by continually raising the issue. Pro-life sermons, special masses or devotions, public statements and actions by churches, and increased mobilization within the churches can all be the result of movement activists' also becoming lay leaders in their church or advocating for the cause with existing leaders.

On the individual level, activism can be an entrée into a new commitment to religious faith. Social movement activity is thus a vehicle for religious renewal or, in some cases, religious conversion. This process is best seen through the stories of the activists themselves. Let me return to Linda, the public outreach activist introduced in chapter 2. Linda became involved in the movement before the *Roe v. Wade* decision was handed down, at a time when the state was holding hearings on the liberalization of abortion laws. She was a leader in the local movement for a time in the late 1970s and 1980s but has since reduced her involvement and focused on research and writing about the issue. Linda was raised in a Catholic home but didn't want much to do with her church for many years. "As a Catholic growing up in the middle sixties, nearly every priest that I knew left the priesthood," she explains, continuing: "And the priests were giving mixed messages. Birth control was becoming a big debate in the Catholic Church, and I thought birth control was the best thing that ever happened to anybody. I mean, I couldn't imagine that people would be opposed to that. What do these old men know? and everything like that. So as soon as I was married, I fell off [from attending mass]." Recall that Linda first came into contact with the movement through a regular office visit to her obstetrician, Fred Mecklenburg, who at that time was a leader in the emerging pro-life movement. He urged her to get involved in the issue, but she was initially skeptical because she thought the movement might be too religious. Mecklenburg was Methodist, which was important to Linda because she then viewed the Catholic leadership as "stodgy" and out of step with the times.

As she became more involved in the movement, she continued to try to keep religion at arm's length. Here she gives an example: "For a while, I was real embarrassed to be with people who would say 'God bless you.' I mean, I thought that was something you said when somebody sneezed but not when you said, 'Good-bye and God bless you.' That was just kind of foreign to me; my family did not talk like that. And I also started meeting evangelical Christians in the pro-life movement who would talk about what the Bible says. And I never knew what the Bible says; Catholics didn't read Bibles." She spent years in the movement with this same basic attitude, feeling "uncomfortable" and "embarrassed" when religious and activist practice overlapped. Nonetheless, her activism brought her into contact with different churches, Bible study groups, prayer breakfasts, and religious vigils. She also worked for years alongside not only evangelical Protestants, as she mentions above, but also devout Catholics. Eventually she decided she needed to start "listening with a different ear" to her friends and colleagues of faith. At the request of a friend in the movement, she attended a conference of Lutherans. Soon afterward she had a conversion experience, which she retells as a highly dramatized, life-altering moment.[10] She then realized: "I'd been trying to earn my way into heaven. If I was a good girl, if I saved the babies, if I was polite to people, if I voted, if I made nice lunches for my kids at school, if I was a good wife to my husband, if my clothes were white on the line, you know. I mean, with all those things, I thought I could get into heaven. I don't rob from the poor, I don't steal, you know, all these things like that. And I realized then that none of that matters. None of that matters at all. What matters is that God loves me just exactly the way I was. He made me. Every sin I have He knows about more than I do. And it was just this amazing grace. . . . And from that moment on, everything started changing." Things did change for Linda, not only in terms of how she thought about the pro-life movement but also in terms of how she related to her family and her attendance at and involvement in church. She is now a committed and active Catholic. "Today, with my faith background," she says, "I would say God had a destiny for me. Maybe that's arrogant, but on the other hand, I've lived it out. That's what I've been living since then."

For Linda, mobilization into the pro-life movement led to a reevaluation of religion and her relationship to Catholicism. Although she never described herself as agnostic or atheist or explicitly rejected God, she did consciously reject both religious institutions and religious ideas. Movement participation, however, put her in contact with people of deep faith and also got her involved in experiences in which religion and activism were both elements. This led to a massive change in her religious faith and commitment to the Church.

In contrast to Linda, twenty-eight-year-old Charleston activist Dana has never felt actively opposed to religious institutions. She, too, was raised in a Catholic family and faithfully attended mass every Sunday with her parents. As an adolescent and a young adult, however, she struggled with her faith, due both to the strong anti-Catholic sentiment in the area and her perception that the Catholics she knew led far more sinful lives than the Protestants around her. She began attending other churches—Presbyterian, Methodist, Baptist—and praying and reading about theology. She found elements of each denomination and congregation that she liked but also never felt entirely comfortable in any of them. She was, in Robert Wuthnow's (1998) terms, a religious seeker.

Meanwhile, Dana first came into contact with the pro-life movement by dating a fellow student who was involved in the movement. She jumped into activism with both feet beginning her senior year in college and has devoted herself full-time to pro-life work since then. Preventing abortion became her burning passion. She spent several years working for a national pro-life organization researching and writing position papers, brochures, and other pro-life information. She is now one of those uncommon activists involved in multiple streams, including working at crisis pregnancy counseling, public outreach, and sidewalk counseling in front of Charleston's abortion clinic.

In the process of learning more about the abortion issue and pro-life movement, she came to see the Catholic Church as the most prominent and uncompromising of all the Christian traditions on the abortion issue. It was this fact that drew her back to Catholicism: "I mean, being on the forefront of the pro-life movement is pretty much what brought me back in. . . . When I started getting involved in the pro-life movement, I realized that the Catholic Church, of Christian churches, was one of the only ones that was on the forefront as a pillar in the world, not just in the United States, for that battle. And that they were willing to go against what the world says regardless and say this is wrong, this is intrinsically evil." Dana never rejected religion but was actively searching for a religious home. Her mobilization into the movement provided her with a key issue through which she could make sense of different religious approaches. She did not participate in the movement due to her Catholic background but rather chose to participate in the Catholic Church on the basis of her pro-life beliefs.

Josh, the direct-action activist introduced in chapter 5, offers an example of yet a third pattern by which individual commitment to religion and the pro-life movement are tied together. Josh grew up in Missouri in a liberal Presbyterian church. He didn't give a lot of thought to religion after leaving home and spent several years bouncing around from college to college and part-time job to part-time job, focusing mostly on friends and earning enough money to have fun. Recall that Josh eventually earned a computer science degree and moved to Oklahoma City with his now longtime friend and college roommate. Neither religion nor abortion was an issue for him at the time. As he explained in chapter 2, he had always believed that women ought to have "the right to choose what they do with their body."

Both Josh and his roommate then began listening regularly to talk radio, which gave them daily exposure to religious messages and pro-life ideas. They would often talk together about the issues raised in these programs and began questioning their current lifestyles and values, including their beliefs about abortion—to this point held largely without conscious reflection on the issue. Josh's roommate then decided to begin attending church and convinced Josh to try out a local Assembly of God congregation. About that same time, they heard ads on the radio for a local pro-life rally and decided it would be a good way to learn more about the issue. The rally opened their eyes to the pro-life moral universe. They returned to their new church and talked to their minister about the issue, asking him if the church would sell fund-raising pins for the movement. The minister told them that he wouldn't sell them but they were welcome to set up a table at the end of services each Sunday and sell the pins themselves. They agreed, and their subsequent pin sales got Josh more involved in the pro-life movement and in his new church.

Josh's participation in the direct-action stream of the movement led to his participating in campaigns to block the entrance to a local abortion clinic. The first time he was arrested for such activity, he had a religious conversion experience sitting in the squad car after his arrest, wondering about his fate. He describes it as a conversation he had with God: "'Hey, God, I don't know what you've got planned for me, but I need you back in my life. Whatever you want, I'll do. I just need you back in me. I need you. I don't know where I'm going right now, but I need you.' So I asked God back in my life, and then somebody was tapping on the window and asking if I had bail money, which I didn't even think of or anything like that." Josh experienced a conversion in a double sense, changing his beliefs about the abortion issue while also discovering a religious faith that had not been a part of his life and was much different from the tradition in which he was raised. His mobilization into the movement and his commitment to religion happened at the same time and mutually reinforced each other. He began by experimenting with a new church and the movement; the sale of pro-life pins in the church reinforced his ties to both. It was then at a crucial turning point in his commitment to the pro-life movement—being arrested for pro-life activity—that he also experienced a momentous deepening of his religious commitment.

The stories of Linda, Dana, and Josh offer examples of three different ways in which religion can be affected at the individual level by social activism. In Linda's case, the relationship is clear: she became mobilized into the movement as a secular person, and the movement then led her to a religious commitment. Religion was always important for Dana, but she went through a period in her life when she was confused about her faith, unsure about the different religious traditions, and shopping for a church. The movement provided her focus, which she used to sort through her confusion; she chose the church she felt was most solidly pro-life. Josh found the movement and a religious faith concomitantly. His involvement and commitment to both grew in a symbiotic relationship with each other.

Religion does not, then, simply impact the pro-life movement; the pro-life movement also affects religion. At the institutional level, it does so by exerting pressure on religious leaders and religious organizations to adopt pro-life beliefs, advocate pro-life positions, commit resources to pro-life groups, and grant them legitimacy. At the individual level, it does so by being a site in which religious commitments are discovered, explored, reaffirmed, and sometimes changed. The regularity with which this occurs is remarkable: roughly 20 percent of all pro-life activists came to their present religious faith only after they began the process of becoming mobilized. The relationship between the movement and religion is thus a complex one, involving not only institutions and beliefs but also practices and influence that operate in both directions.

How Religion Matters

Albert's words at the beginning of the chapter highlight the tight and intricate ways in which the religious sphere and the pro-life sphere are intertwined. This complex relationship is not captured by the standard ways of operationalizing "religion" either as religious institutions such as churches or as bodies of belief. The full relationship between religion and the movement is captured much better by focusing on everyday practice as the mechanism that sustains both social movement activity and religious faith, making each salient and relevant in people's lives. As people fight the battle over abortion, they are also enacting prayerful lives, birth and death rituals, the gathering of the faithful, expressions of faith, understandings of personal sacrifice and persecution, and the doing of God's work on earth. Religion and the pro-life movement, it seems, are not so much discrete, distinct social phenomna in which the former influences the latter but instead are overlapping social processes that impact each other.

Two key points emerge from this analysis. The first is the importance of polysemy in everyday experience. Ideas, events, and behaviors are often seen as having only a single meaning. In scientific analysis, this takes the form of scholars' interpreting a social phenomenon and telling us what it "really" means. Thus, for example, right-wing extremism is often understood as really being about the eroding social status or cultural position of some segment of the population. To those involved in events, the focus on single meanings manifests as a need to explain the reason they believe or act the way they do. Is what I'm doing saving babies, or am I fulfilling my religious obligations? The data show that there is a false dichotomy implicit in these questions. Here we can learn from the anthropological literature that has focused extensively on multivocal symbolism. Experiences can take on multiple meanings; events can take on multiple voices, and behaviors can simultaneously express multiple intentions and beliefs. The issue is not to reduce these manifold meanings to one that is primary or more fundamental but instead to recognize that the polysemy of action can be a major source of social dynamism.

The second key point is that the pro-life movement has been a source of religious negotiation and change. In the relationship between religion and the pro-life movement, the movement is not simply an "effect" caused by religion. Instead, pro-life activism has an impact on religious organizations by tying religious values and language to one of the most divisive social issues in the United States today, controversial enough to cause divisions in conservative Protestant and liberal social justice Catholic congregations alike. Perhaps even more important, the pro-life movement is a site of religious exploration and conversion. A surprisingly large number of activists did not come to understand their activism through a religious lens but instead came to understand their faith through a pro-life lens. This finding can be added to the list of biographical consequences of activism (McAdam 1999) and also reorients the more general discussion of social movement outcomes (Gamson 1990; Andrews 1997; Giugni, McAdam, and Tilly 1999) to consider more than political institutions or the goals of the movement. It suggests religious "spirit" is not just an independent variable but is also something being continually made and remade in contexts such as becoming a pro-life activist.

EIGHT

Becoming an Activist: Ideas and Social Movements

Is it in China or Japan where aborted fetus is a delicacy now? They eat them. They eat humans! That's cannibalism. But it's a delicacy there. I've seen it on television. I've seen it on video.

(JOSH, OKLAHOMA CITY)

I heard this belief expressed by more than one activist, one of a host of fantastic ideas. People carefully laid out for me how Bill Clinton had large runways built in Arkansas to support his international cocaine-smuggling operation, all part of the larger "culture of death" he supports. Others told me how Planned Parenthood manipulates the dosage in the birth control pills it distributes to trick women into getting pregnant and paying Planned Parenthood for their abortions. According to some activists, half the women who have abortions ultimately commit suicide.

These outlandish beliefs fascinate skeptical observers of the pro-life movement. They are the kinds of stories people expect me to tell when they ask me, "So, what do these folks *really* believe?" Some activists do believe these kinds of stories, although only a small minority of pro-lifers hold the most bizarre ideas. Dwelling on such beliefs, however, ultimately trivializes the role of ideas in social movements and seriously underestimates the power of the pro-life moral vision.

Far more common than these tales are stories told with jaws clenched in anger as an activist describes the injustice of abortion or through tears as he or she recounts the innocence of the unborn. Cynthia, a forty-four-year-old

185

Charleston activist, was sobbing as she told me, "It's so hard, so hard not knowing how the end is going to be. But we don't. . . . Every life has meaning, and you know I would hate to take that away. Because I believe that every child's life can have meaning." Activists such as Cynthia are no different from the activists in any other social movement. Some activists have a passion for the pro-life cause that is so strong they have left behind families, friends, and careers to be more involved. The beliefs and moral understandings that produce these kinds of intense emotions and commitment are the ones that most centrally interest me. A common theme running through this study is the varying role of ideas in becoming a pro-life activist. Activists' firmly held and intensely felt beliefs about abortion are much more than just oddities to be accounted for or explained away.

Who Becomes an Activist?

One of the central arguments of this book is that individuals get involved in pro-life activism before they develop solid beliefs or firm ideas about abortion. Individuals mobilized into the pro-life movement in fact begin the mobilization process with a surprisingly diverse range of ideas about the issue. A quarter of those who are now activists were more sympathetic to the movement's opponents when they first became involved, expressing beliefs that abortion should be a woman's right or that abortion is (at least sometimes) morally acceptable. Only after they participated in pro-life movement activities did their views begin to change. Another quarter of all activists first became mobilized with an ambivalent attitude toward the issue. They saw valid arguments on both sides of the controversy and admit they could have been persuaded either way about abortion. Only half of pro-life activists considered themselves pro-life before they got involved. Even among these activists, however, the ideas they held about abortion prior to becoming mobilized are what I call "thin beliefs": poorly thought out, often contradictory, and seldom related to a larger moral vision. The general failure of polling data to differentiate between thin beliefs and more robust ideological commitments is one of the principal reasons that scholars have for so long accepted that grievances are a necessary prerequisite to mobilization.

This argument does not claim that individuals have no ideas about abortion before they get involved in the movement, nor that everyone is equally likely to become mobilized regardless of his or her preexisting beliefs. Some individuals, because of their personal biographies and beliefs, are more likely to know others who are involved in the movement and thus are more likely to come into personal contact with the movement—a key condition in the mobilization process. And although fully a quarter of the activists once held pro-choice views, none of them were strongly invested in this position or were active on the other side of the debate. The point is not that people are completely empty vessels, waiting to be filled with ideas from social movements, but only that our view of social movement activity as expressive behavior that presupposes commitment misses the mark.

I began my research with the intention of understanding the boundary between activists and those who express pro-life beliefs but nonetheless remain uninvolved. Most individual attitudes fall somewhere in between the pro-life position that abortion is always wrong and the pro-choice position that abortion should always be available on demand. Figure 8.1 shows the conventional wisdom on how individual mobilization to activism works. The general population, this view tells us, can be arrayed along a continuum from those who oppose a movement to those who are in the middle or indifferent to a movement to those who sympathize with a movement. The proportion of Americans that falls into each of these positions on the continuum, at least according to public opinion data, is indicated in parentheses in figure 8.1.[1] Given this continuum, social movement mobilization is typically understood to occur on the bottom portion of this figure. Social movement scholars proceed by asking what determines when sympathizers "jump" to becoming active participants in a social movement. I took this conventional wisdom as my own when I began my research: I, too, focused on understanding the arrow in the bottom portion of the diagram. I saw my task as figuring out how to differentiate between pro-life sympathizers and pro-life activists.

My data, however, show that this formulation of the question was misguided. The boundary between activism and nonactivism needs to be redefined because the movement does not draw solely from the segment of the population that already sympathizes with the pro-life message. The arrows in figure 8.2 show a more complex, but more realistic, formulation. Substantial numbers of activists come from the ranks of those who initially expressed either mixed or pro-choice beliefs about abortion. Although these people are certainly less likely to become mobilized, they still represent almost half of the total number of activists in the movement. An important implication of this finding is that the pool of potential activists in the pro-life movement is consider-

8.1 Conventional wisdom on individual mobilization in social movements

ably larger than commonly believed. Although not everyone is equally likely to go through the mobilization process outlined in chapter 3, the pool of potential activists is far from limited to existing conscience adherents.

Understanding individual mobilization as the dynamic, contingent, multistage process outlined here can also help us better understand the historical trajectory of civic participation generally in the United States over the last several decades. Scholars of civic engagement have noted the decline of voluntary associational membership in the United States since the middle of the twentieth century (Putnam 2000; Skocpol, Ganz, and Munson 2000). My findings on the pro-life movement suggest that a key factor behind this decline is a shrinking set of opportunities to come in contact with social movement organizations. As voluntary associations have professionalized, centralized, and placed less emphasis on vibrant local chapters and affiliates (Skocpol 2004), individuals have become much less likely to have the kind of direct, personalized contact with an organization that the model here shows is crucial in the mobilization process. My findings are consistent with what Dana Fisher (2006) found among liberal social movement campaigns: the professionalization of activism reduces grassroots organiz-

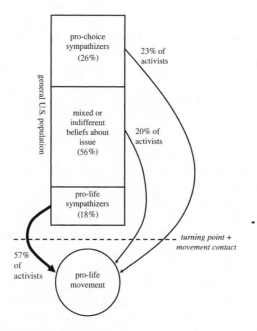

8.2 A new understanding of mobilization

ing, which, in turn, cuts off opportunities to bring more people into the movement. Individual activism requires movement organizations that are actively and visibly engaged with their communities. Activists simply don't mobilize themselves.

How Do Beliefs Matter?

Although beliefs about abortion do not generally lead people into activism or even lead them into contact with pro-life organizations, they remain critically important to the overall movement. Much of what the pro-life movement actually does centers on inculcating a pro-life worldview in its own activists. The wide range of pro-life activities—from meetings and petition drives to rallies and protests—are first and foremost venues in which activists interact with one another and hear new information and new ideas about abortion. This is the mechanism by which pro-life beliefs become articulated through action. Initially vague and inchoate, "thin" ideas about abortion become richer, more coherent, more consistent, and more complex through participation in pro-life work.

As individuals enter the mobilization process, they are exposed to the beliefs of people already active in the movement. At the core of these beliefs is the idea that abortion amounts to killing a child and is thus morally wrong under all circumstances. Beyond this basic idea, however, there is no single movement worldview, master frame, or unified ideology that ties the movement together. Activists differ enormously in their understanding of the abortion issue. In particular, they differ in their beliefs about how to stop abortion and why they believe abortion is wrong.

Beliefs about How to Stop Abortion

The movement is united in a common aim to stop all abortions in the United States, but activists part company in their understanding of the most appropriate strategies for achieving this goal. An important finding of this study is that these differences help constitute the structure of the movement. Beliefs matter because they define different and largely mutually exclusive social movement streams: the politics stream, the direct-action stream, the individual outreach stream, and the public outreach stream. As described in chapters 4 and 5, individuals seldom deliberately choose a movement stream based on their preexisting ideas about the abortion issue. Instead, they happen into contact with a particular stream of the movement and then come to understand the issue from that stream's particular vantage point. Once they are part of a stream, individuals seldom move to other streams of the movement. The beliefs they have learned in the course of becoming mobilized lock them into their existing streams. The structure of the movement, based on differences in ideas, thus has very real implications for both individual activism and the history of the movement.

Understanding how beliefs structure the movement allows us to ask new questions about pro-life activities. For example, the demise of tactics to close abortion clinics by physically blocking access is easily explained through resource mobilization (McCarthy and Zald 1977; Freeman 1977), political opportunity structure (Jenkins and Perrow 1977), or movement interaction (Meyer and Staggenborg 1996) arguments. In each case, the argument would be that pro-life organizations lacked the resources to maintain civil disobedience campaigns in the face of state repression. But why did organizations and activists involved in civil disobedience turn to sidewalk counseling? Understanding the movement in terms of streams helps to answer this question. Streams are distinct sets of groups and individuals with a particular belief about the best means to achieve the movement's goals. Rather than simply adopt a different strategy already existing within the pro-life repertoire of contention (Tilly 1977; Tilly 1978), such as the lobbying of the politics stream, tactical innovation occurred as the organizations and activists of the direct-action stream sought to overcome new laws and pro-choice tactics.

Similarly, understanding the movement as a set of streams can also help explain the movement's recent history and formulate predictive hypotheses about its future. Given the structure of the movement, for example, it is easier to see why the rise of rescue activities in the late 1980s failed to spur on the pro-life movement as a whole (as suggested by some observers, such as Faye Ginsburg [1993] and Sara Diamond [1998]). Similarly, it is unlikely that crisis pregnancy centers (CPCs) will serve as the recruiting grounds for the movement in the future despite the thousands of centers spread throughout the country and the tens of thousands of activists who volunteer in them regularly. The reasoning in both cases is the same: both rescues and CPCs are located in particular streams of the movement that remain separated and distinct from others. Public outreach programs, on the other hand, are much more likely to help mobilize activism because they are commonly conducted outside the movement, in contact with nonactivists living their everyday lives.

Beliefs about Why Abortion Is Wrong

Besides differing in their visions of the best way to end abortion in the United States, activists also differ in their moral understanding of the issue. For some, abortion is wrong because it disrupts God's plan. For others, it is wrong because it is fundamentally racist. Unlike previous work on the pro-life movement, I did not find any single underlying theme or perspective to which all the different ideas in the movement could be reduced. Although control over female sexuality is a concern among some activists, for example, it is entirely absent from the ideas of others in the movement. The moral landscape of the pro-life movement is complex and hosts different and sometimes conflicting ideas about abortion.

Interestingly, divisions in how activists understand abortion do not lead to the same kind of organizationally distinct movement streams as do divisions over the proper means to end abortion. Thus, for example, individuals within the politics stream of the movement have similar beliefs about how abortion should be stopped but differ dramatically in the values they use to make sense of why abortion is wrong in the first place. Different moral understandings coexist within the same organizations and movement streams, further complicating the movement's ideational landscape.

This finding is important because it suggests that movements can cohere even in the face of different visions of the moral status of the movement's object or goal. The pro-life movement does not appear to have any need for a common master frame (Snow and Benford 1992; Benford and Snow 2000) or unified idea about why fellow activists are engaged in what they do. It also suggests that the potential allies and strategic alliances that might be forged between the pro-life movement and other social actors are much wider than commonly perceived. The diversity of moral understandings within the movement provides the means for communication and collaboration with a variety of other social movements, political parties, and religious institutions. The pro-life movement does not necessarily need a close alliance with the Republican Party, for example, even if such an alliance is an important element of the current political landscape. Beliefs in the movement could also resonate with many of the concerns of Democrats. More generally, the moral understandings well represented within the movement are sufficiently diverse as to make multiple ideological interpretations possible.

The wide variety of views within the movement can cause tension within streams. Differences in belief lead to bickering and infighting within the movement, limiting consensus and the ability to focus on external goals. The debate through the 1980s over a human life amendment is an excellent example of the destructive side of these tensions. With the election of Ronald Reagan in 1980, the political climate in the United States made it reasonable to expect that Congress might pass a constitutional amendment banning legalized abortion. Congressional support for such an amendment, however, slowly eroded as fierce debates raged within the pro-life movement over the exact wording of such an amendment. Different wordings spoke to different underlying concerns about abortion and thus different moral understandings of the issue. In the absence of consensus about an amendment even within the movement, congressional passage became impossible.

All of this suggests a danger in scholars' throwing all ideas and beliefs generated by a social movement into the same conceptual pot. Different *kinds* of ideas have very different implications for the trajectory of activism. Clearly, beliefs matter in different ways in the pro-life movement. The development of activists' beliefs is one of the primary results of pro-life organization work; beliefs about strategy help define the contours of the movement's structure; and beliefs about why abortion is wrong help define the potential for both coalition building and united action within the movement. While this finding is consistent with previous work on movement framing that finds that tactical frames are frequently the most contested (Gamson and Meyer 1996), future research is needed to more carefully identify the different kinds of beliefs present within social movements and the differing ways in which such beliefs are important.

What Is the Relationship between the Movement and Religion?

Lurking behind any focus on the pro-life movement in the United States are questions about religion. Opponents and sympathizers alike frequently perceive organized opposition to abortion as an outgrowth of Catholic and conservative Protestant churches. My data show that churches and other religious institutions are important sites of contact between potential activists and the movement. The language and imagery in which many activists express their beliefs are often profoundly religious. The idea that God is behind the movement's work is a powerful belief that is woven into many activists' understanding of the abortion issue.

The role churches play in the pro-life movement is not entirely straightforward, however. Churches provide surprisingly little overt support for the movement; few pro-life organizations receive substantial funding or other material resources from church sources, leadership in the movement is not drawn from religious leadership pools, and even conservative churches are hesitant to support the movement vocally because of the divisiveness of the abortion issue.

Religion's importance is not so much in the direct support it provides but in the meaning-laden practices that it shares with the movement. Movement activists' everyday activities (gathering people together for meetings, singing songs in front of women's clinics, and so forth) frequently overlap with religious ideas and experiences. Christian rituals such as prayer, commemorations of birth and death, the gathering of the flock, and doing God's work in the world all describe common actions in the pro-life movement.

Activists' experiences thus straddle both the religious and the social movement sphere. The result is that the pro-life movement benefits from the legitimacy and meaning that the religious valence of such

193

activities possesses. At the same time, however, the social movement valence of those same practices reflects back on the religious sphere. The pro-life movement has been a source of religious change. On the institutional level, churches have been challenged by the movement to incorporate the pro-life moral universe into their evolving theological worldviews. On the individual level, movement activism has led some people to find or renew a religious faith. Religion thus both affects and is affected by the movement.

This argument has important implications for better understanding the trajectory of conservative Protestantism in the United States over the last several decades (Himmelstein 1990; Diamond 1995; Berlet and Lyons 2000). The sustained focus on how the Christian Right and religion more generally have impacted American politics has blinded us to the opposite pattern: the ways in which politicized social movement activity might be altering religious sensibilities and practices. One possible explanation for the politicization of religion—the chief phenomenon of interest to most scholars of the Christian Right—is that Americans are finding their religious faith through prior commitments to and membership in politicized organizations such as those that make up the pro-life movement. Recall that the central goal of the pro-life movement as a whole is to end legalized abortion in the United States. Given this inherently political objective, we should not be surprised that those who come to their religious faith as a result of pro-life activism have a politicized religious outlook. If a similar pattern holds across other social movements, then perhaps this process of religious development and commitment contributes to the politicization of religious ideas and identities that has been so well documented in recent years.[2]

Lessons to Be Learned

Several of the hunches I had going into this study proved to be false. The line dividing activists and nonactivists is not located simply between those who are involved and those who are merely sympathetic. The level of mobilization and religious characteristics of different cities were not ultimately useful in answering my key questions. However, the research design I used still provided the means to correct my initial hypotheses and answer a number of important questions about the pro-life movement in particular and about contemporary American social movements more generally. In-depth life-history interviewing revealed the diversity of prior beliefs activists brought to the mobilization process. Data collection from four different cities in four different regions of the United States showed that the mobilization process is much the same across the country. The fact that results were similar in all four locations increases the confidence we can place in the robustness of the study's results.

The findings presented here question the conventional wisdom that activists get involved because of the importance of the abortion issue to them. More generally, however, my results question the way in which the literature on social movements has approached the relationship between ideas and activism. Although outrageous pro-life beliefs such as the one that introduced the chapter have excellent shock value, they are ultimately less interesting than the layers of belief that are more commonly at work, and in tension with one another, inside the movement. The model here also questions more general theories about the nature of political participation. It suggests scholars need to focus more on experiences and practices than on interests or preferences in understanding where and how participation occurs.

Throughout this study, I have drawn comparisons to other movements, past and present. Many of my findings are similar to what others have found in studying other movements, including the critical importance of social networks and personal ties, the relevance of religion to mobilization, and the key role played by the movement's existing organizational infrastructure. Other findings here, however, are at odds with what has been reported about other movements, including the absence of a single core, unifying set of beliefs; sharp boundaries among movement streams seldom crossed by activists; and, of course, a mobilization process not predicated on preexisting movement sympathy.

How much can we generalize from the results here? Although a case study of a single movement is inadequate to prove the point, I am confident that subsequent research will support the basic finding that social movements are the crucibles in which activists form beliefs about issues. This conclusion is likely less true, however, among material beneficiaries of social movement activity (such as blacks in the case of the civil rights movement or gay and lesbian members of the gay and lesbian movement). My findings are also based on examination of a movement that is already well established. The model here may be less relevant to understanding mobilization in a movement that is itself still emerging or that lacks an organizational infrastructure. Finally, the basic beliefs of the pro-life movement are consistent with the expressed opinions of a broad, if not majority, segment of the U.S.

population. The mobilization process may be different in movements with less widely accepted beliefs, such as is the case with the racialist movement or black separatists.

Even in these cases, however, this analysis suggests that new questions need to be asked about the way in which ideas are interwoven into social movement activity. The frame analysis that has been the hallmark of thinking about ideas and social movements since the 1990s only scrapes the surface of the many ways in which scholars must consider the impact of ideas. What are the normal limits of movement shaping of an individual's existing beliefs? To what extent are beliefs controlled by movement leaders versus rank-and-file activists? How much ideational diversity is possible before a movement falls apart? How do shifts in movement beliefs occur? Why do beliefs about action create more divisiveness than beliefs about why or how an issue is important? Taking the beliefs of pro-life activists seriously has generated several theoretical payoffs in understanding the pro-life movement and suggesting avenues for further research on other social movements. Subsequent work will be able to answer these kinds of questions.

"Do what you can," says Carol, a fifty-two-year-old activist in Charleston, as she explains her approach to activism. "You can make a difference to someone. You can't do it all, but do the best that you can with what you have. Even if it is a little bit or a lot, whatever gift you have of yourself, whatever gift you have—whether it's small or large— helps and you make a difference." Carol's motto could be the rallying cry of any contemporary social movement. My hope is that by taking seriously what pro-life activists have to say, exploring their beliefs, carefully questioning their stories, and comparing their trajectories into the movement, this work has shed light on the pro-life movement and offers tools that will be useful in understanding other movements in the United States and around the world.

Appendix

Study Methodology

I met Betty for an interview in an old donut shop in St. Paul. Betty, sixty-six years old, is a homemaker and mother of seven. I began the interview with basic questions about where she was born and raised, where she went to high school, and so forth. Although she gave a skeletal story of these years in her life, she quickly turned the focus of the conversation to the story of her own unplanned pregnancy. She became pregnant soon after graduating from high school, a young woman still living at home and afraid to tell her parents. She fled to Florida to stay with an old friend and soon thereafter met her future husband, who was both supportive and keen to convince her of the importance of her pregnancy and the preciousness of human life. She carried her pregnancy to term, gave the child up for adoption, and six months later was married to the man. This experience galvanized her, and since that time, she and her husband have been ardent pro-life activists, involved in rallies, protests, letter-writing campaigns, and other pro-life activity wherever they have lived.

This is Betty's mobilization story, centered on her own pregnancy crisis and focused on her long-standing opposition to abortion. She tells the story as a longtime activist explaining how it all began. As the interview progressed, however, and I was able to probe more narrowly about various events in her life, a much different mobilization process emerged. Although her husband has been involved in the pro-life movement throughout their marriage, she herself had never participated until very recently—more than forty years after the story she offered at the beginning of the interview. Moreover, she and her husband have not been the fellow activists she implied as she first told her story. Her husband's activism has in fact been a severe source of tension in their family, and over the years, she has consulted both priests and physicians for help in moderating his pro-life activities and views. Their long-standing arguments over his involvement and its effect on the family have led her to one halfhearted suicide attempt and many thoughts of divorce over the course of the last fifteen years. In other words, while Betty tells a convincing and concise mobilization story, the actual history of her relationship to the movement is decidedly more complex.

The kinds of stories activists tell to explain their involvement are important elements in their overall set of beliefs about the issue. They are the stories of mobilization as understood by the activists themselves and legitimated by the movement in which they are embedded. As Betty's story shows, however, such accounts can be distinct from the actual sociological process that takes place in becoming an activist. Many of the activists I spoke to offered these kinds of narratives as their own explanations for involvement. Any study of individual mobilization into a social movement thus faces a challenge: how does one gather detailed biographical data on those who mobilize that can be separated from the subjective stories of mobilization that activists commonly offer?

Two qualities of the interviews I conducted help to meet this challenge. First, the interviews were long, all of them lasting at least two hours and the majority lasting three hours or more. This interview length provided time for me to develop a more comfortable rapport with interview participants than might have been possible in shorter interviews. Stories such as Betty's are part of the public face of an individual's activism, frequently offered unprompted at the beginning of an interview. In many cases, it was only later, after we had talked for some time, that the more mundane and less morally adorned information about how an individual became involved in the movement emerged.

Second, my strategy in the interviews focused on probing into specific events, decisions, and feelings individuals experienced in the course of their lives. By directing interview participants to reconstruct their trajectory into the movement step by step, I allowed for much less interpretation and narrative construction on the part of the participants than would have been possible if the questions had been more general. Ultimately, the issue is not one of second-guessing participants' accounts or uncovering "hidden" motives and actions behind their stories. Interviews lasting several hours simply allow for a greater level of communication, and a focus on questions that refer to narrow, specific times and events elicits more accurate information than would shorter and more general inquiries (Weiss 1994; Seidman 1998).

Interviews covered a wide variety of topics and were designed to start with general background information and become increasingly specific to the individuals' pro-life beliefs and activism. I began by asking about their parents, upbringing, early schooling, and so forth. I then asked about their religious background, both as children and today. It was only after we had covered these topics that I brought up the abortion issue, generally more than an hour into the interview. I asked them specific questions about when they first heard of abortion, conversations they'd had about abortion, times when they had thought about abortion, and the first experiences they had had with pro-life organizations or other pro-life activists. I also asked them about their abortion beliefs, probing how they understood the abortion issue and why they believed legalized abortion was wrong and needed to be stopped. I collected basic demographic data and also administered a short written survey at the very end of the interview session. The final interview protocol I used is reproduced in table A.1.

I conducted most interviews in people's homes. The visits often gave me the opportunity to meet spouses, children, parents, and siblings. It also allowed me to make observations about interviewees' lives or gave me ideas for interview questions that would not otherwise have been possible. When meeting in an interviewee's home was impossible, I held the interview at a bookstore, public library, local café, or other location where we could sit uninterrupted for several hours. At the end of every interview, I asked the person to share the names of others, both in and outside the movement, whom I might also contact as part of the study. Often the interviewees contacted such people personally for me, vouching for me and allaying any fears or suspicions they might have had about the project.

All interviews were taped and fully transcribed, resulting in more than four thousand pages of transcripts, which were then coded in their entirety and analyzed using the software package ATLAS.ti. ATLAS.ti assists researchers in generating and applying complex coding schemes, links among passages in different transcripts, memos relating to transcripts, codes and other aspects of data analysis, and conceptual maps of the different ideas being developed in the study. It permits the

Table A.1 Interview protocol

Interview Protocol 3.0

GENERAL BIOGRAPHY

- Born, raised, siblings, married, where lived, children
- Parents' occupation, education, politics
- Schooling

RELATIONSHIP TO RELIGIOUS INSTITUTIONS AND IDEAS

- What, where, how often, range of activities
- Development of relationship to church:
  - Times in your life that you have fallen away from your faith?
  - Times in your life when your faith has changed or deepened?
- Relationship with church ideas:
  - What are the most important teachings of your faith?
  - Are there teachings at your church with which you disagree?

DEVELOPMENT OF ACTIVISM

- First time ever heard of or thought about abortion
- First time ever did something about abortion
- Development of activism—different organizations/phases
- How has the abortion issue touched your life personally?
  - Personal experiences with abortions, adoptions, miscarriages, premature births, children with disabilities
- Relationship between activism and religion
- Relationship of family, friends, and colleagues to movement
- Previous activism/organizational involvement of any kind

---

analyst to order and link passages in complex ways and incorporate far more information than is possible manually.

An initial coding system was developed using transcripts from the three pretest interviews I conducted with activists in Orange County, New Jersey. The coding system was then developed further alongside the data collection and analysis. The purpose of the coding was not to impose a rigid system of classification upon the data to produce quantitative counts and frequencies (although with some of the codes, this is possible). Instead, coding was used to "fracture" (Maxwell 1996) the data to develop theoretical models as well as winnow down the thousands of pages of information to the most important empirical

Table A.1 (*Continued*)

ATTITUDINAL POSITION ON ABORTION AND PRO-LIFE MOVEMENT

- Are there situations in which abortion is justified?
- How do we know abortion is wrong?
- What is the range of ways people can be involved in this issue?
- Tell me about your last conversation, meeting, or talk on the issue.
- Strategy:
  - How effective are different forms of activism? (1) politics / political lobbying, (2) crisis pregnancy centers, (3) sidewalk counseling, (4) rescues/blockades/protests, (5) attacking equipment/clinics, (6) prayer
  - What is the best means to reach others on this issue?
- Sources of information and ideas:
  - How have your ideas about abortion developed?
  - Where have you learned the most about this issue?
  - What are the best sources of information on this issue?
- Questioning of beliefs or ideas
- Ideas about birth control, parental consent laws, live-and-let-live people

OTHER CIVIC ENGAGEMENT (highlight for nonactivists)

- Politics
- Social, fraternal
- Kids (familial)
- Moral: Are there other moral issues as important as abortion today?

---

components (Lofland and Lofland 1995). I included codes for different beliefs about the issue (for example, "abortion as a civil rights issue," "importance of responsibility"), different aspects of involvement in the movement (for example, "first experience with activism," "social reasons for participation"), discussions about specific organizations or people (for example, "Planned Parenthood," "Bill Clinton"), and more analytic codes for passages that reflect well-known existing concepts in the scholarly literatures on social movements and the sociology of religion (for example, "biographical availability," "political opportunities," "religious authority"). Almost two hundred different codes were eventually generated and used in the analysis.

My choice of the four sites in which to conduct research was based on ensuring variation in the relative levels of pro-life mobilization and religious composition of the sites, as outlined in chapter 1. Relative levels of mobilization in different cities are a difficult thing to gauge or quantify. Pro-life organizations seldom keep reliable membership figures, and the few numbers that are available are almost impossible to compare.[1] Data collected on picketing and other forms of street activism are aggregated to the national level to protect the identity of individual abortion clinics and are thus deliberately unhelpful in identifying mobilization in particular areas. I therefore used two alternative measures of contentious opposition to abortion in each community. As a rough indicator of the level of mainstream pro-life mobilization, I counted the number of "abortion alternative organizations" (such as crisis pregnancy centers, or CPCs) located within twenty-five miles of the city center and listed in the yellow pages of the city's 1998 phone book. As a measure of more militant mobilization, I looked at the number of acts of violence directed at facilities that provide abortion services in each city, using data drawn from Blanchard and Prewitt (1993) and the U.S. Bureau of Alcohol, Tobacco, and Firearms (MSNBC 1998).

The four cities I visited have clearly different levels of pro-life mobilization as gauged by these two measures. The Twin Cities and Oklahoma City both have more abortion alternative organizations in absolute and per capita terms than does either Boston or Charleston (thirty-five and twenty-two, compared to sixteen and six, respectively). In terms of violence, clinics in the Twin Cities had experienced a total of ten bombings, arsons, attempted arsons, and attempted bombings when this research began, whereas Oklahoma City had four. By contrast, Boston had experienced only one bombing in addition to the well-publicized 1994 Brookline clinic shooting spree by John Salvi. There are no reports of abortion-related violence anywhere in South Carolina at any time in the twenty years preceding my study. State legislative activity in 1998 provides further confirmation that the pro-life movement is better mobilized in Minnesota and Oklahoma than it is in Massachusetts or South Carolina. In both of the former states, 1998 state legislatures enacted new laws further regulating or restricting abortion services, but no such legislation was passed in either of the latter states (NARAL Legal Department 1998; Alan Guttmacher Institute 1998). The pattern was similar in 2006 (NARAL 2007). My estimation of relative levels of mobilization in each city is thus consistent across several different measures.

Differing religious composition is the second dimension of variation

Table A.2 Research site information

Oklahoma City	
number of abortion alternative centers	22
number of violent incidents	4
pro-life legislation in 1998?	Y
Catholic (%)	6.7
fundamentalist Protestant (%)	38.2
population	958,839
per capita income ($)	26,883
foreign born (%)	3.2
white (%)	81.3
college degree or higher (%)	21.6

Minneapolis/St. Paul	
number of abortion alternative centers	35
number of violent incidents	10
pro-life legislation in 1998?	Y
Catholic (%)	32.5
fundamentalist Protestant (%)	4.7
population	2,464,124
per capita income ($)	36,565
foreign born (%)	3.5
white (%)	92.2
college degree or higher (%)	27.1

Charleston	
number of abortion alternative centers	6
number of violent incidents	0
pro-life legislation in 1998?	N
Catholic (%)	5.9
fundamentalist Protestant (%)	17.5
population	506,875
per capita income ($)	28,066
foreign born (%)	2.1
white (%)	67.9
college degree or higher (%)	18.9

Boston	
number of abortion alternative centers	16
number of violent incidents	2
pro-life legislation in 1998?	N
Catholic (%)	26.2
fundamentalist Protestant (%)	1.6
population	4,171,747
per capita income ($)	40,666
foreign born (%)	10.4
white (%)	89.0
college degree or higher (%)	30.7

I identified as important in selecting research sites. I chose locations with very different populations of Catholics and Protestant fundamentalists, frequently identified as the key constituencies for pro-life ideas (Granberg and Granberg 1980; Ginsburg 1993; Wilcox 1994). Data on the religious composition of different cities are available through the Glenmary Research Center (1990). In the Twin Cities and Boston, Catholics are the single largest religious group (33 percent and 26 percent of the population, respectively), while neither city is home to large numbers of fundamentalist Protestants (5 percent in the Twin Cities, 2 percent in Boston).[2] In Oklahoma City and Charleston, these numbers are reversed: overall, 38 percent of the population in Oklahoma City and 18 percent in Charleston belong to fundamentalist denominations, while Catholics make up no more than 7 percent of the population in either city.

The four locations thus fall into a classic two-by-two table, with the Twin Cities and Oklahoma City representing cities with high mobilization and Boston and Charleston representing those with low mobilization. The Twin Cities and Boston are cities with a high proportion of Catholics, and Oklahoma City and Charleston have a high proportion of fundamentalist Protestants. Table A.2 shows the four locations arrayed on these two dimensions along with basic demographic information on each city drawn from the 1990 U.S. Census.[3] As described in chapter 1, the variation each of these cities exhibits turned out to have little impact on the mobilization process. While the mix of organizations in different movement streams affected the relative number of people who engaged in different kinds of activism, the process of becoming an activist looked the same in all four sites. This does not mean the variation was unimportant to the study, however, because it acted as an important control that suggests the model here might be generalized beyond the specific sites in which I collected data.

Notes

CHAPTER ONE

1. All activist names throughout the book are pseudonyms.

2. *Partial-birth abortion* is a political, not medical, term. Its meaning has been contested and reframed by both sides in the abortion controversy (Esacove 2004). The actual medical procedures covered by the term remain vague (Cohen and Saul 1998).

3. Even the name of the movement opposed to legalized abortion—the pro-life movement—is a subject of controversy. Pro-choice activists insist the label is an unfair one, calling the movement instead "antichoice" or "antiabortion." The media also consistently uses the term *antiabortion* instead of *pro-life* (Shaw 1990). What to call contentious opposition to abortion is a central part of the struggle taking place over the issue. The labeling is not trivial, as the power to name something is also the power to "rhetorically accomplish" it (Aho 1994). The truth is that none of the terms used by either side in the debate are completely accurate labels for the movement; each is misleading in one way or another. Here I will adopt the names preferred by those who are themselves being labeled in the controversy and refer to the movement to end legalized abortion as "pro-life" and the movement supporting legal access to abortion as "pro-choice."

4. Jacoby 1998 is an important exception.

5. For specific applications of this approach to the abortion debate, see Burns 2005, Esacove 2004, and Ferree et al. 2002.

CHAPTER TWO

1. There is a vast literature on abortion attitudes in the general population that also focuses on attitudinal and demographic predictors of such beliefs. Measures of conservatism in personal

morality and levels of religiosity, for example, are statistically significant predictors of pro-life attitudes (Granberg and Granberg 1980; Tamney, Johnson, and
Burton 1992; Cook, Jelen, and Wilcox 1992; Hout 1999). Among demographic
variables, education is the most closely correlated with abortion beliefs: the
lower the education level, the more likely a person is to express pro-life ideas
(Granberg and Granberg 1980; Jelen 1994; Cook, Jelen, and Wilcox 1992; Jelen
and Wilcox 2003). These studies are tangential to the question here, however,
because they focus only on attitudes toward abortion in the general public, not
among those who become activists. Moreover, attitudinal and demographic
variables have proved to be very poor overall predictors of abortion attitudes.
Measures of conservative personal morality account for only a modest amount
of variation—24 percent in Donald Granberg and Beth Wellman Granberg's
1980 study. Demographic variables fare even worse. Even when a kitchen sink's
worth of demographic measures are included—education, income, occupational
prestige, age, race, sex, region, and rurality combined—such variables explain
a paltry 9 percent of the variance in public abortion attitudes (Granberg and
Granberg 1980; Cook, Jelen, and Wilcox 1992; Guth et al. 1993).

2. In fact, this assumption appears to be built into the way Maxwell (2002)
addressed abortion with her interview participants. She reports organizing her
interviews around five topics, the first two of which are "How did you become
pro-life?" and "How did you come to act on your beliefs?" (p. 6). The linear process from beliefs to action that she reports may thus be the result of interview
questions that presume the linear process.

3. Data on the marital status and average number of children of participants
in the Jacoby study are not available either in published sources or directly
from the author.

4. Chapter 4 focuses on the history of the pro-life movement.

5. Perhaps the self-selection bias of those willing to return surveys in each
study partly accounts for these latter findings. The differences, however, are
overwhelming and certainly call into question common stereotypes of the pro-
life movement or the Christian Right in general as being "poor, uneducated
and easy to command" (Weisskopf 1993).

6. More than 70 percent of the activists I spoke to expressed opposition to
capital punishment. See table 2.2.

7. This is a frequent problem in studies generally that seek to explain one attitude or set of beliefs by reference to other attitudes or beliefs.

8. As with the previous example of beliefs about capital punishment, different opinions on these two issues may be the result of pro-life activism itself,
because the pro-life movement ties each of them strongly to the abortion issue.
For example, consider what Elizabeth, a twenty-one-year-old activist in Boston,
says in support of increased welfare spending: "I think it is very tied in to life
issues, because you have single mothers or poor families that are trying to support children. . . . We just need to support the welfare system, and in that way
people will feel more secure, and I think that will prevent a lot of abortions."

9. Birthright is a national federation of crisis pregnancy centers (CPCs), which seek to convince abortion-minded pregnant women to carry their pregnancies to term. CPCs are discussed in detail in chapter 5.

10. Disentangling these mobilization stories from other data in the interviews is discussed in the appendix.

11. For some activists, the word *conversion* might be appropriate. Like Maxwell (2002), I found that many activists experienced a religious conversion after becoming involved in the movement. This issue is taken up in detail in chapter 7.

12. Bernard Nathanson, for example, was a national pro-choice figure and helped found the National Association for the Repeal of Abortion Laws (NARAL) before switching to pro-life activism. Norma McCorvey, the anonymous plaintiff identified as "Jane Roe" in the *Roe v. Wade* Supreme Court decision, has since become a pro-life activist. Carol Everett is well known within the pro-life movement for having once run a number of abortion clinics before becoming a pro-life activist.

13. My exact question was, "Do you think abortion should be illegal in all circumstances?"

14. In a May 2007 poll conducted by the *Gallup Report,* for example, 94 percent of respondents indicated they were either "pro-life" or "pro-choice" with respect to the abortion issue, as opposed to having either mixed feelings or no opinion. This result has been replicated literally hundreds of times in different kinds of surveys with differently worded questions.

CHAPTER THREE

1. See Jasper and Poulsen (1995) and McAdam and Paulsen (1993) for helpful reviews as well as critique of this literature.

2. I discuss the relationship between religion and the movement in detail in chapter 7.

3. She contrasts this finding with her analysis of pro-choice mobilization, which she attributes to "consciousness-raising" activity on the part of pro-choice organizations.

4. I classified individuals as "self-starters" if they did not explicitly articulate their motivation for attending a pro-life event, at least in part, in terms of a personal relationship—even if they admitted they went to the event with someone from their workplace, congregation, neighborhood, and so forth or knew such a person at the event.

5. I believe focused probing in the remaining ten interviews would have revealed turning points in those cases as well, although I cannot demonstrate this empirically with my existing data.

6. Schools obviously vary enormously in the extent to which they expose students to diversity and challenging ideas. Such qualities are not limited to selective liberal arts colleges, however. Even the most politically conservative or

technical schools draw on a larger population and host a greater range of ideas than individuals are typically exposed to in their childhood.

7. Chapter 5 more fully examines the development and lock-in of activists' pro-life beliefs and compares those beliefs with beliefs expressed by nonactivists.

CHAPTER FOUR

1. Many commentators have pointed out that the *Roe v. Wade* decision was as much about providing maximum professional autonomy to physicians as it was about the privacy rights of women. See Heimer and Staffen 1998 for a discussion of how conflicts over professionalization and authority have played out more generally in the field of medicine. Scott Frickel and Kelly Moore's edited volume (2006) provides a series of snapshots of the role of power and the state in making scientific claims.

2. In 1974, the National Council of Catholic Bishops founded another organization, the National Committee for a Human Life Amendment, to advocate and lobby for the Catholic Church's official antiabortion position.

3. NARAL Pro-choice America reports that state legislatures considered almost twenty-seven hundred and adopted almost five hundred "antichoice" measures between 2001 and 2005 alone (NARAL 2006).

4. Exceptions to this prohibition are made for cases of rape, incest, and when the life of the mother is endangered by a continued pregnancy.

5. The movement itself has fiercely debated what the exact wording of such an amendment should be. An example of a human life amendment that addresses abortion directly is the version introduced in 1981 by Senator Orrin Hatch: "A right to abortion is not secured by this Constitution. The Congress and the several states shall have the concurrent power to restrict and prohibit abortions: Provided, that a law of a state which is more restrictive than a law of Congress shall govern" (Forsythe 1999, 20). The human life amendment supported by the American Life League, a national pro-life advocacy organization, provides an example of wording that avoids the term *abortion:* "The paramount right to life is vested in each human being from the moment of fertilization" (American Life League 2000).

6. The common view that rescues originated with Terry or were his brainchild (for example, Staggenborg 1991, 131) is not supported by the evidence. Clinic blockades and the ideological rationale behind them had been well developed and regularly used for years before Terry entered the pro-life movement. See Risen and Thomas 1998 and Maxwell 2002 for a historical account of this aspect of the movement.

7. This includes only those arrests documented and reported by the Bureau of Alcohol, Tobacco, and Firearms (ATF); see National Abortion Federation 2005. Media reports put the estimate much higher, between forty thousand and fifty thousand.

8. The NRLC has in the past claimed more than 1.6 million members, a figure that is almost certainly exaggerated. The organization no longer releases any membership information. It does estimate, however, that its regular news-letter has "almost" 400,000 subscribers, which is probably very close to its actual number of members.

9. In addition to these so-called single-issue organizations, there are several other national groups that focus a considerable proportion of their energy and resources on pro-life activism. These include the Christian Coalition (whose current president, Roberta Combs, was once a pro-life activist in Charleston, South Carolina), Concerned Women for America, and the Family Research Council.

10. The movement also includes several national pro-life federations, mostly focused on creating and maintaining crisis pregnancy centers (CPCs) around the country. The largest of these federations are Care-Net, Birthright, and the National Institute of Family and Life Advocates. All three also have multimil-lion-dollar annual budgets, but they offer guidance and support for local pro-life groups rather than recruiting individual members themselves. CPCs are dis-cussed in more detail in chapter 5.

11. The organizational infrastructure of the pro-life movement is consistent with the literature on civil society that has found the idea of a vast sea of lo-cal groups to be largely a myth; many local organizations are in fact tied in to larger state, regional, or national federations (Skocpol 1999; Skocpol, Ganz, and Munson 2000).

12. This perspective follows Michael Young's argument (2002) regarding the social construction of protest and grievances in the United States in the mid-nineteenth century.

CHAPTER FIVE

1. Oklahoma Repentance and Rescue is now defunct.

2. The larger moral universe of pro-life activists is analyzed in detail in chapter 6.

3. 2006 General Social Survey, variable ABDEFECT; results from other surveys on this issue are similar.

4. Twenty-one-year-old Elizabeth's comments are typical of this attitude: "You know that [abortion to preserve the life of the mother] is such a small percentage. I don't think most women have major issues when they're giving birth. So I don't think that's such a big consideration. I don't think most mothers are in danger of [losing] their lives when they're pregnant. So I think that's like a lame excuse. And it's just such a small percentage that that is their [pro-choicers'] entire argument." Approximately 4 percent of women seeking abortions in 2004 cited their physical health as the primary reason for their decision (Finer et al. 2005). The number of women whose life is threatened by a pregnancy, however, is certainly much lower.

5. This particular statement was made by a man, but the belief that abortion is never justified even when the life of the mother is in jeopardy is equally distributed among men and women; however, married people are more likely than single people to believe this is an acceptable justification for abortion.

6. As discussed in the previous chapter, *Roe v. Wade* and *Doe v. Bolton* are companion cases, both handed down on the same day, that together deal with the legal status of abortion. Although overturning these Supreme Court decisions is a central aim of the politics stream of the movement, few activists understand that doing so would merely eliminate federal protection of abortion rights; it would not make abortion illegal. The legal status of abortion would then be decided by individual states. For the legal implications of the Supreme Court's overturning these landmark rulings, see Hull and Hoffer 2001 and Craig and O'Brien 1993.

7. As noted in chapter 1, *partial-birth abortion* is a political, not medical term. The actual medical procedures covered by the term remain vague (Cohen and Saul 1998), and its meaning has been contested and reframed by both sides in the abortion controversy (Esacove 2004).

8. FACE, for example, provides for criminal fines of up to ten thousand dollars and six months in jail for an individual's first nonviolent violation of the law's provisions, in addition to civil penalties. No arrests have been made for clinic rescues since 1999, although the National Abortion Federation reports there have been more than fifty rescues nationwide since then (National Abortion Federation 2005).

9. Reports from pro-choice activists and the media indicate that some women are subjected to even more extreme forms of confrontation, including being physically jostled, chased, spit at, and blocked from leaving or entering their cars. While I did not personally witness any of these kinds of tactics, they are consistent with descriptions that even pro-life activists give of some protest experiences.

10. Sidewalk counseling does not persuade many women to continue their pregnancies to term. Even those involved in this form of activism readily admit the vast majority of women don't even stop to speak to them, much less consider changing their minds about an abortion. Some pro-lifers in other streams of the movement see it as entirely ineffectual and agree with pro-choice advocates that it is tantamount to harassment. Opponents of sidewalk counseling, both within and outside the movement, also point out that even those few women who are turned away from the clinic by counselors often return later and have the abortion procedure. These critics, however, fail to recognize direct-action activists' understanding of the abortion issue, an understanding that is not based on such statistics. Margaret, a seventy-three-year-old in the Twin Cities, reflects this view well when she says, "If every one of them [the activists] combined to only save one baby, then it is worth it. Because that's how much value I place on even one human life. I think it's absolutely precious."

11. Freestanding clinics are facilities that operate primarily for the purpose of providing abortion services and are physically separate from larger hospitals or medical care providers. There were only 447 such clinics nationwide in 2000, but they performed 71 percent of all abortions (Finer and Henshaw 2003).

12. The pro-life movement has recently begun trying to change the term used for CPCs to avoid the word *crisis,* preferring instead the term *pregnancy help centers.*

13. Most CPCs keep careful statistics on a number of different aspects of their efforts. Interestingly, only about one-third of the women who come into such clinics actually turn out to be pregnant. Tracking the clinics' effectiveness in persuading pregnant women not to abort is trickier. Many of the women who use the clinics have never considered abortion as a choice. Of those who are "abortion-minded," meaning they have admitted to considering abortion on a clinic entrance form, many do not return to the clinic and are not reachable by phone—hence, the CPC doesn't know what decisions they made. Furthermore, many women who do decide to abort report miscarriages to the pro-life activists who make follow-up calls. Evaluations of the clinics' "success" in terms of actually convincing women not to abort are thus mainly anecdotal.

14. Birthright is an international Catholic organization that was begun in Canada in 1968 and today claims more than 400 centers worldwide, most in the United States. Care-Net was founded in 1975 as the Christian Action Council and today claims more than 850 affiliates in the United States and Canada (Entsminger 2005). NIFLA was founded in 1993 and claims more than 950 individual CPC affiliates in forty-eight states (National Institute of Family and Life Advocates 2005).

15. For more information about the medical evidence for and against post-abortion trauma, see Joyce 1997.

16. Here is how one activist involved in the division described it: "We all got thrown off the board [of MCCL]. They threw us all off the board. We called it the Saint Joseph's Day massacre. And it was the best thing that ever happened. Best thing that ever happened, because MCCL is an affiliate of the National Right to Life Committee. And they are no longer what I would call the authentic pro-life movement. They have sold away some of the basic concepts."

17. This interview took place in the summer of 2000, before George W. Bush was elected.

18. The description also gets the history of the pro-life movement wrong. Clinic blockades actually preceded the widespread diffusion of sidewalk counseling as a tactic.

19. This finding is supported by Maxwell's (2002) analysis of the Direct Action League (DAL), a pro-life group organized in St. Louis, Missouri, in the 1980s. She found that most of the founding members of DAL did not come from other groups involved in other strategies; most were new to the movement as a whole.

NOTES

CHAPTER SIX

1. According to 2006 General Social Survey data, 73 percent of Americans support legal abortion in cases in which there is a "strong chance of serious defect" in the fetus. Support is greater only for cases in which a pregnancy is the result of rape or seriously endangers a woman's health. By contrast, only 39 percent support legal abortion "if the woman wants one for any reason."

2. According to 2006 General Social Survey data, women are indeed slightly less likely than men to support legalized abortion. The difference, however, is quite small.

3. There are no definitive social science data on the incidence of regret over previous abortion decisions. A 2000 *Los Angeles Times* poll of Americans who know a woman who has had an abortion, however, shows that 26 percent believe that the woman regretted the decision later, a substantial proportion but far less than the 94 percent cited by the activist in this passage (Armet 2000).

4. Black women are more than twice as likely to terminate a pregnancy as white women in the United States (Jones, Darroch, and Henshaw 2002).

5. Overall, only 12 percent of the Catholic activists in my sample support capital punishment, while 75 percent of Protestants activists do. In the general U.S. population, 64 percent of Catholics and 73 percent of Protestants support capital punishment (according to the 2006 General Social Survey).

CHAPTER SEVEN

1. Christian churches make up the vast majority of the religious institutions in contact with the pro-life movement. I focus in this chapter solely on Christian organizations and traditions because the role of Judaism, Islam, and other faiths is negligible.

2. *The Silent Scream* is a well-known video documentary that shows ultrasound images of an abortion.

3. Interestingly, the lay leaders in charge of the Catholic Church's pro-life efforts in each of the cities I visited saw their role as being largely about broadening the pro-life issue to include not only abortion but also opposition to euthanasia, capital punishment, and support for a living wage and other economic positions of the Church.

4. Note the similarity between Richard's search for a cause in which to get involved and the stories of other activists who sought out volunteer opportunities or organizations to join without a clear sense that pro-life activism in particular was important to them. The sequence of motivations and experiences in each of these cases supports the larger argument that passionate pro-life beliefs are seldom the proximate "cause" of individual mobilization. This finding is also supported by the interviews conducted by Maxwell (2002) with direct-action activists in St. Louis, Missouri. She documents that a number of the early activists in her study were "looking for a cause" (p. 34).

5. Ben is referring here to a pro-life vigil once held annually in Charleston—a "Life Chain," in which individuals would stand silently along a major thoroughfare holding pro-life signs.

6. The fact that the churches would come together to actively oppose video poker and not abortion is particularly galling to activists because nobody would argue that the moral weight of the former exceeds that of the latter. The very different ways in which churches have handled the two issues is a vivid demonstration that the divisiveness and controversy surrounding abortion limit churches' involvement. There is no controversy, by contrast, over the appropriate stance toward video poker.

7. This conclusion is predicated, of course, on trying to understand how individuals become activists in the contemporary pro-life movement. Historically, churches—and, in particular, the Catholic Church—have played an important role in the development of the movement as a whole, as chapter 4 showed. For an account of the religious roots of similar movements that emerged in the nineteenth century, see Young 2002 and 2006.

8. A focus on experience, rather than institutions or theology, as the foundation of religious life is not new. Here I follow Marshall Berman (1982), who, in turn, draws on both Karl Marx and Søren Kierkegaard in highlighting the experiential component of religion. This approach is also not so different from that of Blaise Pascal in his *Pensées* (1669/1995), when he privileges "habits" over beliefs.

9. I use the term *practice* here in its most straightforward and pedestrian meaning. Practices are activities in which individuals are physically involved and in which the actions themselves mean something to participants and observers alike. My use of the term does not carry with it the theoretical baggage common in the tradition of Pierre Bourdieu (1977, 1984) or the moral baggage with which it has been discussed specifically in relation to religion (for example, Stout 1988; MacIntyre 1984). For a helpful discussion of the use of "practice" as a concept in the social sciences, see Bender 2003.

10. Such conversion (or "born-again") narratives are common in some Protestant traditions (for example, Baptist) but are relatively rare among Catholics.

CHAPTER EIGHT

1. Results vary depending on question wording and the timing of the poll, but the results reported in figure 8.1 are typical. They come from a Gallup poll conducted in May 2007. The exact question asked was "Do you think abortions should be legal under any circumstances, legal only under certain circumstances, or illegal in all circumstances?"

2. This process would also be consistent with recent work on secularization in the United States, which has found that the authority of religious ideas and institutions has declined (Chaves 1994) even as religion as a source of identity claims has remained important (Ammerman 2003).

1. What constitutes a "member" varies enormously. Some groups count only those who regularly pay some kind of yearly membership fee. Others count as members anyone on their mailing list or anyone who has attended a group-sponsored event.

2. Fundamentalist Protestants were measured by denomination, based on the typologies used by Laurence Iannaccone (1994) and Christian Smith (1998).

3. 2000 Census data were not yet available when this project began.

References

Aho, James. 1994. *This Thing of Darkness: A Sociology of the Enemy.* Seattle: University of Washington Press.

Alan Guttmacher Institute. 1998. "The Status of Major Abortion-Related Laws and Policies in the States." New York: Alan Guttmacher Institute. http://www.agi-usa.org/pubs/abort_law_status.html (accessed Dec. 14, 1998).

American Life League. 2000. "American Life League—Philosophy." http://www.all.org/about/policy2.htm (accessed Apr. 21, 2000).

Ammerman, Nancy T. 2003. "Religious Identities and Religious Institutions." In *Handbook for the Sociology of Religion,* ed. M. Dillon, 207–24. New York: Cambridge University Press.

———, ed. 2006. *Everyday Religion: Observing Modern Religious Lives.* New York: Oxford University Press.

Andrews, Kenneth. 1997. "The Impacts of Social Movements on the Political Process: The Civil Rights Movement and Black Electoral Politics in Mississippi." *American Sociological Review* 62, no. 5 (Oct.): 800–819.

———. 2002. "Movement-Countermovement Dynamics and the Emergence of New Institutions: The Case of 'White Flight' Schools in Mississippi." *Social Forces* 80:911–36.

Appiah, Kwame Anthony. 2004. *The Ethics of Identity.* Princeton, NJ: Princeton University Press.

Armet, Elizabeth. 2000. "Poll Analysis: Americans Lean More Conservative on Social Issues." *Los Angeles Times,* June 18. http://www.latimes.com/news/nationworld/timespoll/la-000618abortpoll-442pa2an,1,7894326.htmlstory (accessed Mar. 13, 2008).

Armstrong, Elizabeth A. 2002. *Forging Gay Identities: Organizing Sexuality in San Francisco, 1950–1994.* Chicago: University of Chicago Press.

Bader, Eleanor J., and Patricia Baird-Windle. 2001. *Targets of Hatred: Anti-abortion Terrorism*. New York: Palgrave Macmillan.

Bellah, Robert, Richard Madsen, Ann Swidler, William Sullivan, and Steven Tipton. 1985. *Habits of the Heart: Individualism and Commitment in American Life*. Los Angeles: University of California Press.

Bender, Courtney. 2003. *Heaven's Kitchen: Living Religion at God's Love We Deliver*. Chicago: University of Chicago Press.

Benford, Robert D. 1993. "Frame Disputes within the Nuclear Disarmament Movement." *Social Forces* 71, no. 3 (Mar.): 677–701.

Benford, Robert D., and David A. Snow. 2000. "Framing Processes and Social Movements: An Overview and Assessment." *Annual Review of Sociology* 26:611–39.

Berlet, Chip, and Matthew N. Lyons. 2000. *Right-Wing Populism in America: Too Close for Comfort*. New York: Guilford Press.

Berman, Marshall. 1982. *All That Is Solid Melts into Air: The Experience of Modernity*. New York: Simon and Schuster.

Birnbaum, Jeffrey H. 1999. "Follow the Money." *Fortune*, Dec. 6, 206–8.

Blanchard, Dallas A. 1994. *The Anti-abortion Movement and the Rise of the Religious Right: From Polite to Fiery Protest*. New York: Twayne Publishers.

Blanchard, Dallas A., and Terry J. Prewitt. 1993. *Religious Violence and Abortion: The Gideon Project*. Gainesville: University of Florida Press.

Blee, Kathleen. 2002. *Inside Organized Racism: Women in the Hate Movement*. Los Angeles: University of California Press.

Boldt, David R., and Anne Hobald. 1970. "Police, Abortion Opponents Clash in March on GW Hospital Clinic." *Washington Post*, sec. A, June 7, 1.

Bourdieu, Pierre. 1977. *Outline of a Theory of Practice*. New York: Cambridge University Press.

———. 1984. *Distinction: A Social Critique of the Judgement of Taste*. Cambridge, MA: Harvard University Press.

Burns, Gene. 2005. *The Moral Veto: Framing Contraception, Abortion, and Cultural Pluralism in the United States*. New York: Cambridge University Press.

Caniglia, Beth Schaefer, and JoAnn Carmin. 2005. "Scholarship on Social Movement Organizations: Classic Views and Emerging Trends." *Mobilization* 10, no. 2 (June): 201–12.

Chaves, Mark. 1994. "Secularization as Declining Religious Authority." *Social Forces* 72, no. 3:749–74.

Clemens, Elisabeth S. 1997. *The People's Lobby: Organizational Innovation and the Rise of Interest Group Politics in the United States, 1890–1925*. Chicago: University of Chicago Press.

Cohen, Susan A., and Rebekah Saul. 1998. "The Campaign against 'Partial-Birth' Abortion: Status and Fallout." *Guttmacher Report on Public Policy* 1, no. 6 (Dec.): 6–10.

Connors, Joseph M. 1989. "Operation Rescue." *America*, Apr. 29, 400–403.

Cook, Elizabeth Adell, Ted G. Jelen, and Clyde Wilcox. 1992. *Between Two Absolutes: Pubic Opinion and the Politics of Abortion*. Boulder, CO: Westview Press.

Craig, Barbara Hinkson, and David M. O'Brien. 1993. *Abortion and American Politics*. Chatham, NJ: Chatham House.

Curtis, Russell L., Jr., and Louis A. Zurcher Jr. 1973. "Stable Resources of Protest Movements: The Multi-organizational Field." *Social Forces* 52, no. 1 (Sept.): 53–61.

Dalton, Russell J. 2006/1988. *Citizen Politics: Public Opinion and Political Parties in Advanced Industrial Democracies*. Washington, DC: Congressional Quarterly Press.

Darnell, Alfred, and Darren E. Sherkat. 1997. "The Impact of Protestant Fundamentalism on Educational Attainment." *American Sociological Review* 62, no. 2 (Apr.): 306–15.

Davis, James A., Tom W. Smith, and Peter V. Marsden. 2007. *General Social Surveys, 1972–2006 (Cumulative File)*. MRDF (machine-readable data file). Chicago: National Opinion Research Center.

DeVries, Julian. 1962. "Pill May Cost Woman Her Baby." *Arizona Republic* (Phoenix), July 23, A1, A4.

Diamond, Sara. 1995. *Roads to Dominion: Right-Wing Movements and Political Power in the United States*. New York: Guilford Press.

———. 1998. *Not by Politics Alone: The Enduring Influence of the Christian Right*. New York: Guilford Press.

DiMaggio, Paul, John Evans, and Bethany Bryson. 1996. "Have Americans' Social Attitudes Become More Polarized?" *American Journal of Sociology* 102, no. 3 (Nov.): 690–755.

Elder, Glen H., Jr. 1985. "Perspectives on the Life Course." In *Life Course Dynamics*, ed. G. H. Elder Jr., 23–49. Ithaca, NY: Cornell University Press.

Eliasoph, Nina. 1998. *Avoiding Politics: How Americans Produce Apathy in Everyday Life*. New York: Cambridge University Press.

Encyclopedia of Associations. 1978. *National Organizations of the United States*. Detroit: Gale Research.

Entsminger, Kurt. 2005. "Care-Net: Who We Are." Washington, DC. http://www.care-net.org/aboutus/index.html (accessed Sept. 27, 2005).

Esacove, Anne W. 2004. "Dialogic Framing: The Framing/Counterframing of 'Partial-Birth' Abortion." *Sociological Inquiry* 74, no. 1 (Feb.): 70–101.

Evans, John H. 2003. "Have Americans' Attitudes Become More Polarized? An Update." *Social Science Quarterly* 84, no. 1 (Mar.): 71–91.

Eyerman, Ron, and Andrew Jamison. 1991. *Social Movements: A Cognitive Approach*. University Park: Pennsylvania State University Press.

Faludi, Susan. 1991. *Backlash: The Undeclared War against American Women*. New York: Crown.

Ferree, Myra Marx, William A. Gamson, Jurgen Gerhards, and Dieter Rucht. 2002. *Shaping Abortion Discourse: Democracy and the Public Sphere in Germany and the United States*. New York: Cambridge University Press.

Fields, Karen E. 1985. *Revival and Rebellion in Colonial Central Africa*. Princeton, NJ: Princeton University Press.

Finer, Lawrence B., Lori F. Frohwirth, Lindsay A. Dauphinee, Susheela Singh, and Ann M. Moore. 2005. "Reasons U.S. Women Have Abortions: Quantitative and Qualitative Perspectives." *Perspectives on Sexual and Reproductive Health* 37, no. 3 (Sept.): 110–18.

Finer, Lawrence B., and Stanley K. Henshaw. 2003. "Abortion Incidence and Services in the United States in 2000." *Perspectives on Sexual and Reproductive Health* 35, no. 1 (Jan.–Feb.): 6–15.

Fisher, Dana. 2006. *Activism, Inc.: How the Outsourcing of Grassroots Campaigns Is Strangling Progressive Politics in America*. Palo Alto, CA: Stanford University Press.

Forsythe, Clarke D. 1999. "A New Strategy." *Human Life Review* 25, no. 4 (Fall): 15–27.

Freeman, Jo. 1977. "Resource Mobilization and Strategy: A Model for Analyzing Social Movement Organization Actions." In *The Dynamics of Social Movements*, ed. M. N. Zald and J. D. McCarthy, 167–89. Cambridge, MA: Winthrop Publishers.

Frickel, Scott, and Kelly Moore, eds. 2006. *The New Political Sociology of Science: Institutions, Networks, and Power*. Madison: University of Wisconsin Press.

Gallup, Inc. 2008. "Abortion." Gallup.com. http://www.gallup.com/poll/1576/abortion.aspx (accessed Mar. 10, 2008).

Gamson, William A. 1990. *The Strategy of Social Protest*. Belmont, CA: Wadsworth Publishing Company.

Gamson, William A., and David Meyer. 1996. "Framing Political Opportunity." In *Comparative Perspectives on Social Movements: Political Opportunities, Mobilizing Structures, and Cultural Framings*, ed. D. McAdam, J. D. McCarthy, and M. N. Zald, 275–90. New York: Cambridge University Press.

Gerlach, Luther P. 1970. *People, Power, Change: Movements of Social Transformation*. Indianapolis: Bobbs-Merrill.

Ginsburg, Faye. 1989/1998. *Contested Lives: The Abortion Debate in an American Community*. Berkeley: University of California Press.

———. 1993. "Saving America's Souls: Operation Rescue's Crusade against Abortion." In *Fundamentalisms and the State: Remaking Politics, Economies, and Militance*, ed. M. Marty and R. S. Appleby, 557–88. Chicago: University of Chicago Press.

———. 1998. "Rescuing the Nation: Operation Rescue and the Rise of Antiabortion Militance." In *Abortion Wars: A Half Century of Struggle, 1950–2000*, ed. R. Solinger, 227–50. Los Angeles: University of California Press.

Giugni, Marco, Doug McAdam, and Charles Tilly, eds. 1999. *How Social Movements Matter*. Minneapolis: University of Minnesota Press.

Glenmary Research Center. 1990. *Churches and Church Membership in the United States, 1990*. MRDF (machine-readable data file). Storrs, CT: Roper Center for Public Opinion Research (producer).

Gold, Rachel Benson. 2003. "Lessons from before *Roe:* Will Past Be Prologue?" *Guttmacher Report on Public Policy* 6, no. 1 (Mar.): 8–11.

Goodwin, Jeff, James Jasper, and Francesca Polletta, eds. 2001. *Passionate Politics: Emotions and Social Movements.* Chicago: University of Chicago Press.

Gorney, Cynthia. 1998. *Articles of Faith: A Frontline History of the Abortion Wars.* New York: Simon and Schuster.

Granberg, Donald. 1981. "The Abortion Activists." *Family Planning Perspectives* 12, no. 5 (July–Aug.): 157–63.

Granberg, Donald, and Beth Wellman Granberg. 1980. "Abortion Attitudes, 1965–1980: Trends and Determinants." *Family Planning Perspectives* 12, no. 5 (Sept.–Oct.): 250–61.

Guth, James L., Corwin E. Smidt, Lyman A. Kellstedt, and John C. Green. 1993. "The Sources of Anti-abortion Attitudes: The Case of Religious Political Activists." *American Politics Quarterly* 21, no. 1:65–80.

Hannigan, John A. 1991. "Social Movement Theory and the Sociology of Religion: Toward a New Synthesis." *Sociological Analysis* 52, no. 4:311–31.

Hart, Stephen. 1996. "The Cultural Dimension of Social Movements: A Theoretical Reassessment and Literature Review." *Sociology of Religion* 57, no. 1 (Spring): 87–100.

Heimer, Carol A., and Lisa R. Staffen. 1998. *For the Sake of the Children: The Social Organization of Responsibility in the Hospital and the Home.* Chicago: University of Chicago Press.

Henshaw, Stanley K. 1998. "Abortion Incidence and Services in the United States, 1995–1996." *Family Planning Perspectives* 30, no. 6 (Nov.–Dec.): 263–70, 287.

Himmelstein, Jerome L. 1990. *To the Right: The Transformation of American Conservatism.* Berkeley: University of California Press.

Hondagneu-Sotelo, Pierrette, Genelle Gaudinez, Hector Lara, and Billie C. Ortiz. 2004. "'There's a Spirit That Transcends the Border': Faith, Ritual, and Postnational Protest at the U.S.-Mexico Border." *Sociological Perspectives* 47, no. 2 (Summer): 133–59.

Hout, Michael. 1999. "Abortion Politics in the United States, 1972–1994: From Single Issue to Ideology." *Gender Issues* 17, no. 2 (Spring): 3–34.

Hull, N.E.H., and Peter Charles Hoffer. 2001. Roe v. Wade: *The Abortion Rights Controversy in American History.* Lawrence: University Press of Kansas.

Iannaccone, Laurence R. 1994. "Why Strict Churches Are Strong." *American Journal of Sociology* 99, no. 5 (Mar.): 1180–1211.

Inglehart, Ronald. 1977. *The Silent Revolution: Changing Values and Political Styles among Western Publics.* Princeton, NJ: Princeton University Press.

Jacoby, Kerry N. 1998. *Souls, Bodies, Spirits: The Drive to Abolish Abortion since 1973.* Westport, CT: Praeger.

Jasper, James M. 1997. *The Art of Moral Protest: Culture, Biography, and Creativity in Social Movements.* Chicago: University of Chicago Press.

Jasper, James M., and Jane D. Poulsen. 1995. "Recruiting Strangers and Friends: Moral Shocks and Social Networks in Animal Rights and Anti-nuclear Protests." *Social Problems* 42, no. 4 (Nov.): 493–512.

Jelen, Ted, ed. 1994. *Perspectives on the Politics of Abortion*. Westport, CT: Praeger.

Jelen, Ted G., and Clyde Wilcox. 2003. "Causes and Consequences of Public Attitudes toward Abortion: A Review and Research Agenda." *Political Research Quarterly* 56, no. 4 (Dec.): 489–500.

Jenkins, J. Craig. 1983. "The Transformation of a Constituency into a Movement." In *The Social Movements of the Sixties and Seventies*, ed. J. Freeman 52–70. New York: Longman.

Jenkins, J. Craig, and Charles Perrow. 1977. "Insurgency of the Powerless: Farm Worker Movements, 1946–1972." *American Sociological Review* 42 (Apr.): 249–68.

Jenkins, Philip. 1999. "Fighting Terrorism as If Women Mattered: Anti-abortion Violence as Unconstructed Terrorism." In *Making Trouble: Cultural Constructions of Crime, Deviance, and Control*, ed. J. Ferrell and N. Websdale, 319–46. New York: Aldine de Gruyter.

Jones, Rachel K., Jacqueline E. Darroch, and Stanley K. Henshaw. 2002. "Patterns in the Socioeconomic Characteristics of Women Obtaining Abortions in 2000–2001." *Perspectives on Sexual and Reproductive Health* 34, no. 5:226–35.

Jones, Rachel K., Mia R. S. Zolna, Stanley K. Henshaw, and Lawrence B. Finer. 2008. "Abortion in the United States: Incidence and Access to Services, 2005." *Perspectives on Sexual and Reproductive Health* 40, no. 1:6–16.

Joyce, Arthur. 1997. "The Psychological After-effects of Abortion: The Real Story." *The Humanist* 57, no. 2 (Mar.–Apr.): 7–9.

Klandermans, Bert. 1984. "Mobilization and Participation: Social/Psychological Expansions of Resource Mobilization Theory." *American Sociological Review* 49:583–600.

———. 1997. *The Social Psychology of Protest*. Cambridge, MA: Blackwell Publishers.

———. 2004. "The Demand and Supply of Participation: Social Psychological Correlates of Participation in Social Movements." In *The Blackwell Companion to Social Movements*, ed. D. A. Snow, S. A. Soule, and H. Kriesi, 360–79. Malden, MA: Blackwell Publishing.

Larana, Enrique, Hank Johnston, and Joseph R. Gusfield, eds. 1994. *New Social Movements: From Ideology to Identity*. Philadelphia: Temple University Press.

Lawler, Philip F. 1992. *Operation Rescue: A Challenge to the Nation's Conscience*. Huntington, IN: Our Sunday Visitor.

Lee, Ellie. 2003. *Abortion, Motherhood, and Mental Health: Medicalizing Reproducing in the United States and Britain*. New York: Aldine de Gruyter.

Lee, Taeku. 1999. "The Sovereign Status of Survey Data." Manuscript, John F. Kennedy School of Government, Harvard University, Sept.

Lichbach, Mark I. 1994. "Rethinking Rationality and Rebellion: Theories of Collective Action and Problems of Collective Dissent." *Rationality and Society* 6, no. 1 (Jan.): 3–39.

Lin, Vitoria, and Cynthia Dailard. 2002. "Crisis Pregnancy Centers Seek to Increase Political Clout, Secure Government Subsidy." *Guttmacher Report on Public Policy* 2:4–5.

Lo, Clarence. 1982. "Countermovements and Conservative Movements in the Contemporary U.S." *Annual Review of Sociology* 8:107–34.

Lofland, John, and Lyn H. Lofland. 1995. *Analyzing Social Settings: A Guide to Qualitative Observation and Analysis.* New York: Wadsworth Publishing Company.

Lofland, John, and Rodney Stark. 1965. "Becoming a World-Saver: A Theory of Conversion to a Deviant Perspective." *American Sociological Review* 30, no. 6 (Dec.): 862–75.

Luker, Kristin. 1984. *Abortion and the Politics of Motherhood.* Los Angeles: University of California Press.

MacIntyre, Alasdair. 1984. *After Virtue: A Study in Moral Theory.* Notre Dame, IN: University of Notre Dame Press.

Mason, David T. 1984. "Individual Participation in Collective Racial Violence: A Rational Choice Synthesis." *American Political Science Review* 78, no. 4 (Dec.): 1040–56.

Maxwell, Carol J. C. 2002. *Pro-life Activists in America: Meaning, Motivation, and Direct Action.* New York: Cambridge University Press.

Maxwell, Joseph A. 1996. *Qualitative Research Design: An Interactive Approach.* Thousand Oaks, CA: Sage Publications.

McAdam, Doug. 1982. *Political Process and the Development of Black Insurgency, 1930–1970.* Chicago: University of Chicago Press.

———. 1986. "Recruitment to High-Risk Activism: The Case of Freedom Summer." *American Journal of Sociology* 92, no. 1:64–90.

———. 1988. *Freedom Summer.* New York: Oxford University Press.

———. 1999. "The Biographical Impact of Activism." In *How Social Movements Matter,* ed. M. Giugni, D. McAdam, and C. Tilly, 119–46. Minneapolis: University of Minnesota Press.

McAdam, Doug, and Ronnelle Paulsen. 1993. "Specifying the Relationship between Social Ties and Activism." *American Journal of Sociology* 99:640–67.

McCarthy, John D., and Mayer N. Zald. 1977. "Resource Mobilization and Social Movements: A Partial Theory." *American Journal of Sociology* 82:1212–41.

Media Matters. 2005. "Religious Conservatives Claim Katrina Was God's Omen, Punishment for the United States." http://mediamatters.org/items/200509130004 (accessed Oct. 28, 2007).

Melucci, Alberto. 1989. *Nomads of the Present: Social Movements and Individual Needs in Contemporary Society.* Philadelphia: Temple University Press.

Meyer, David S. 2007. *The Politics of Protest: Social Movements in America.* New York: Oxford University Press.

Meyer, David S., and Suzanne Staggenborg. 1996. "Movements, Countermovements, and the Structure of Political Opportunity." *American Journal of Sociology* 101, no. 6 (May): 1628–60.

Mohr, James C. 1978. *Abortion in America: The Origins and Evolution of National Policy, 1800–1900.* New York: Oxford University Press.

Moon, Dawne. 2004. *God, Sex, and Politics: Homosexuality and Everyday Theologies.* Chicago: University of Chicago Press.

Morris, Aldon D. 1981. "Black Southern Student Sit-in Movement: An Analysis of Internal Organization." *American Sociological Review* 46 (Dec.): 755–67.

———. 1984. *The Origins of the Civil Rights Movement: Black Communities Organizing for Change.* New York: Free Press.

Morris, Jim. 2000. "Democrats Promise to Fight Recount Denial." CNN.com, Nov. 16. http://www.cnn.com/2000/ALLPOLITICS/stories/11/15/president.election.03/index.html (accessed Nov. 17, 2000).

MSNBC. 1998. "Abortion Clinic Violence." Redmond, WA: MSNBC.com. http://www.msnbc.com/modules/clinics/default.asp (accessed Oct. 26, 1998).

Muller, Edward N., and Karl-Dieter Opp. 1986. "Rational Choice and Rebellious Collective Action." *American Political Science Review* 80, no. 2 (June): 471–87.

Munson, Ziad. 2006. "When a Funeral Isn't Just a Funeral: The Layered Meaning of Everyday Action." In *Everyday Religion: Observing Modern Religious Lives,* ed. N. T. Ammerman, 121–36. New York: Oxford University Press.

NARAL. 2006. *Who Decides? The Status of Women's Reproductive Rights in the United States.* Washington, DC: NARAL Pro-choice America.

———. 2007. *Who Decides? The Status of Women's Reproductive Rights in the United States.* Washington, DC: NARAL Pro-choice America.

NARAL Legal Department. 1998. "1998 Activity in State Legislatures." Memo, National Abortion and Reproductive Rights Action League, Washington, DC. http://www.naral.org/publications/facts/stateactivity.html (accessed Nov. 3, 1998).

National Abortion Federation. 2008. "Incidents of Violence and Disruption against Abortion Providers in the U.S. & Canada." http://www.prochoice.org/about_abortion/violence/violence_statistics.html (accessed Mar. 10, 2008).

National Institute of Family and Life Advocates. 2005. "About NIFLA." Fredericksburg, VA: National Institute of Family and Life Advocates. http://www.nifla.org/aboutnifla.asp (accessed Sept. 27, 2005).

National Right to Life Committee. 2000. "National Right to Life: Taking a Stand . . . Making a Difference." http://www.nrlc.org (accessed Apr. 20, 2000).

O'Bannon, Randall K. 2000. "What Do We Know about America's Crisis Pregnancy Centers?" Paper presented at the Annual Convention of the National Right to Life Committee, Milwaukee, WI, June 24–26.

Oberschall, Anthony. 1973. *Social Conflict and Social Movements.* Englewood Cliffs, NJ: Prentice-Hall.

Oliver, Pamela E., and Hank Johnston. 2000. "What a Good Idea! Ideologies and Frames in Social Movement Research." *Mobilization* 4, no. 1 (Spring): 37–54.

Paige, Connie. 1983. *The Right-to-Lifers.* New York: Summit Books.

Pascal, Blaise. 1669/1995. *Pensées.* Trans. A. Krailsheimer. Reprint, New York: Penguin Classics.

Passy, Florence, and Marco Giugni. 2001. "Social Networks and Individual Perceptions: Explaining Differential Participation in Social Movements." *Sociological Forum* 16, no. 1: 123–53.

Pierce, Roy, and Philip E. Converse. 1990. "Attitudinal Sources of Protest Behavior in France: Differences between Before and After Measurement." *Public Opinion Quarterly* 54, no. 3 (Autumn): 295–316.

Polletta, Francesca. 2002. *Freedom Is an Endless Meeting: Democracy in American Social Movements.* Chicago: University of Chicago Press.

Press, Eyal. 2006. *Absolute Convictions: My Father, a City, and the Conflict That Divided America.* New York: Holt and Co.

Putnam, Robert D. 2000. *Bowling Alone: The Collapse and Revival of American Community.* New York: Simon and Schuster.

Reagan, Leslie J. 1997. *When Abortion Was a Crime: Women, Medicine, and Law in the United States, 1867–1973.* Los Angeles: University of California Press.

Reiter, Jerry. 2000. *Live from the Gates of Hell: An Insider's Look at the Antiabortion Underground.* New York: Prometheus Books.

Risen, James, and Judy L. Thomas. 1998. *Wrath of Angels: The American Abortion War.* New York: Basic Books.

Sampson, Robert J., and John H. Laub. 1993. *Crime in the Making: Pathways and Turning Points through Life.* Cambridge, MA: Harvard University Press.

Schussman, Alan, and Sarah A. Soule. 2005. "Process and Protest: Accounting for Individual Protest Participation." *Social Forces* 84, no. 2 (Dec.): 1083–1108.

Segers, Mary C. 1995. "The Catholic Church as a Political Actor." In *Perspectives on the Politics of Abortion,* ed. T. Jelen, 87–130. Westport, CT: Praeger.

Seidman, Irving. 1998. *Interviewing as Qualitative Research: A Guide for Researchers in Education and the Social Sciences.* New York: Teachers College Press.

Shaw, David. 1990. "Abortion Bias Seeps into News." *Los Angeles Times,* sec. A, July 1, 1.

Shepard, Charles E. 1991. "Operation Rescue's Mission to Save Itself." *Washington Post,* sec. A, Nov. 24, final edition, 1.

Skocpol, Theda. 1999. "How Americans Became Civic." In *Civic Engagement in American Democracy,* ed. T. Skocpol and M. P. Fiorina, 27–80. Washington, DC: Brookings Institution Press.

———. 2004. *Diminished Democracy: From Membership to Management in American Civic Life.* Norman: University of Oklahoma Press.

Skocpol, Theda, Marshall Ganz, and Ziad Munson. 2000. "A Nation of Organizers: The Institutional Origins of Civic Voluntarism in the United States." *American Political Science Review* 94, no. 3 (Sept.): 527–47.

Smilde, David. 2003. "Skirting the Instrumental Paradox: Intentional Belief through Narrative in Latin American Pentecostalism." *Qualitative Sociology* 26, no. 3 (Fall): 313–29.

———. 2004. "Popular Publics: Street Protest and Plaza Preachers in Caracas." *International Review of Social History* 49, suppl., 179–95.

Smith, Christian. 1996. *Resisting Reagan: The U.S. Central America Peace Movement.* Chicago: University of Chicago Press.

———. 1998. *American Evangelicalism: Embattled and Thriving.* Chicago: University of Chicago Press.

Snow, David A., and Robert D. Benford. 1992. "Master Frames and Cycles of Protest." In *Frontiers in Social Movement Theory,* ed. A. D. Morris and C. M. Mueller, 135–55. New Haven, CT: Yale University Press.

Snow, David A., E. Burke Rochford Jr., Steven K. Worden, and Robert D. Benford. 1986. "Frame Alignment Process, Micromobilization, and Movement Participation." *American Sociological Review* 51 (Aug.): 464–81.

Solinger, Rickie. 1994. *The Abortionist: A Woman against the Law.* New York: Free Press.

———, ed. 1998. *Abortion Wars: A Half Century of Struggle.* Berkeley: University of California Press.

Staggenborg, Suzanne. 1991. *The Pro-choice Movement: Organization and Activism in the Abortion Conflict.* New York: Oxford University Press.

Steinberg, Marc W. 1999. "The Talk and Back Talk of Collective Action: A Dialogic Analysis of Repertoires of Discourse among Nineteenth-Century English Cotton Spinners." *American Journal of Sociology* 105, no. 3 (Nov.): 736–80.

Stevens, Mitchell L. 2002. "The Organizational Vitality of Conservative Protestantism." In *Social Structure and Organizations Revisited,* ed. M. Lounsbury and M. J. Ventresca, 337–60. Boston: JAI.

Stout, Jeffrey. 1988. *Ethics after Babel: The Languages of Morals and Their Discontents.* Boston: Beacon Press.

Strauss, Anselm, and Juliet Corbin. 1990. *Basics of Qualitative Research: Grounded Theory Procedures and Techniques.* Newbury Park, CA: SAGE Publications.

Swidler, Ann. 1986. "Culture in Action: Symbols and Strategies." *American Sociological Review* 51 (Apr.): 273–86.

———. 2001. *Talk of Love: How Culture Matters.* Chicago: University of Chicago Press.

Tamney, Joseph B., Stephen D. Johnson, and Ronald Burton. 1992. "The Abortion Controversy: Conflicting Beliefs and Values in Society." *Journal for the Scientific Study of Religion* 31, no. 1 (Mar.): 32–46.

Tarrow, Sidney. 1994. *Power in Movement: Social Movements and Contentious Politics.* New York: Cambridge University Press.

Tatalovich, Raymond. 1997. *The Politics of Abortion in the United States and Canada.* Armonk, NY: M. E. Sharpe.

Tatalovich, Raymond, and Byron W. Daynes. 1981. *The Politics of Abortion: A Study of Community Conflict in Public Policy Making.* New York: Praeger.

Taylor, Verta. 1989. "Social Movement Continuity: The Women's Movement in Abeyance." *American Sociological Review* 54, no. 5 (Oct.): 761–75.

Thomas, Cal, and Ed Dobson. 1999. *Blinded by Might: Can the Religious Right Save America?* Grand Rapids, MI: Zondervan Publishing House.

Tilly, Charles. 1977. "Repertoires of Contention in America and Britain, 1750–1830." In *The Dynamics of Social Movements,* ed. M. N. Zald and J. D. McCarthy, 126–55. Cambridge, MA: Winthrop Publishers.

———. 1978. *From Mobilization to Revolution.* New York: Addison-Wesley.

Tribe, Laurence H. 1990. *Abortion: The Clash of Absolutes.* New York: Norton.

Turner, Victor W. 1969. *The Ritual Process: Structure and Anti-structure.* Chicago: Aldine Publishing Company.

Van Gelder, Lawrence. 1973. "Cardinals Shocked—Reaction Mixed." *New York Times,* Jan. 23, 1, 20.

Verba, Sidney, Kay Lehman Schlozman, and Henry E. Brady. 1995. *Voice and Equality: Civic Voluntarism in American Politics.* Cambridge, MA: Harvard University Press.

Walsh, Edward J. 1981. "Resource Mobilization and Citizen Protest in Communities around Three Mile Island." *Social Problems* 29, no. 1:1–21.

Warren, Mark R. 2001. *Dry Bones Rattling: Community Building to Revitalize American Democracy.* Princeton, NJ: Princeton University Press.

Weber, Max. 1958. *The Protestant Ethic and the Spirit of Capitalism.* New York: Charles Scribner and Sons.

Weick, Karl. 1979/1969. *The Social Psychology of Organizing.* New York: McGraw-Hill.

———. 1995. *Sensemaking in Organizations.* Thousand Oaks, CA: SAGE Publications.

Weiss, Robert S. 1994. *Learning from Strangers: The Art and Method of Qualitative Interview Studies.* New York: Free Press.

Weisskopf, Michael. 1993. "Energized by Pulpit or Passion, the Public Is Calling." *Washington Post,* Feb. 1, final edition, A1.

Wilcox, Clyde. 1994. "The Sources and Consequences of Public Attitudes toward Abortion." In *Perspectives on the Politics of Abortion,* ed. T. Jelen, 55–86. Westport, CT: Praeger.

Wilder, Marcy J. 1998. "The Rule of Law, the Rise of Violence, and the Role of Morality: Reframing America's Abortion Debate." In *Abortion Wars: A Half Century of Struggle, 1950–2000,* ed. R. Solinger, 73–94. Los Angeles: University of California Press.

Williams, Rhys H. 1996. "Religion as Political Resource: Culture or Ideology?" *Journal for the Scientific Study of Religion* 35, no. 4:368–78.

———. 1999. "Visions of the Good Society and the Religious Roots of American Political Culture." *Sociology of Religion* 60, no. 1:1–34.

Wood, Richard L. 1999. "Religious Culture and Political Action." *Sociological Theory* 17, no. 3 (Nov.): 307–32.

———. 2002. *Faith in Action: Religion, Race, and Democratic Organizing in America.* Chicago: University of Chicago Press.

Wuthnow, Robert. 1998. *After Heaven: Spirituality in America since the 1950s.* Berkeley: University of California Press.

Young, Michael. 2006. *Bearing Witness against Sin: The Evangelical Birth of the American Social Movement.* Chicago: University of Chicago Press.

Young, Michael P. 2002. "Confessional Protest: The Religious Birth of Two U.S. National Social Movements." *American Sociological Review* 67, no. 5 (Oct.): 660–89.

Zald, Mayer. 1992. "Looking Backward to Look Forward: Reflections on the Past and Future of the Resource Mobilization Research Program." In *Frontiers in Social Movement Theory,* ed. A. D. Morris and C. McClurg Mueller, 326–48. New Haven, CT: Yale University Press.

Index

abolitionists, 88, 145. *See also* slavery

abortion: availability, 78–80, 90, 95; duty to have, 143; effects on society, 140–42; emotional harm to women from, 64–65, 115, 142–45; funding for, 87, 88; as killing of life, 134–36; legal requirements for, 88; maternal fatalities from, 80; rationales for, 79, 100 (*see also* pregnancies); as stemming from irresponsibility, 137–38 (*see also* responsibility); as symptom of bigger problem, 132; as taboo topic, 163; terminology, 135, 161–62 (*see also* pro-life movement: terminology); "therapeutic" (*see* pregnancies: problem; "therapeutic" abortions); as threat to medical progress, 141; in United States today, 89–95

"abortion alternative" clinics/organizations, 114, 202. *See also* crisis pregnancy centers (CPCs)

abortion debate, evolution, 87–89

abortion laws, 42, 78–83, 95, 108. *See also* Congress, U.S.; Constitution, U.S.; politics stream; Supreme Court decisions

abortion providers, 114, 148; counties with no, 90; deceit of, 148–51, 153; direct-action activities against, 88, 89, 126, 127; financial greed as motiva-

tion behind, 148–51; illegal, 79, 80; information given to women by, 143; murders of, 88; number of, 113; positive views of, 151; threats against, 88, 127; viewed as murderers, 136; who have renounced pro-choice views, 115. *See also* physicians: who perform abortions

abortion statistics, 89–90

abortion survivors, 115

action mobilization, 21. *See also* mobilization

action precedes belief model, 5–6, 32–36, 64, 186; social networks and, 52–53; turning conventional wisdom on its head, 20–21, 27, 43–45. *See also* mobilization: stories of

adoption, 58, 104, 113

African Americans, 145, 212n4

American Citizens Concerned for Life, 86

American Law Institute (ALI), 80

American Life League, 91–92

"antiabortion," 205n3

Appiah, Kwame Anthony, 54

arson, 127

Baptists, 8, 81, 152, 165, 166, 168

beliefs: and actions reinforcing each other, 68; as a component of motivation, 5; irrational/paranoid, 185; about legality of abortion, 42; role in social movements, 5; that life begins

Morality and Society Series

EDITED BY ALAN WOLFE

The Necessity of Politics: Reclaiming American Public Life
CHRISTOPHER BEEM, WITH A FOREWORD BY JEAN BETHKE ELSHTAIN

Childerley: Nature and Morality in a Country Village
MICHAEL MAYERFELD BELL

Heaven's Kitchen: Living Religion at God's Love We Deliver
COURTNEY BENDER

Heartwood: The First Generation of Theravada Buddhism in America
WENDY CADGE

Beyond Caring: Hospitals, Nurses, and the Social Organization of Ethics
DANIEL F. CHAMBLISS

The First Year Out: Understanding American Teens after High School
TIM CLYDESDALE

More Than Victims: Battered Women, the Syndrome Society, and the Law
DONALD ALEXANDER DOWNS

The End of the Line: Lost Jobs, New Lives in Postindustrial America
KATHRYN MARIE DUDLEY

*Playing God? Human Genetic Engineering and the Rationalization of Public
Bioethical Debate*
JOHN H. EVANS

Rationality and Power: Democracy in Practice
BENT FLYVBJERG (TRANSLATED BY STEVEN SAMPSON)

Democracy in Latin America, 1760–1900: Volume 1, Mexico and Peru
CARLOS A. FORMENT

Healing Powers: Alternative Medicine, Spiritual Communities, and the State
FRED M. FROHOCK

Moral Communities in Medical Science: Managing Risk in Early Human Experiments
SYDNEY HALPERN

*Cultural Dilemmas of Progressive Politics:
Styles of Engagement among Grassroots Activists*
STEPHEN HART

MORALITY AND SOCIETY SERIES

For the Sake of the Children:
The Social Organization of Responsibility in the Hospital and the Home
CAROL A. HEIMER AND LISA R. STAFFEN

Money, Morals, and Manners:
The Culture of the French and the American Upper-Middle Class
MICHÈLE LAMONT

Streets of Glory: Church and Community in a Black Urban Neighborhood
OMAR MAURICE MCROBERTS

God and Government in the Ghetto:
The Politics of Church-State Collaboration in Black America
MICHAEL LEO OWENS

The Catholic Social Imagination:
Activism and the Just Society in Mexico and the United States
JOSEPH M. PALACIOS

Citizen Speak: The Democratic Imagination in American Life
ANDREW J. PERRIN

Speaking of Abortion: Television and Authority in the Lives of Women
ANDREA L. PRESS AND ELIZABETH R. COLE

The Ironies of Affirmative Action: Politics, Culture, and Justice in America
JOHN DAVID SKRENTNY

Public and Private in Thought and Practice: Perspectives on a Grand Dichotomy
EDITED BY JEFF WEINTRAUB AND KRISHAN KUMAR

Soft Patriarchs, New Men: How Christianity Shapes Fathers and Husbands
W. BRADFORD WILCOX

Faith in Action: Religion, Race, and Democratic Organizing in America
RICHARD L. WOOD